D0874082

Stephen Spender
Works and Criticism

Garland Reference Library of the Humanities (Vol. 43)

Stephen Spender
Works and Criticism
An Annotated Bibliography

H. B. Kulkarni

/ / /

Garland Publishing, Inc., New York & London

1976

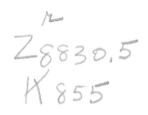
Library of Congress Cataloging in Publication Data

Kulkarni, Hemant Balvantrao, 1916-
    Stephen Spender, works and criticism.

    (Garland reference library of the humanities ; v. 43)
    Includes index.
    1. Spender, Stephen, 1909-   --Bibliography. I. Ti-
tle.
Z8830.5.K855   [PR6037.P47]   016.821'9'12   75-24090
ISBN 0-8240-9960-5

Printed in the United States of America

CONTENTS

PREFACE

The earliest reference in this bibliography is dated 1925 and the latest, September 1975. Attempt has been made to make the listings of Spender's works within the period of these fifty years fairly exhaustive without reference to their quality as literature. Even ephemeral writing, I believe, has a place in the comprehensive literary history of a writer like Stephen Spender whose creative interests have been as wide as life itself. He appears not too happy with some of his writings, but his sincerity even in casual compositions produced under the stress of financial need or otherwise is never doubted. By means of this outstanding quality he seems to have succeeded in elevating casual and ephemeral writings to the status of serious literature. Perhaps it is too early to evaluate this impressive career which fortunatly has not yet come to a close. Spender continues to write, and as he himself says: "It is not yet too late." I wish him health and peace of mind and hope that he may continue to produce beautiful works of art out of these dark and chaotic times.

I had to omit Spender's letters from inclusion here for want of space. But I may have overlooked some other items either because I was unaware of them or because they were unavailable at the time this bibliography was being compiled. The listings as they appear here may not be entirely free from errors. The reader is requested to point them out to me for correction in future impressions of this book.

I acknowledge with gratitude my indebtedness to all who have helped me in preparing this bibliography. First of all, I thank Mr. Spender for his introduction and the photograph which he has kindly provided for this book. I thank my wife who spent as much time as I did in the library and helped me at every step in the prosecution of my task. Even my sons and their wives deserve my special thanks for the many little ways in which they came to my assistance. The librarians and their staff at the Humanities Research Center, University of Texas at Austin, and the Bancroft Library (Special Collections), University of California at Berkeley placed their Spender material at my disposal. I thank them for their generosity and friendship. I am grateful to Utah State University Research Council for granting me financial assistance to work on this project.

Finally, I owe a debt of gratitude to Mr. Geoff Gillie and Ms. Lana Gregory for typesetting my manuscript with care and diligence and the editors of Garland Publishing, Inc., for their patience and understanding during the long time I have taken in completing my work.

H. B. Kulkarni
Department of English
Utah State University

Logan, Utah
August 9, 1976

INTRODUCTION

by

Stephen Spender

Receiving this excellently compiled Bibliography of my writings, from the assiduous Mr. Kulkarni, I am left wondering what of their works, and of works about their works, writers most enjoy reading. Would Shakespeare enjoy reading a Shakespeare Concordat? A few pages perhaps, for the laugh. James Joyce would probably be pleased to spend several millenia of eternity reading a Variorum Edition of *Finnegans Wake*—a work of which Cyril Connolly reports him to have remarked that the least he expected of the reader was that he should devote his whole life to reading it.

Before the war, a friend of mine going on a night journey from Paris to Madrid found himself alone in a railway compartment with Julien Benda. He noticed that all the philosopher had with him for the journey was a bulging briefcase. As soon as the train left Paris, Julien Benda opened this and, chuckling from time to time, contentedly read throughout the night from the dozens or so volumes it contained. They were all works by Julien Benda.

W.H. Auden used to read and reread his poems: but he did so with a view to correcting, rewriting and cutting poems or sections of poems out of the Auden Canon.

But it would take a writer with a very clear literary conscience to be happy reading his own bibliography. When I read mine, I feel "Would that there were but six pages containing but six items: fifty poems, a handful of stories, *World Within World, Trial of a Judge* (an unsatisfactory but genuinely felt work), a few essays, such as the one called The Making of a Poem, some translations. This already seems quite a list."

If one is a poet with a family to support, one does have to do things other than write poetry to make money. When my friends and I were young poets we used to discuss this problem of the "deuxieme metier," and we usually agreed that it would be better to do something "real," such as being a truck driver, than write prose simply to make money to support one's poetry. However most of us became teachers. So we reviewed books and wrote critical essays.

Looking back on my own life, I regret my critical writings more than I do the pure and ephemeral journalism. This it would be futile to regret since there was a certain inevitability about work written from dire need.

Usually one had to write an aritcle or review, in order to pay some debt. But serious critical works required much time and dictated what one read as well as what one wrote. They also absorbed creative energies which might certainly have gone into poems, stories, plays. Moreover, commitments to write criticism built up a backlog of obligations, some of which I have never fulfilled.

So, at the age of 67, glancing through my bibliography, to me it provides a moral lesson: *"I had better start writing seriously. Perhaps it is not too late."* Doing so will provide more material for bibliography, but only a very few pages: pages perhaps which will, I hope, make those that precede it seem irrelevant to the real work.

S.S.

A

WORKS BY

STEPHEN SPENDER

"Incense and wine avail me nothing. When I sit down and write a poem I am nearer God than when I kneel in a church blazing with light and smelling of incense. And when I stand in a green meadow and hear the murmuring of the bees, the song of birds and see the varied flowers, and the deep blue of the sky melting into the pale horizon, I can understand the wonder of God's creation, through my poetry the better."

—From Spender's Diary
(1925).

a)   *First edition:*

NINE EXPERIMENTS / by S.H.S. [Stephen Harold Spender] / [rule] / Being Poems Written at the Age of Eighteen / [rule] / 1928 / Printed at No. 10, Frognal, Hampstead, N.W. 3.

3 leaves, 7-21, 1 leaf, 2 end leaves. 20.5 x 13 cm. Green paper jacket printed in black on front: NINE EXPERIMENTS / By S.H.S. / Edges untrimmed.

Published by the poet himself; copies distributed free among friends and relatives. Thirty copies of each sheet of poems were printed and eighteen made up. Each copy was numbered by hand.

Dedication: To W.E.P.

Contents: Invocation—Appeal—Epistle (near the canal): 1. for G.C., 2. I Must Repress, 3. Boiling the Desperate Coffee, 4. Come, Let Us Praise the Gasworks—From Enshrinement of the Ideal. Part: IV—Gilles—Evening on the Lake (Dolce)—Ovation for Spring—Made Sober—The Farewell.

Notes: At the age of eighteen Spender was studying at University College School, Frognal, N.W. 3 (London). He printed these poems on a small hand-press he had bought. But soon he became dissatisfied with his venture and tore up all the sheets and the copies he could get. Copies Nos. 6 and 9 were examined. In copy No. 6, these words appear under his signature: "Here is this invaluable work."

b)   *Second impression (Facsimile edition):*   1964

NINE EXPERIMENTS / By S.H.S. / [rule] / Being Poems Written at the Age of / Eighteen / [rule] / 1928 / Printed at No. 10, Frognal, Hampstead, N.W. 3.

4 leaves, 5-21 [22] pp. 2 leaves. 22 x 13.5 cm. Hardboards in green cloth; on the front, title and author's initials stamped in black type.

Published by Elliston Poetry Foundation, University of Cincinnati, Cincinnati, Ohio. A photo-litho-graphic facsimile by the Earl D. Printing Co., Cincinnati, Ohio. Printed from copy No. 1 in possession of the George Elliston Collection of the twentieth century poetry. Edition limited to 500 copies.

Contents: The same as the first edition.

Notes: This edition carries a special foreword by Stephen Spender in which he states that his volume of *Nine Experiments* was printed earlier than the Auden *Poems.*

Although in a fit of dissatisfaction he tried to destroy all the copies of his book he could retrieve, he now realizes that he owes it his first recognition, which came from Mr. Untermeyer.

First edition:

TWENTY POEMS / BY STEPHEN SPENDER / BASIL BLACKWELL
BROAD STREET OXFORD [ENGLAND]

3 blank leaves, 1-23 [24] pp., 3 blank leaves. 18.5 x 13 cm. White paper
wrapper on paper jacket. On the front of the wrapper title and author's
name printed in black: TWENTY POEMS; The second line in smaller type:
BY STEPHEN SPENDER; at bottom in still smaller type: BASIL BLACK-
WELL BROAD STREET OXFORD; back of wrapper is blank; cover and
titlepage, same. Printed on hand-made woven paper. Edges untrimmed.

Published in 1930 by Basil Blackwell at Broad Street, Oxford, England.
Copyright reserved by the poet. "Of this edition one hundred and thirty
copies have been printed of which seventy-five are signed and numbered."
P. [24].

Contents: I. At the Edge of Being–The "Marston" Poems: II. Discovered
in Mid-Ocean–III. The Dust Made Flesh–IV. His Figure Passes–V. Not to
You I Sighed–VI. Marston, Dropping It in the Grate–VII. Acts Passed Beyond the Boundary of Mere Wishing–VIII. Hearing from Its Cage–IX. Lying Awake at Night–X. Constant April–XI. Saying "Good Morning" Becomes Painful–XII. The Port. Other Poems: XIII. Written Whilst Walking
Down the Rhine–'I' Can Never Be Great Man–XV. Different Living–XVI.
Always Between Hope and Fear–XVII. The Swan–XVIII. I Hear the Cries
of Evening–XIX. That Girl Who Laughed and Had Black Eyes–XX.
Beethoven's Death Mask.

Notes: The poems have been printed almost in the order of their composition between the Winter of 1928 and the Summer of 1930, except the first
poem.
	Although a second edition of this book was not published, most of
the poems included here appear in the next volume and in his *Collected
Poems.*

a)	*First edition:*

POEMS / BY / STEPHEN SPENDER / LONDON / FABER & FABER / 24
RUSSELL SQUARE

2 blank leaves, 2 leaves, 7-57 [58] pp., 4 blank leaves. 23 x 15 cm. Hard-
boards in black cloth with title, author, and publisher printed in gold
down the spine. Cream colored paper for dust jacket: on the front STEPH-
EN SPENDER in black large type, then underneath, the title: POEMS, in
red in slightly larger type; at bottom in smaller type, the publisher's name
in black; in the center, a commendatory note on the poet, continued on

the front flap. On the back of the wrapper is Faber's advertisement of its poetry publications. On the wrapper spine, title, author, and publisher's initials in red. The book is printed on cream-colored paper by R. Maclehose and Company Limited, at the University Press, Glasgow. All rights are reserved. Price: 5s. net.

Contents: He Will Watch the Hawk with an Indifferent Eye—Rolled over on Europe—Marston, Dropping It in the Grate, Broke His Pipe—Not to You I Sighed. No, Not a Word—Acts Passed Beyond the Boundary of Mere Wishing—I Hear the Cries of Evening—Different Living Is Not Living in Different Places—An 'I' Can Never Be a Great Man—Beethoven's Death Mask—Never Being, but Always at the Edge of Being—My Parents Kept Me from Children Who Were Rough—What I Expected—In 1929—The Port—Moving Through the Silent Crowd—Who Live under the Shadow of a War—How Strangely This Sun Reminds Me of My Love—Your Body Is Stars Whose Million Glitter here—The Prisoners—Without That Once Clear Aim, the Path of Flight—Oh Young Men, oh Young Comrades—I Think Continually of Those Who Were Truly Great—After They Have Tired—The Plyons—Those Fireballs, Those Ashes—From All These Events—Not Palaces, an Era's Crown.

Notes: The publisher describes Spender as "a young poet whose work has already created an unusual interest in a small circle." The fact that he comes from Oxford and belongs to the generation of Auden is noted. His lyrical qualities and technical excellence have been praised.

Some of these poems had been earlier published in magazines: *Criterion, Adelphi, 20th Century, New Statesman, Listener, Neue Schweizer Rundschau, Cahiers du Sud,* and especially in *New Signatures.*

The following poems have been taken from his earlier volume, *Twenty Poems,* some with minor changes: Never Being, but Always at the Edge of Being—No, Not to You I sighed. No, Not a Word—He Will Watch the Hawk with an Indifferent Eye—Marston, Dropping It in His Grate, Broke His Pipe—Acts Passed Beyond the Boundary of Mere Wishing—I Hear the Cries of Evening—An 'I' Can Never Be a Great Man—Beethoven's Death Mask—The Port—Written Whilst Walking Down the Rhine, with a new title 'In 1929'—Different Living Is Not Living in Different Places.

This volume is also noteworthy for some of what are known as "programme" poems.

b)   *Second (revised and enlarged) edition:*   1934

POEMS / BY / STEPHEN / SPENDER / LONDON / FABER & FABER / 24 RUSSELL SQUARE

1 blank leaf, 3 leaves, 7-69 [70] pp., 2 blank leaves. 23 x 15 cm. Hard boards with black cloth with title, author, and publisher printed in gold on the spine. Blue colored paper wrapper with STEPHEN SPENDER printed in black in large type and POEMS printed in red underneath in a slightly

larger type. At bottom is printed in red in two lines: "second edition, revised and enlarged" followed by publisher's name in black. At the center of the wrapper is the trade description of the edition and poet. On the front flap are selected extracts from reviews. The spine carries title, author's name, and publisher's initials in red. The book is printed on thick cream-colored paper; edges are untrimmed.

Published September 1934 at 5s. *On verso of title leaf*: "First published in MCMXXXIII..., second impression in May MCMXXXIII, second edition September MCMXXXIV; printed in Great Britain by R. Maclehose and Company Limited, The University Press Glasgow. All Rights Reserved."

Dedication inscribed to Christopher Isherwood.

Contents: He Will Watch the Hawk with an Indifferent Eye—Rolled Over on Europe: The Sharp Dew Frozen to Stars—Marston, Dropping It in the Grate, Broke His Pipe—Not to You I Sighed. No, Not a Word—Acts Passed Beyond the Boundary of Mere Wishing—At the End of Two Months' Holiday—Different Living Is Not Living in Different Places—An 'I' Can Never Be a Great Man—Beethoven's Death Mask—Never Being, but Always at the Edge of Being—My Parents Kept Me from Children Who Were Rough—After Success, Your Little Afternoon Success—Alas, When He Laughs It Is Not He—What I Expected—In 1929—The Port—Moving Through the Silent Crowd—Who Live under the Shadow of a War—Shapes of Death Haunt Life—How Strangely This Sun Reminds Me of My Love—Your Body Is Stars Whose Million Glitter Here—For T.A.R.H.—The Prisoners—Van der Lubbe—Without That Once Clear Aim, the Path of Flight—Passing Men are Sorry for Birds in Cages—Oh Young Men, oh Young Comrades—I Think Continually of Those Who Were Truly Great—After They Have Tired—Perhaps—The Funeral—The Express—The Landscape Near An Aerodrome—The Pylons—Abrupt and Charming Mover—In Railway Halls—Those Fireballs, Those Ashes—New Year—From All These Events—Not Palaces, an Era's Crown.

Notes: The first edition had thirty-three poems, whereas the new edition contains forty poems. After running through two impressions, the second edition provides a definitive edition. Spender removed two poems included in the first edition: "I Hear The Cries of Evening," "My Parents Quarrel in the Neighbour Room," and added nine more: At the End of Two Months' Holiday—After Success, Your Little Afternoon Success—Alas, When He Laughs It Is Not He—Shapes of Death Haunt Life—For T.A.R.H. —Van der Lubbe—Passing Men are Sorry for Birds in Cages—Perhaps—New Year.

The present volume contains "all that the author wishes to preserve" of his work up to September 1934.

The reviews are very enthusiastic and consider these poems to be "an unmistakable declaration of genius." The synthesis of traditional and revolutionary values and techniques in his poetry is repeatedly mentioned.

c)   *Second impression of the second edition:*   1935

The same as the second edition in all details.

Published in December 1935.

d)   *American edition:*   1934

POEMS by / STEPHEN / SPENDER / [gold ornamental design inset for title and author] Random House: New York, 1934

4 blank leaves, 2 leaves 5-68 pp., 4 blank leaves. 23.5 x 15 cm. Hard board with blue textured cloth with title inset in ornamental gold leaf design. Title, author, and publisher in gold letters on the spine. Printed on white paper; edges untrimmed.

Published by Random House, New York, 1934; price not given. Printed in U.S.A. (Walpole Printing Office, New Rochelle). Copy right (1934) by The Modern Library, Inc.

Dedicated to Christopher Isherwood.

Contents: The same as in the second edition with the addition of two poems: "I Hear the Cries of Evening" and "My Parents Quarrel in the Neighbour Room"; these two poems which appeared in the first edition of *Poems* had been omitted in its second English edition.

Notes: This is Spender's first book published in the United States.

A4   **PERHAPS**   [1933]

PERHAPS / BY / STEPHEN SPENDER / [Privately printed]

[8] pp. 16.5 x 11.5 cm. Wall-paper jacket designed in blue, white, and gold with 5.5 x 2.5 cm silver paper glued on it for title and author printed in black. Sewn with blue thread.

Privately printed. "Twenty-two copies of this edition were printed for the author." No price indicated, perhaps meant for free distribution.

Contents: The poem "Perhaps," with the opening line: "The explosion of a bomb."

Notes: The copy examined was a "trial copy on rice paper, intended to test the quality of the printing." This statement written in long hand is signed: "F.P." [Fredric Prokosch].

The poem later appears in *Poems* and also in its revised and enlarged edition.

POEM / [stars] / STEPHEN / SPENDER / [stars] / XMAS / 1934

1 blank leaf, [4] pp., one blank leaf. Delicate wall-paper flower design on cover. Title and author's name printed in black on 5 x 3 cm. pale gray paper and then glued to the front cover. Printed on white thin paper and sewn with black thread.

Colophon: "Twenty-two copies of this poem were printed for the author: five on Halle, numbered 1-5; five on Arnold, numbered I-V; five on Japan vellum, numbered a-e; five on green vellum, numbered A-E; and two on Imperial vellum, numbered x and xx."

The copy examined was "one of two special copies on Dresden."

First Edition:

VIENNA / by / Stephen / Spender / London / FABER AND FABER / 24 RUSSELL Square

3 blank leaves, 3 leaves, 9-43 [44] pp. 2 blank leaves. 22.5 x 14.5 cm. Hard-bound in red cloth; title and author's name in gold on the spine. Dust jacket in plain grey with VIENNA in large black type on top and at bottom, A poem by, in small type and author's name in two lines in black capital letters; in the center, a red cross. Back of the wrapper has a list of poetry publications by Faber.

Published by Faber and Faber Ltd., London, at 3s 6d. net in November 1934. *On the verso of the title leaf:* First published . . . Printed in Great Britain by R. Maclehose and company Limited, The University Press, Glasgow. All rights reserved. *On verso* of half-title; also by Stephen Spender: POEMS.

Dedication to Muriel.

Contents: The poem is divided into four parts: Arrival at the City—Parade of the Executive—The Death of Heroes—Analysis and Statement.

Notes: On page [11] there is a quotation from Wilfred Owen:

They will be swift with swiftness of the tigress,
None will break ranks, though nations trek from progress.

Proof copy was also examined. Printer's name stamped with date: 4 Oct. 1934.

AT / NIGHT / [STAR] / STEPHEN / SPENDER / [STAR] / Christmas / 1935 / [privately printed]

one blank leaf, [4] pp., one blank leaf. 16.5 x 11.5 cm. Printed on hand-made paper, cover of the same paper, wrappers in different colors of wall-paper design, label of different colors in size, 4.5 x 3 cm. pasted on front with title and author, printed in black. Sewn with colored thread.

A note on p. [4]: "Twenty-two copies of this poem were printed for the author: five on Arches, numbered 1-5; five on Ingres, numbered I-V; five on Fabriano, numbered a-e; five on Brussels parchment, numbered A-E; and two on red florentine, numbered x and xx."

Proof copy carries a hand-written note: Printed by the Cambridge University Press, Cambridge, England, in December, 1935," Signed F.P. [Fredric Prokosch]

Contents: The poem "At Night" beginning wih: "Rather death's monolith" ends with "Dumb, the decisions made for iron death."

Notes: The poem with the same title published in *Ruins and Visions* is different.

a)   *First edition:*

THE DESTRUCTIVE ELEMENT / A Study of Modern Writers / and Beliefs / By / STEPHEN SPENDER / [Device] / JONATHAN CAPE / THIRTY BEDFORD SQUARE / LONDON

1 blank leaf, 2 leaves, 5-284 pp., end leaf. 20.5 x 14 cm. Hard-boards in brown cloth with title printed on front in luminous green and on spine title, author, and publisher in the same color. Edges rough trimmed. Dust-jacket in pale brown with STEPHEN / THE / DESTRUCTIVE ELEMENT / [ornament] / a study of / modern writers / and beliefs / SPENDER / on front: author's name in double lines and large type. Printing down the spine in black. Front flap has a note on Spender and the book.

First published in 1935 by Jonathan Cape Ltd., 30 Bedford Square, London, and 91 Wellington Street West, Toronto at 8s 6d. net. Printed in Great Britain by J. and J. Gray, Edinburgh. Paper made by John Dickinson and Co. Ltd. and bound by A.W. Bain and Co. Ltd. On *verso* of half-title: Other works by the author. Note, p.8 Index, pp 281-84.

Dedicated to Rosamond and Wogan.

Contents: PART ONE: HENRY JAMES: Introduction—I. The School of Experience in the Early Novels of Henry James—II. Life as Art and Art as

Life—III. The Unconscious—IV. The Ivory Tower and the Sense of the Past. PART TWO: THREE INDIVIDUALISTS: V. A Bridge—VI. Yeats as a Realist—VII. T.S. Eliot in His Poetry—VIII. T.S. Eliot in His Criticism—IX. Notes on D.H. Lawrence. PART THREE: IN DEFENCE OF A POLITICAL SUBJECT: X. Henry James and the Contemporary Subject—XI. The Great Without—XII. Poetry and Pity—XIII. Writers and Manifestos—XIV. Upward, Kafka and Van Der Post—XV. The airman, politics, and psychoanalysis—Epilogue. Index.

Note: The book has been described as "the first critical work of a young writer whose poetry has already made him a representative figure of the youngest generation ... The whole is a striking expression of new points of view, and is certain to arouse lively discussion." (Trade blurb on front flap).

b)   *American edition:*   1936

THE DESTRUCTIVE ELEMENT / A Study of Modern Writers and Beliefs / By STEPHEN SPENDER / BOSTON AND NEW YORK / HOUGHTON MIFFLIN COMPANY / 1936

1 blank leaf, 2 leaves, 5-284 [6, 7, 9, 10] pp., 1 blank leaf. 20.5 x 13.5 cm. Hard-bound in cream colored cloth with decorative horizontal black lines between title, author and publisher on the spine. Edges rough trimmed.

Published by Houghton Mifflin Company, Boston and New York in 1936. Printed in Great Britain (on *verso* of title-leaf); on *verso* of half-title, information about other works by Spender. Index.

Dedication to Rosamond and Wogan.

Contents: Part One: Introduction—The School of Experience in the Early Novels of Henry James—Life as Art and Art as Life—The Unconscious—The Ivory Tower and The Sense of the Past. *Part Two*: Three Individualists: A Bridge—Yeats as a Realist—T.S. Eliot in His Poetry—T.S. Eliot in His Criticism—Notes on D.H. Lawrence. *Part Three*: In Defence of a Political Subject—The Great Without—Poetry and Pity—Writers and Manifestos—Upward, Kafka and Van der Post—The Airman, Politics and Psychoanalysis—Epilogue—Index.

Notes: "The idea for a book on James gradually resolved itself ... in my mind into that of a book about modern writers and beliefs, or unbeliefs; which turned again into a picture of writers grouped round the 'destructive element,' wondering whether or not to immerse themselves."

Parts of this book had appeared in The *Criterion, Hound and Horn, The London Mercury*, and *Left Review*.

c)   *Third edition:*

THE LIFE AND LETTERS SERIES NO. 87 / [thick rule] / STEPHEN SPENDER / THE DESTRUCTIVE ELEMENT / LONDON-JONATHAN

CAPE-TORONTO

1 blank leaf, 2 leaves, 5-284 pp., 2 blank leaves, 1-20: list of books in The Life and Letters Series, end leaf. Hard-boards in green cloth; front: wavy gold lines / THE DESTRUCTIVE / wavy lines / second line, long wavy gold lines with ELEMENT in the center; left hand bottom corner has gold lined ornament. Spine has gold printing of title. author separated by ornament and at bottom publisher's name. Dust-jacket in white paper, front and spine in green with title and author and ornament in white. Some recent additions to Life and Letters Series on the back of the wrapper, and on front flap a note on the book and the series.

First published in the Life and Letters Series in 1938 by Jonathan Cape Ltd., 30 Bedford Square, London and 91 Wellington Street West, Toronto. First published in 1935; second impression in August 1935; third impression in January 1937; reissued in this series in 1938. Printed in Great Britain by J. and J. Gray, Edinburgh and bound by A.W. Bain & Co. Ltd. Paper made by John Dickinson & Co. Ltd. Priced at 4s. 6d. net.

Contents: The same as previous impressions and other editions.

d)   Paperback edition: 1953

THE DESTRUCTIVE ELEMENT / A Study of Modern Writers / and Beliefs / By / STEPHEN SPENDER / 1953 / Philadelphia / ALBERT SAIFER

2 leaves, 5-284pp., 2 blank leaves. 17.5 x 10.5 cm. Soft-bound, front in yellow framed in black strips for boxes; top: Stephen Spender, middle: Title in three lines on the right and on the left, names of authors discussed: Henry James, T.S. Eliot, Kafka, Yeats, D.H. Lawrence, James Joyce. Back of the cover has a quotation selected from the introduction and publisher's name and address.

Published by Albert Saifer: Publisher, Box 7791, Philadelphia 1, Pa. Reprinted by permission of Jonathan Cape, London. Manufactured in U.S.A.

Contents: The same as the English edition.

A9   THE BURNING CACTUS   1936

a)   First edition:

THE BURNING CACTUS / by / STEPHEN SPENDER / [ornamental design of a burning cactus] / LONDON / FABER & FABER LIMITED / 24 Russell Square

2 blank leaves, 3 leaves, 9-265 pp. [266] p. blank, 2 blank leaves. 19.5 x 12.5 cm. Hard-bound in blue cloth, stamped in gold letters downward on spine with vignette in red and gold. Cream dust-wrapper printed in black with vignette of a burning cactus in red. On the front flap, the author's note on the five stories included in the volume with additional comments

by the publisher. At the end of the note,: by the same author: *Poems, Vienna*. On the back of the jacket a list of the Faber Library, uniform with this volume.

First published in April 1936 by Faber and Faber Ltd., at 7s. 6d. On *verso* of the title-leaf: First published . . . Printed in Great Britain by Latimer Trend and Co., Plymouth. All rights reserved. On *verso* of half-title: by the same author: *The Destructive Element, Vienna, Poems*.

Dedication to W.H. Auden and to T.A.R. Hyndman.

Contents:

The book contains 5 stories—The Dead Island—The Cousins—The Burning Cactus– Two Deaths–By the Lake.

Notes: "The Burning Cactus," published in *Best Short Stories* (1934), earlier in *Hound and Horn*, January-March 1934, New York; "By the Lake," in a second version, published in *New Stories* has been altered for this volume. "Two Deaths" appeared in *The London Mercury* under the name of "The Strange Death."

"The Burning Cactus" was written in 1933, and the other three stories: "The Dead Island," "Two Deaths," and "The cousins" written in 1935.

b)   *First American edition:*   1936

THE BURNING CACTUS / by / STEPHEN SPENDER / [ornamental device of a burning cactus] / Random House: New York

2 blank leaves, 3 leaves, 9-265 [266] pp., end papers. 19.5 x 12.5 cm. Hard-bound in red cloth stamped in gold on the spine. Cream-colored dust jacket, title, author, publisher stamped in black, with the vignette of a burning cactus in red. On the back of the wrapper, a list of recent Random House fiction.

Published by Random House, New York, at $2.00. On the *verso* of the title-leaf: 1936, Printed in Great Britain.

Dedication, contents etc. are the same as in the English edition.

Notes: The wrapper describes Spender as "foremost among the younger generation of writers in England." He has already won "critical and public acclaim" as a poet and essayist. These stories add to Spender's "prestige as a versatile talent."

c)   *Second edition:*   1955

THE BURNING CACTUS / by / STEPHEN SPENDER / FABER AND FABER LIMITED / 24 RUSSELL SQUARE / LONDON

One blank leaf, 3 leaves, 9-265 [266] pp., end paper. Same size as that of the first edition. Hard-bound in blue cloth with gold letters on the spine with the vignette of a burning cactus in red and gold. Plain yellow wrapper with printing in black. On *verso* of the title-leaf: First published in MCMXXXVI . . . Printed in Great Britain by Bradford and Dickens, London W.C.1. All rights reserved. Price: 12s.6d.

Dedication and contents the same as the first edition.

Notes: On the front flap of the wrapper, information about how well the book was received. Included are reviews by *TLS* and The *Observer*.

A10   FORWARD FROM LIBERALISM   1937

a)   *First edition:*

FORWARD FROM LIBERALISM / by / STEPHEN SPENDER / LONDON / VICTOR GOLLANCZ LTD / 1937

1 blank leaf, 3 leaves, [7] 8-196 pp., 1 blank leaf. 19 x 13 cm. Hardbound in black cloth, title author and publisher stamped in gold on the spine. Plain yellow paper-wrapper with bold black letters for title, underlined in purple. Author's name in smaller type. Purple lines for ornament all around the front.

Published by Victor Gollancz Limited, London in 1937 at 7s. 6d. Printed in Great Britain by The Camelot Press Ltd., London and Southampton. On *verso* of half-title, information about other books by the writer is given, classified under poetry, cirticism, stories, and poetic drama (The *Death* of *a Judge*, in preparation).

Contents: The book is divided into three parts: *Part One*: Journey Through Time: Goal of an Unpolitical Age—The Liberal Idealist—The Liberal Politician—International Socialism the Basis of Collective Security. *Part Two*: The Inner Journey: Questions and Answers: Statement. *Part Three*: The Means and the Ends: The Means—The Ends.

Notes: In this book Spender presents what he calls "a personal approach to communism," but with a more general application, specially for liberals like himself who believe in freedom for all. He describes his experiences that led him to a belief in communism. He develops his thesis into three journeys: one that explores the past for reasons for the failure of liberalism, the second through the present, and the third, an inner journey which examines his own doubts concerning communism and the efficacy of his approach to politics.

b)   *Left Book Club edition:*   *1937

FORWARD FROM LIBERALISM / By / STEPHEN SPENDER / LONDON / VICTOR GOLLANCZ LTD / 1937

1 blank leaf, 3 leaves, [7] 8-295 [296] pp., one blank leaf. 18.5 x 12.5 cm. Soft-bound in orange cloth with title, author, and publisher in black on

the spine and on front after title and author, at bottom:
LEFT BOOK CLUB EDITION / NOT FOR SALE TO THE PUBLIC.

Printed and published: the same as the hard-bound edition. Priced at 2s. 6d. for members of the Left Book Club. Perhaps this edition preceded the hard-bound edition.

Contents: The same as in the general edition.

c) *American edition:*   1937

FORWARD / from / LIBERALISM / STEPHEN SPENDER / [Publisher's device] / NEW YORK / RANDOM HOUSE

2 blank leaves, 3 leaves, vii-x, [1-2] 3-281 [282] pp., 2 blank leaves. Hardbound in tan cloth, decorative design on front with brown and black rectangles with title between STEPHEN and SPENDER; similar design on the spine for author, title, and publisher's trade-mark. Cream paper wrapper with title and author printed in black letters and description: A Random House Book. On the front flap information about the poet and publications by Random House. On the back flap description of The Modern Library.

Published by Random House New York, at $2.00 in 1937. Publisher holds copyright (1937). Printed in U.S.A. on *verso* of title-leaf, among other books by Stephen Spender is a poetic drama in preparation: *The Death of a Judge*. (Its title was later changed to *Trial of a Judge*).

Contents: The same as in the English editions, but the chapter headings have been decorated with black horizontal lines.

Notes: The front flap of the wrapper describes Spender as being "in the foremost ranks of English poets" with Auden and Day-Lewis. "In *Forward from Liberalism* Mr. Spender states his philosophy with the deep feeling and conviction that one would expect from a poet of great quality."

d) *French edition:*   [1945]

ÉCRITS POLITIQUES / STEPHEN SPENDER / AU DELA / DE LIBÉR-ALISME Forward form Liberalism TRADUIT DE L'ANGLAIS / PAR MARIE-JEANNE VIEL / [Publisher's emblem] / LES ÉDITIONS NAGEL, 47, RUE BLANCHE, PARIS (IXe) / [1945]

3 leaves, VII-XIII [XIV-XV], 1-182 [183] pp., [184] blank, 2 leaves. 22.5 x 14 cm. Paper-back in white, front decorated with red and black border lines: ÉCRITS POLITIQUES / STEPHEN SPENDER / in black type; title in red in two lines. TRADUIT DE L'ANGLAIS PAR MARIE-JEANNE VIEL in black; then down publisher's emblem in red and white decoration followed by NAGEL. Advertisement on back and front flap, a brief note on Spender and the book; back flap has advertisement about publications in the same series. Edges untrimmed.

Published by Les Éditions Nagel, Paris, in December 1945. Copyright by Les Éditions Nagel, 1945: "Tous droits réservés pour tous pays." Printed "sur les presses de l'Imprimerie Wallon, Vichy-Paris."

Introduction: An essay on Spender and his works pp. VII-XIII.

A11   TRIAL OF A JUDGE   1938

a)   *First edition:*

by Stephen Spender / TRIAL / OF A JUDGE / a tragedy / in five acts / Faber and Faber Limited / 24 Russell Square / London

1 blank leaf, 2 leaves, 5-115 [116] pp., 1 blank leaf. 22.5 x 14.5 cm. Hard-boards in red cloth with gold letters printed on the spine. Paper-wrapper ornamented in yellow and purple, title and author printed in purple letters, *Trial of a Judge* described as "A tragic statement in five acts."

Published by Faber and Faber in March 1938 at 5s. On *verso* of title-leaf: First published . . . Printed in Great Britain by R. Maclehose and Company Limited, The University Press, Glasgow. All rights reserved. On the *verso* of the half-title leaf, information about other books by Spender and on p.5: *Trial of a Judge* was written for the Group Theatre, and first produced by Rupert Doone with decor by John Piper. On front flap of the dust-jacket is a trade-blurb on the play and on the backflap, selections from reviews of *Poems, Vienna, & The Burning Cactus*. On the back is a list of poetry publications by Faber and Faber. At the head of title page: by Stephen Spender; then the title follows.

Dedication: A poem addressed to T.A.R.H. (T.A.R. Hyndman)

Contents: Each Act of this five-act play is titled—1. Illusion and Uncertainty, 2. The Small Scene, 3. The Large Scene, 4. The Trial, 5. The Three Cells.

Notes: Spender had been working on this play for three years. Although political on the surface, it has deeper levels of meaning where it becomes a struggle of conscience. It is a verse-drama and deserves comparison with contemporary dramatists responsible for revival of poetic drama in modern times. A play for the study as well as the stage.

    One of the author's autograph copy in the possession of Humanities Research center, The University of Texas at Austin carries this interesting note: To Rex from Stephen, March 18th 1938: "If it is a debate, it is an unfairly melodramatic one . . . if it is poetry . . . its clotted conceits clog the ear and its packed imagery dams the flow of the mind . . . if it is drama, ought it to be so wearisome?"—Lionel Hale. The intended title of the play before publication. *The Death of a Judge.*

b)   *Second edition:*   1955

by Stephen Spender / TRIAL / OF A JUDGE / A Tragic Statement in
Five Acts / Faber and Faber Limited / 24 Russell Square / London

The same as the first edition, but price changed from 5s to 12s 6d. On
verso of the title-leaf, First published in March MCMXXXVIII, by . . . second impression May MCMXXXVIII, Third impression May MCMXLIII,
Fourth impression June MCMXLV, Fifth impression November
MCMXLVIII, Sixth impression March MCMLV. Printed in Great Britain
by Bradford and Dickens, London W.C.1. All rights reserved.

On page 9, in addition to the list of characters in the play, there is a note:
—Producers are not expected to follow too closely the details of sound
(drums), lighting, and scene—shifting, which are written by the author
partly as suggestions, partly for the benefit of readers who have not seen
the play acted.

More books are added under the title: *also* by Stephen Spender, both on
the *verso* of half-title and the back-flap of the wrapper.

On the front flap of the wrapper, a selection from Nevill Coghill's review
in *The Spectator* states: "Mr. Spender will astonish even his admirers by
this extraordinary performance . . . this play certainly contains the most
moving poetry he has yet published." Rose Macaulay in the *News Chron-
icle* describes it as "a remarkable achievement" and calls its verse . . .
"closely packed, reasoned, often passionate, sometimes beautiful."

A12   FRATERNITY   1939

FRATERNITY / [Star] / Poem by / STEPHEN SPENDER / Traduction
de / LOUIS ARAGON / Engravings by / JOHN BUCKLAND-WRIGHT /
STANLEY WILLIAM HAYTER / JOSEF HECHT / DALLA HUSBAND /
WASSILY KANDINSKY / RODERICK MEAD / JOAN MIRO / DOLF
REISER / LUIS VARGAS / [Star] / MARCH 1939

No pagination, printed part: 12 pp., engravings: 9 plates. 22.5 x 16 cm.
Unbound book. Printed on hand-made art-paper; same paper for cover on
which the title: FARTERNITY and the names of collaborating artists are
printed in black. Edges are untrimmed.

Colophon: "The printing of the typography was completed the 1st March
1939 by Gonzalo More; the engravings printed by Atelier 17 and Henri
Hecht. The edition is limited to 101 copies printed on Montval hand-made
paper of which the No. 1 contains the states of the plates, the manuscript
of the poem and the original drawings; plus twelve copies lettered A to L
for the collaborators."

Contents: A poem called "The Fall of a City" and its French translation
by Louis Aragon; plus 9 engravings by collaborating artists.

Notes: Two boxed copies at HRC (copy No. 28 and 30) were examined. Box has label with a decorative sketch with words FRA / TER / NI / TY printed in separate places. Sketch on the label is signed Hayter 39.

A13   THE NEW REALISM   1939

THE NEW REALISM / *A DISCUSSION* / STEPHEN SPENDER / [device] / THE HOGARTH PRESS / 52 TAVISTOCK SQUARE / LONDON, W.C.1. / 1939

2 leaves, 5-24 pp. 18.5 x 12 cm. Gray paper cover with author: Stephen Spender, title: THE NEW REALISM, A DISCUSSION, and Hogarth Sixpenny Pamphlets, Number Two, printed in blue on front. Sewn with white thread.

First published by Hogarth Press in 1939. priced at 6d. Printed in Great Britain by the Garden City Press Ltd., at Lechworth, Hertfordshire. On the *recto* of the first leaf: HOGARTH SIXPENNY PAMPHLETS: NO. 2 / THE NEW REALISM / A DISCUSSION, in three separate lines. On *verso*, the following information appears: "This essay was originally delivered as a lecture to the Association of Writers for Intellectual Liberty . . ."

Dedicated to Margaret and Humphrey Spender.

Notes: Starting with a comment on the artist's conscience, the lecturer maintains that realism "involves not an imitation but an analysis of the society in which we are living "and that is bound to be revolutionary. He disagrees with Caudwell's judgement of many of the modern masters, for he takes a partisan view of literature. Literature should be evaluated in terms of the amount of life it portrays with truth and honesty.

A14   THE STILL CENTRE   1939

First edition:

THE STILL CENTRE / by / STEPHEN SPENDER / FABER & FABER LTD / 24 Russell Square / London

2 blank leaves, 3 leaves, 9-107 [108] pp., 3 blank leaves. 21.5 x 14.5 cm. Hard-bound in red cloth printed in gold on the spine. Cream-colored wrapper with title on front inscribed within a red circle with white circular lines surrounding the title and "poems by" printed on the edge of the circle and author's name at bottom outside the circle in black. On the front flap of the wrapper publisher's blurb and on the back flap trade notices of Spender's other works. On the back flap, a list of Faber poetry publications.

First published in May 1939 by Faber & Faber Ltd., at 6s. net. Printed in Great Britain by Western Printing Services Ltd., Bristol. All rights reserved.

Dedicated to Inez.

Contents: The book opens with a foreword and is divided into 4 parts. *Part One*: Polar Exploration—Easter Monday—Experience—Exiles from Their Land, History Their Domicile—The Past Values—An Elementary School Class Room in a Slum—The Uncreating Chaos. *Part Two*: Hoelderlin's Old Age—Hampstead Autumn—In the Street—The Room Above the Square—The Marginal Field—A Footnote (*From Marx's Chapter on The Working Day*)—Thoughts During an Air Raid. *Part Three*: View from a Train—The Midlands Express—The Indifferent One—Three Days—Two Armies—*Ultima Ratio Regum*—The Coward—A Stopwatch and an Ordnance Map—War Photograph—Sonnet—Fall of a City—At Castellon—The Bombed Happiness—Port Bou. *Part Four*: Darkness and Light—The Human Situation—The Separation—Two Kisses—The Little Coat—Variation on My Life: The First: Variations on My Life, The Second: Napoleon in 1814—The Mask—Houses at Edge of Railway Lines—To a Spanish Poet.

Notes: The publisher *predicts* that this volume "will prove to be one of the most interesting literary events of the year 1939. Although prolific in other areas, Spender seems to have been "parsimonious" in his production of poetry. A kind of unity may be experienced in these poems as their purpose, as Spender describes it, is to explore the 'human condition.' Spender's Foreword to the book throws much light upon the poems and the philosophy that has inspired them. The poems have been arranged in an order of development from political to personal concerns. "Poetry does not state truth, it states the conditions within which something felt is true." Although the pressure of external events and their violence is tremendous, Spender has consciously chosen to be more personal in his recent poems.

Many of the poems included here appeared in different "versions" in *The Listener, New Statesman and Nation, New Verse, New Writing, The London Mercury, Poetry, The Year's Poetry, The Faber Book of Modern Verse*, and *Poems of Spain*. Some of the poems written between 1934-39 are entirely rewritten and some eliminated.

A15   SELECTED POEMS   1940

a)   *First edition:*

SELECTED POEMS / by / STEPHEN SPENDER / FABER AND FABER / 24 Russell Square / London

1 blank leaf, 2 leaves, 5-76 pp., 2 blank end-leaves. 19.5 x 12.5 cm. Hardboard bound in yellow paper with title and author on front and title, author, and publisher on the spine printed in bright red. Green paper for dust-jacket with title and author in brown letters separated by a star. Brown decorative border.

First published by Faber and Faber in February 1940. Printed in Great Britain by Western Printing Services Ltd., Bristol. All rights reserved. On page 5, a select bibiography of Spender's Works with publication details is given. On front flap of the wrapper, title and author, and on back flap other works by Spender. The back of the wrapper has a list of books uniform with this volume in the new series called "Sesame Books" by Faber, meant to introduce works of contemporary poets.

Contents: I. From *Poems*: He Will Watch the Hawk with an Indifferent Eye—Rolled over on Europe: The Sharp Dew Frozen to Stars—Different Living Is Not Living in Different Places—Beethoven's Death Mask—What I expected—In 1929—Moving Through the Silent Crowd—Who Live Under the Shadow of a War—Van der Lubbe—Oh Young Men Oh Young Comrades—Perhaps—Not Palaces, an Era's Crown. II. From *The Still Centre*: Polar Exploration—Exiles from Their Land, History Their Domicile—The Uncreating Chaos—Hoelderlin's Old Age—The Room above the square— Thoughts During an Air Raid—Two armies—Ultima Ratio Regum—The Coward—A Stopwatch and an Ordnance Map—War Photograph—Fall of a City—Port Bou—Darkness and Light—The Human Situation—Variations on My Life—Napoleon in 1814—To a Spanish Poet. From *Trial of a Judge*: Act I: "So far from gentle, he is the danger"—Act II: "How strange it seems::—Act III: "When Petra slept with me"—Act IV: "I speak from the centre of a stage"—Act V: "Dear friend, your world is the antipodes."

Notes: This book was chosen for inclusion in the new series by Faber called "Sesame Books" designed to be an introduction to the work of contemporary poets. Other poets in the series: T.S. Eliot, W.H. Auden, Louis MacNeice etc.

b)   *American edition:*

Stephen Spender / Selected Poems / [on verso of half-title] : / Random House / [Publisher's emblem] / New York

One blank leaf, 3 leaves, vii-xi [xii], [1,2] 3-81 [82] pp., one leaf, end leaf. 22 x 13.5 cm. Hard boards in brown cloth, with gold printing on the spine. Cream-colored dust-jacket; on front: a circle of flower design, title in black type and author in brown.

Published by Random House, Inc., New York in ·1964. First printing. Manufactured in the United States of America by Kingsport Press, Inc., Kingsport, Tennessee. Design by Betty Anderson. All rights reserved under International and Pan-American Copyright conventions. Copyright, 1964, by Stephen Spender, Copyright 1942, 1946, 1947, 1949, 1955 by Stephen Spender. Introduction, p. vii (Jan 5, 1964). Price: $4.00.

Dedicated to Natasha, Matthew and Lizzie.

Contents: Introduction. PART ONE. FIRST POEMS: Icarus—Not to You —Waiting—Trigorin—Beethoven's Death Mask—Rough—What I expected— Souvenir de Londres—In 1929—The Shadow of a War—Remembering—The

Express—The Truly Great—Perhaps—Van der Lubbe—The Landscape Near an Aerodrome—The Pylons—Not Palaces. PART TWO. 1934-1939: Polar Exploration—An Elementary School Classroom in a Slum—A footnote (From Marx's chapter, *The Working Day*)—The Room Above the Square—Thoughts During an Air Raid—Ultima Ratio Regum—A Stopwatch and an Ordnance Map. PART THREE. 1939-1947: The Flask of Tears—Song—The Double Shame—The War God—Air Raid Across the Bay at Plymouth—Human Drama—*From* Explorations—Daybreak—Seascape—The Barn. PART FOUR. LATER POEMS: The Trance—Word—In Attica—To My Daughter—Nocturne—Subject: Object: Sentence—Earth-Treading Stars That Make Dark Heaven Light—One More New Botched Beginning.

Notes: Some of the poems published earlier appear here with alterations. Spender has added three poems which have not previously been published in volume form: 1. Subject: Object: Sentence; 2. Earth-Treading Stars That Make Dark Heaven Light; 3. One More New Botched Beginning.

Spender's note on *Selected Poems:* "In making a *Collected Poems* one feels—I don't know quite why—under an obligation to put in nearly everything. Selecting poems is a happier situation. One can cut away all the things about which one is most doubtful."

c)   *Second American edition:*   1964
      Also available in paperback.

d)   *Second English edition:*   1965

These two editions have slightly different introductions and include three previously uncollected poems.

A16   THE BACKWARD SON   1940

THE / BACKWARD SON / A NOVEL by / STEPHEN SPENDER / THE HOGARTH PRESS / 37 MECKLENBURGH SQUARE, / LONDON, W.C.1 / 1940

1 blank leaf, 5 leaves, 11-266 pp., end-papers. 18.5 x 12.5 cm. Hard-boards in yellow cloth printed in red on the spine. Brown dust-jacket designed in mellon leaves and fruit by Robert Buhler.

First published by The Hogarth Press in 1940 at 7s. 6d. Made and printed in Great Britain by The Garden City Press Limited at Letchworth, Hertfordshire.

Dedicated to Peter Watson.

Notes: This is Spender's first novel. It deals with the unique experiences of his childhood which incidentally provide "an imaginative history of his generation."

a)   *First edition:*

RUINS AND VISIONS / Poems by / STEPHEN SPENDER / FABER & FABER LIMITED / 24 Russell Square / London / [1942]

2 blank leaves, 2 leaves, 7-84 pp., one blank leaf. 22 x 14.5 cm. Hardbound in blue cloth, printed in gold on the spine; dust-cover in orange with title and author's name printed in purple on the front and on the spine with the addition of the publisher's initials. On the front flap title and author's name, on the back flap a list of sesame Books and selections from reviews of Spender's *The Burning Cactus*. The back of the wrapper carries Faber's list of poetry publications.

First published in 1942 by Faber and Faber at 6s. net. Printed in Great Britain by Western Printing Services Ltd., Bristol. All rights reserved. Proof copy of this book is dated, however, *November 1941*.

Contents: The book is divided into 4 parts. *Part One: A Separation:* Song —A Separation—The Vase of Tears—The Double Shame—The Journey—A Hall of Mirrors—No Orpheus, No Eurydice—A Wild Race. *Part Two: Ironies of War:* The War God—To Poets and Airmen—The Air Raid Across the Bay—Winter and Summer—In Memorium—June 1940. *Part Three: Deaths:* The Ambitious Son—*Tod Und das Maedchen*—The Drowned— Wings of the Dove—The Fates. *Part Four: Visions:* At Night—The Barn—In a Garden—A Childhood—Into Life—The Coast Dusk—Daybreak—To Natasha.

b)   *American edition:*   [1942]

Ruins and Visions / POEMS 1934-1942 / by *Stephen Spender* / [Publisher's emblem] / RANDOM HOUSE. NEW YORK

2 blank leaves, 2 leaves, 5-138 pp., 3 blank leaves. 21 x 14 cm. Hardboards in red cloth, printed in white letters on front at bottom: Ruins and Visions / POEMS 1934-1942 / and publisher's emblem on the right hand side. On the spine downwards in white; Ruins and Visions. Poems 1934-1942. Stephen Spender and publisher's emblem. Dust-jacket in red and white; front: Stephen Spender in white on red, title in red within a white strip. Downward: Poems 1934-1942 and a note on Spender that continues on front flap. At bottom: Random House with the trade emblem. On the spine, author's name, title and publisher. On the back of the jacket is a list of Random House Poetry. Front and back flap has selections from Reviews of Spender's works by Macleish, Peter Monro Jack, J.G. Fletcher and others.

Published by Random House in 1942. First printing. Copyright, 1942, by Stephen Spender. Manufactured in the United States of America by American Book-Stratford Press, Inc., New York, N.Y.

Dedication: To Inez.

Contents: Combines two in one volume:
  Ruins and Visions and *The Still Centre*.

Foreword—the same as for the English edition of *The Still Centre*, with one or two minor verbal alterations. Same poems, except three poems from Part Three have been put into Part Two. *Ruins and Visions* has the same poems as the English edition.

Notes: Interesting comment by Archibald Macleish: "As a spectator who loves poetry I listen only for that clean sharp stroke which is heard when the axe goes into the living wood. In Mr Spender's poems at their best I hear it."

c)   *Second edition:*   1947

The same as the first edition, except that it is hard-bound in turquoise cloth and the dust-jacket has pale blue paper.

On *verso* of the title leaf: First published in 1942; second impression September 1942; and third impression February 1947.

A list of Spender's books is given on the back flap of the wrapper.

A18   LIFE AND THE POET   1942

First edition:

LIFE AND THE POET / [by] / STEPHEN SPENDER / SEARCHLIGHT / [emblem] / BOOKS / LONDON / SECKER & WARBURG / 1942

2 leaves, [5] 6-127 [128] pp., 18 x 11 cm. Soft-paper cover in white printed in blue; on front, title and author with publisher's searchlight emblem in the center. On the spine in blue author, title, and publisher's initials "S.B." and No. 18 of the book in the series. Paper wrapper in white and blue with title and author printed in black on the upper white half; the lower half is blue with a large searchlight emblem and underneath on a white strip words: "SEARCHLIGHT BOOKS" printed in black. On the spine, title, author the price 2s. net and publishers' initials and the No. 18 printed in black. On front flap a brief note on Spender with the price 2s. net and at bottom: Jacket design by Zec. Back flap has a list of books by Spender and the back of the wrapper, a list of Searchlight Books.

First published in March 1942 by Martin Secker & Warburg Ltd., 22 Essex Street, London, W.C.1. Made and printed in Great Britain by Morrison and Gibb Ltd., London and Edinburgh, priced at 2s. net. This is number 18 of Searchlight Books; of them The Times Educational Supplement says (printed on *verso* of half-title): "One central conviction these writers hold: They believe in the England of the English people. For that reason, if for no other, these books are an important contribution to the study of current affairs."

Dedicated to: "The Young Writers in the Armed Forces, Civil Defence and the Pacifist Organisations of Democracy: in the hope that this tribute may encourage them to write."

Contents: I. The Position of the Poet—II. The Technique of Living—III. The Criticism of Life—IV. Voyagers to the Moon—V. Poets Must Be Truthful—VI. The Furthest Future.

Notes: The front flap of the wrapper notes that Spender belongs to the group of Oxford poets who became well-known in the early thirties, at a time of economic crisis and unemployment. The note adds: "During the present war there are signs of the emergence of a younger generation of writers in the armed forces, or working on the land, or in civil defence and in the factories. This book is written for them by a slightly older writer. It is an attempt to state the importance of poetic values in the present time, and to defend the status of the poet in society.

At present Spender is himself a member of the National Fire Service. As a fireman, he attempts to carry on his work as poet and critic."

A19   SPIRITUAL EXERCISES   1943

STEPHEN SPENDER / [ornamental rule] / SPIRITUAL EXERCISES / (To Cecil Day Lewis) / LONDON / *Privately Printed* /1943

1 leaf, 3-7 [8] pp., end leaf. 19 x 14.5 cm. Soft-bound in white art-paper, the same used for contents, wrapped in paper of wall-paper design, with white thin paper 6.5 x 9 cm. glued on front, title and author written by hand.

Colophon: "125 copies of these poems printed at the Curwen Press Plaistow as a greeting for Christmas and the New Year 1944 for their friends from Stephen and Natasha Spender." Each copy is numbered by hand.

Contents: We Fly Through a Night of Stars—I. Beneath Our Nakedness, We Are Naked Still—II. You Were Born, Must Die; Were Loved, Must Love. III. Since We Are What We Are, What Shall We Be—IV. That Which Divides, Joins Again in Belief—V. The Immortal Spirit Is That Single Ghost —VI. I Am That Witness Through Whom the Whole—VII. Outside, the Eternal Star—Tall Mountains Gleam—VIII. Transparent Light.

Notes: Appears as "Part Three: Spiritual Explorations" in *Poems of Dedication* (1947), except VII. "Transparent Light" It is replaced by a new poem "Light," which seems to be the final version of the same poem. In Spender's work book there are about 20 versions of this poem, whose rough draft begins with "shadowless light."

First edition:

CITIZENS / IN WAR — AND AFTER / STEPHEN SPENDER / [rule] / FOREWORD BY / HERBERT MORRISON / M.P.P.C. / Home Secretary / Minister of Home Security / [rule] / 48 color PHOTOGRAPHS BY / JOHN HINDE / [Publisher's emblem] / GEORGE G. HARRAP & CO. LTD / LONDON TORONTO BOMBAY SYDNEY / [1945]

1 blank leaf, 2 leaves, 5-112 pp., 1 blank end leaf. 23 x 16.5 cm. Hardbound in grey cloth with author, title and publisher downward on the spine. Dust-jacket in thick colored paper; on front the title and author in white with a colored photograph of a fireman filling the whole page and sideways in white: "Colour photographs by John Hinde." On the spine the same with the addition of: Foreward by the Rt. Hon. Herbert Morrison, M.P. and the publisher. On the back of the wrapper a list of books under the series entitled "America and Britain." On the front and back flap, a note on the author and the book.

First published in 1945 by George G. Harrap and Co., Ltd., 182 High Holborn, London, W.C.1. Copyright. All rights reserved. This book is produced in complete conformity with the authorized economy standards. Printed in Great Britain by W.S. Cowell Ltd., Ipswich and London. Designed and produced by Adprint Limited, London. Priced at 15s, net.

Contents: Foreword by H. Morrison—Preface by Spender and Hinde—A poem: Almond Blossom in War-Time (by Spender)—I. War and Peace—II. The Problem of Civil Defence—III. The Ranker in Civil Defence—IV. The Individual Civil Defence Worker—V. During the Blitz—VI. After the Blitz—VII. People in Civil Defence—VIII. Portrait: Doctor—Epilogue: Epilogue to a Human Drama (A Poem).

Color Plates: Development and Training: I. A Member of the Warden's Service Fitting a Gas-Mask—II. A Blood Donor at a Civil Defence First-Aid Station III. An Evacuee Arriving at Her New Temporary Home with the Billeting Officer—IV. W.V.S. Worker Demonstrating How to Build an Emergency Oven—V. Auxiliary Fire—Service Men Hauling the Trailer-Pump—VI. Welsh Firemen in a Strategic Position above the Pit-Head and Railway—VII. The Building Squad of the N.F.S.—VIII. River Firemen Knitting Bags —IX. Firemen in Training at a Water Jump—X. Heavy Rescue Workers Going into Training—XI. An Ambulance with Wardens Helping in an Emergency—XII. A First-Aid Party Training in the Furnace Room of an Iron Foundry. *Civil Defense in Action:* XIII. A Member of The Royal Observer Corps on the Cliffs of England—XIV. The Control Room of a Civil Defence Centre—XV. A Fire Engine with a Turn-Table Ladder-Pump—XVI. A Fire-Fighting—XVII. A Medical Officer Directing the Medical Services of a London Borough—XVIII. Heavy Rescue Workers Saving a Victim—XIX. A Shelter Concert in the Crypt of a Church—XX. A family Emerging from the Anderson Shelter—XXI. Fighting Incendiary Bombs in the Street—XXII. Inquiring of the Incident Officer about Relatives—XXIII. A Victim of an Air Attack—XXIV. Troops cooperating with Civil Defence Wardens in Salvage Work—XXV. A Father and Daughter Saving Their Belongings—XXVI. The Life and Soul of W.V.S. of Her District—XXVII. A W.V.S. Worker Selecting a Frock for a Little Girl—XXVIII. A Hostel for the Bombed-out in Scotland—*Portraits*: XXIV. A Warden in the East End—XXX. A Fire Guard—XXXI. An Ambulance Attendant—XXXII. A Police-man- XXXIII. A Heavy Rescue Man—XXXIV. A Canadian Fireman—Off Duty—XXXV. A Professional Fireman—XXXVI. A Telephonist of the N.F.S. *Welfare*: XXXVIII. A Mobile Canteen at The Docks—XXXIV. Res-cue Workers Playing Basket-Ball at a Depot—XL. Gardening at a Depot—XLI. Tea at a Mobile Unit of the Fire Service—XLII. Paddles for Rescue Dinghies Made by River Fire Service Men—XLIII. Discussion Circle at a Fire Station—XLIV. A Civil Defence Artists' Exhibition—XLV. Making Toys at a Fire Station—XLVI. A Tactical Table Made by Men of the Aux-iliary Fire Service—XLVII. Evacuees in the Grounds of Their Hostel—XLVIII. A Game of Darts: Civil Defence Workers' Recreation.

Notes: This is an account of the 'great experiment in the direct applica-tion of citizenship to the tasks of war by Spender as "he himself has ex-perienced and seen it." "The thesis of the text is revealed in the photo-graphs. It is that Civil Defence is an awakening of the consciousness of civilians all over Britain, before and during the Second World War, which will affect the life of our towns and countryside in time of peace."

A21   EUROPEAN WITNESS   1946

a)   *First edition:*

EUROPEAN / WITNESS / BY / STEPHEN SPENDER / [rule] / [Pub-lisher's emblem] / HAMISH HAMILTON LTD / LONDON / [1946]

1 blank leaf, 2 leaves, [5] 6-241 pp., 19 x 12.5 cm. Hard-bound in greenish grey cloth, printed in gold on the spine. Dust-jacket in cream colored paper, front decorated in red, framed in black lines and flowery design, with title and author in cream-colored print and publisher in black. The wrapper spine is red, title and publisher's emblem in cream and author in black. The back of the wrapper has a list of Hamilton's publications. Trade-blurb on front flap and price.

First published•by Hamish Hamilton in 1946, at 10s. 6d. net. Printed in Great Britain by Morrison and Gibb Ltd., London and Edinburgh. Intro-duction, p.6.

Dedication: To José

Contents: RHINELAND JOURNEY (July and August 1945): I. Bad Oeynhausen—II. A Journey—III. Cologne—IV. Conversations—V. Bonn—VI. Polish Displaced persons—VII. A Student—VIII. Interpreter—IX. Concentration Camp Inmate—X. A Day in Cologne—XI. Nausea—XII. Lieutenant Arran—XIII. Rudi Bach—XIV. Displaced persons' Concert—XV. Dinner Party. FRENCH INTERLUDE (May, August and October 1945)—JOURNEYS THROUGH THE BRITISH ZONE (September and October 1945): I. An Officer's Mess—II. The Film Unit—III. My Driver—IV. Libraries—V. Bonn—VI. Jung's Interview—VII. Joachim Bender—VIII. Wupertal—IX. Goebbels- X. Newspapers—XI. Fire and Blood—XII. The Student Aulach Again—XIII. Ernst Junger—XIV. Hamburg—XV. Berlin.

Notes: This book, says Spender, is "a Travel Book of a conventional kind," written from journals made on journeys through post-war Germany and France in 1945. Spender was sent on a mission to find out what had survived of German intellectual and imaginative life after war. He brings to his meditations on post-war Europe a poet's sympathies and a critic's understanding and judgement.

Spender says that the names of the people he had met have been altered and incidents and characters invented. "It is the general picture which counts . . ."

b)　*First American Edition:*　　　　　　　　　　　　　　1946

Stephen Spender / Eurpean Witness / Reynal & Hitchcock, New York

1 blank leaf, 3 leaves, VII—[X], 1-246 pp., end leaf. Hard-boards in brown cloth with printing down the front and spine in black.

Published by Reynal & Hitchcock of New York. Printed in U.S.A. by the Cornwall Press, Inc., Cornwall, N.Y. Priced at $2.50. Copyright 1946 by Stephen Spender.

Dedication and *Contents* the same as the English edition.

The book ends with the date: 26th March 1946.

c)　*French edition:*　　　　　　　　　　　　　　　　1947

STEPHEN SPENDER / UN TÉMOIN / DE L'EUROPE / traduit de L'anglais par / MARCELLE SIBON / [Device] / FONTAINE / PARIS

1 blank leaf, 4 leaves, 9-242 [243-46] pp. 19 x 11.5 cm. Paperback with author, title, translator, and publisher on front; and title and publisher on the spine. Back cover carries other titles in "Editions de la revue Fontaine" of collections of English literature.

Published in Paris: "Editions de la revue Fontaine," Printed: "Impremeries Parisiennes Reunies, 10, Faubourg Montmartre, 10, on the 15th of January 1947. All rights of reproduction in French language reserved.

Note: Translated from the edition of *European Witness*, published by Hamish Hamilton, London.

First edition:

POETRY SINCE 1939 / By / STEPHEN SPENDER / *ILLUSTRATED* / Published for / The British Council / by LONGMANS GREEN & CO. / LONDON, NEW YORK, TORONTO /

2 leaves, V-VII [VIII] 9-70 pp., 1 leaf. 20.5 x 14 cm. Soft-cover in gray with a colored picture of "lyre-birds" by Moore on front, title and author printed in white below. Title, author, and price in black on the spine. On the back of the cover, a list of books of the British Council, uniform with this volume in the series: The Arts in Britain.

First published in 1946 by Longmans Green and Co. Ltd., 6 & 7 Clifford Street, London, W.1, for the British Council at 2s. net. Printed in Great Britain by R. & R. Clark, Limited, Edinburgh. This booklet is produced in complete conformity with the authorised economy standards. On p. [8]: "The opinions expressed in this book are the author's and not necessarily those of the British Council." Illustrated. Frontispiece is an illustration by John Coxon to "Poem" by W.H. Auden.

Select Bibliography on the works of the poets included here, compiled by W.M., pp. 65-70.

Dedication to HENRI HELL, souvenir of Paris in June 1945.

Contents: I. Introductory—II. Conditions in which poets have worked—III. Conditions of British poets in war compared with those of poets in Europe—IV. T.S. Eliot's "Four Quartets"—V. Miss Edith Sitwell—VI. Other Poets of an Elder Generation—VII. Robert Graves—VIII. Edwin Muir—IX. W.H. Auden and the Poets of the 'Thirties'—X. Day Lewis, MacNeice, and Spender—XI. William Empson and Others—XII. Dylan Thomas, George Barker, David Gascoyne—XIII. Poets who have become known since 1939—XIV. Regionalism—XV. Summing up.

Illustrated with pictures of poets in black and white facing pages 16, 17, 20, 21, 28, 29, 32, 33, 48, 49, 64, 65.

Notes: Copy examined was a presentation copy autographed by Stephen [Spender] who has crossed the publisher's commemdatory note on him and added these words: "For Edith, with apologies for the inadequacy and impermanence of my critical remarks and with love, Stephen."

The question asked is: "What has Britain produced during the five years of war?" Spender answers this question with regard to poetry. The editor wishes to remind the readers that Spender "is one of the most distinguished of our younger poets in England today."

a)   *First edition:*

POEMS / OF DEDICATION / by / Stephen Spender / Faber and Faber Limited / 24 Russell Square / London [1947]

one blank leaf, 2 leaves, 5-58 [7-10, 24-26, 37-38, 48-50] pp., 2 blank end-leaves 22.5 x 14.5 cm. Hard-bound in slate-colored cloth, printed in silver on the spine. Pale-green paper wrapper printed in red on front and spine with decorations. Back of the wrapper has a list of Faber poetry publications. On front flap, trade-blurb and on back other books by Spender. Edges untrimmed.

First published in 1947 by Faber and Faber at 6s. net. Printed in Great Britain by R. Maclehose and Company Limited at The University Press Glasgow. All rights reserved. Note, p. 58.

Dedication: "These poems are inscribed to the memory of Margaret Spender who died on Christmas day, 1945."

Contents: Part One: Elegy for Margaret: 'Darling of Our Hearts, Drowning' —'Dearest and Nearest Brother'—'From a Tree Choked by Ivy, Rotted'— 'Poor Girl, Inhabitant of a Strange Land'—'Already You are Beginning to Become'—'The Final Act of Love. *Part Two*: Love, Brith, and Absence: Summer—Four Eyes—The Dream—Man and Woman—The Trance—Absence —Lost. *Part Three*: Spiritual Explorations: 'We Fly Through a Night of Stars'—'You Were Born; Must Die; Were Loved; Must Love'—'Since We Are What We Are, What Shall We Be'—'We Divided, Join Again in Belief'—'The Immortal Spirit Is That Single Ghost'—'I Am That Witness Through Whom the Whole'—'Outside, The Eternal Star-Tall Mountains Gleam'—'Light.' *Part Four*: Seascape and Landscape: Midsummer—Seascape—Meeting.

Notes: On front flap of the wrapper: "This is Mr. Spender's first volume of poems for five years. It represents only a part of his work during that time, but a part which forms a unity by itself and which must therefore appear as a volume by itself."

Note on p. 58: 1. Versions of poems III & IV in *Elegy for Margaret* appeared in *Ruins and Visions*. 2. A sketch of *Spiritual Explorations* (then called *Spiritual Exercises* was privately printed at Christmas 1944. It was also published in *New Writing, Daylight*, and *The Neue Schweizer Rundschau*, where it appeared together with a translation by Professor E.R. Curtius.

Earlier versions of some of these poems appeared in *New Writing, New Writing & Daylight, Penguin New Writing*.

Part Two is dedicated to Natasha, *Part Three*, To Cecil Day Lewis, and The Poem 'Midsummer' to Edith Sitwell and the poem 'Meeting' has a headnote, which is a quotation from Apollinaire.

b)   *Second impression:*   1947

Second impression was printed in February 1947. The same as the first
edition except the description on the front flap of the wrapper: The first
group of poems dedicated to Margaret Spender commemorate death, the
second deals with themes of birth, love and separation, whereas the third is
"the most sustained attempt by the author to integrate a view of the iso-
lated situation of the individual, with an heroic idea of the re-creation of
modern man's conception of life." The fourth group goes beyond the
personal and achieves a wider detachment.

A selection from a review follows: "Spender has achieved maturity and a
poetry more hard and brilliant, its images more concentrated and exact,
than any of his previous work . . . ."

c)   *American edition:*   1947

Poems / of / Dedication / by / STEPHEN SPENDER / [Publisher's em-
blem] / RANDOM HOUSE: NEW YORK / [Framed in decorative design]

2 blank leaves, 5 leaves, 11-60 pp., 2 blank leaves. 24.5 x 15 cm. Hard-
bound with leather spine, and wall-paper cover. Printing on the spine in
gold. Blue paper wrapper, center of the front designed in cream-color with
title, author, and publisher printed in black with brown trade-emblem and
a frame of flower-design. Printed on the spine in cream-color. Jacket
design by Meyer Wagman. Trade-blurb on front-flap and selections from
reviews on the back-flap. A list of Random House poetry publications on
the back of the wrapper. Pages in the book are decorated with flower design at the top. Trimmed edges.

Published by Random House in 1947. Manufactured and printed in the
United States of America. Copy-right, 1947, by Stephen Spender.

Contents: The same as in the British edition, including note on p. 58.

Notes: These poems have been described as "a spiritual intellectual and
lyrical advance over his two distinguished books of verse. "In substance, in
location, in gravity of feeling, they are among the finest poetic utterances
of our day."

A24   RETURNING TO VIENNA 1947   1947

RETURNING TO VIENNA 1947 / NINE SKETCHES BY STEPHEN
SPENDER / THE BANYAN PRESS / [PAULET, VERMONT]

1 blank leaf, 2 leaves, [5-10] pp., 20 p. blank, 22 p. blank, end leaf. 21
x 15.5 cm. Soft-bound in English hand-made paper, used both for cover
and contents. Wrapper in wall-paper design, with title printed on white
label 10.5 x 4 cm glued on front, double rule on top and bottom.

Printed and published in the United States by The Banyan Press in December 1947. Copyright, 1947 by The Banyan Press. *Colophon*: This poem was set by hand in Bodoni faces and printed on English handmade paper at The Banyan Press in December 1947. The edition is limited to one hundred and fifty copies for friends of the author and three hundred and fifty for sale.

Dedication to William Jay Smith.

Notes: The copy examined was copy No. 55 presented to Miss Rose Macaulay signed on Christmas Day 1947 with the inscription: To Rose / with Love / from / Stephen and Natasha, Stratford Road, Scarsdale, New York.

A25   THE EDGE OF BEING   1949

a)   *First edition* (1949):

2 blank leaves, 3 leaves, 9-57 [58] pp., 4 blank end-leaves. 22.5 x 14 cm. Hard-bound in chocolate cloth. Dust-jacket of yellow paper with bold black letters for author and title on front and spine. The front is decorated with red line around the title. The back of the wrapper has a list of Faber poetry publications. Back flap, works by Spender.

Published by Faber and Faber in 1949 at 7s. 6d. Printed in Great Britain by R. Maclehose and Company Limited, at The University Press Glasgow. All rights reserved.

Dedication to Natasha.

Contents: O Omega, Invocation—O Night, O Trembling Night—On the Third Day—Awakening—Faust's Song—Judas Iscariot—Ice—Returning to Vienna 1947—Weep, Girl, Weep—The Angel—Epilogue to a Human Drama —Rejoice in the Abyss—A Man-Made World—The Conscript—Almond Tree in a Bombed City—Responsibility: The Pilots Who Destroyed Germany, Spring 1945—Tom's A-Cold—Word—Empty House—Madonna—Epithalamion—Memento—Speaking to the Dead in the Language of the Dead—We Cannot Hold onto the World—Time in Our Time. Acknowledgements and Note, p. 57. (signed S.S.).

Notes: "Returning to Vienna 1947" was published earlier as a separate volume in a limited edition by The Banyan Press, Paulet, Vermont. Some of the poems included here were previously published in his prose-work *Citizens in War and After*. An earlier version of "Speaking to the Dead . . ." was read at the Harvard *Phi Beta Kappa* celebrations in June 1948, and "Tom's A-Cold" at Columbia University, *Phi Beta Kappa* celebrations.

Previously published poems which appear here have been considerably altered.

Publisher's note says that this selection "will fully support his reputation and satisfy his admirers."

b)   *American edition:*

THE / EDGE / OF / BEING / POEMS by / STEPHEN SPENDER / Random House / New York / [decorative rule down the left-hand side of the page] .

2 blank leaves, 4 leaves, 9-57 [58 blank] pp., 3 end leaves. 24 x 15.5 cm. Hard-bound in gray paper with black spine, printed in gold. Dust-jacket in gray and gold paper, printing in black. Jacket designed by Meyer Wagman. Back of the wrapper Random House Poetry publications. Front-flap carries trade-blurb. Inside pages decorated with a flowing line down the page on the left. Edges trimmed.

Published in New York by Random House and simultaneously in Toronto, Canada, by Random House of Canada Limited. Manufactured in the United States of America; designed by Meyer Wagman. Copyright, 1949, by Stephen Spender; all rights reserved under International and Pan-American Copyright Conventions. Price. $2.50.

Contents, acknowledgements and *note*: the same as in the British edition.

Notes: Publisher's note describes Spender as "one of three leading living poets of England," *The Edge of Being* is marked by "greater maturity" than his previous publications. "A lyrical advance over his three earlier books of verse," this volume is "a profession of faith, a re-appraisal of the influences and impressions of youth and the record of a mind's coming of age."

A26   WORLD WITHIN WORLD   1951

a)   *First edition:*

WORLD / WITHIN / WORLD / THE AUTOBIOGRAPHY OF / STEPHEN SPENDER / [Publisher's emblem] / HAMISH HAMILTON / LONDON

1 blank leaf, 3 leaves, VII-IX, [X] , 1-349, [350] pp., end leaf. 22.5 x 14 cm. Hard-bound in blue cloth with title, author, and publisher's emblem printed on the spine in gold. Dust-jacket in grey printed in blue: "Stephen Spender's Autobiography / World Within World. / Has red ornamental design in the center on front, "Book Society Choice" on top in red, publisher's note about the book on the front flap. The back of the wrapper has selections from reviews on Spender's *European Witness*.

First published by Hamish Hamilton, London, on the 9th April 1951 at 15s. net. Made and printed in England by Staples Printers Limited at their Rochester, Kent, establishment. Book Society Choice. Facing copyright and dedication page is a poem from *The Still Centre* (1935): "Darkness and Light."

Introduction, pp. VII-IX; Index, pp-337-349.
Frontispiece: Photograph of the author in 1932 by Humphrey Spender.

Dedication: To Isaiah Berlin.

Notes: Parts of the book were written in Taos, New Mexico, at the Lawrence ranch.

Dates of composition: 1947—May 10, 1950.

Spender states that his autobiography is composed around themes of love, poetry, politics, the life of literature, childhood, travel, and the development of certain attitudes towards moral problems.

Publisher's note: "... Besides the light it throws on Mr. Spender's own point of view, this book is particularly illuminating on the relationship between literature and politics in England during the thirties. It contains vivid portraits of Virginia Woolf, T.S. Eliot, Lady Ottoline Morrell, W.H. Auden, Christopher Isherwood and other outstanding literary figures of the time." Spender also analyses the motives that drove the youth of his generation into the politics of communism.

An examination of the proof copy indicates that the book was ready for publication in 1950.

b)   *Second impression:*   April 1951

The same as the first edition.

c)   *First American edition:*   [1951]

Stephen Spender / WORLD / WITHIN [small type] / WORLD / Harcourt, Brace and Company / New York

1 blank leaf, 2 leaves, V-VII [VIII], 1-312 pp., end-leaf. Hard-bound in grey cloth printing on front and spine in black. Dust-jacket made of yellow paper with double picture of author's photograph, reproduced from the British edition, one of them shaded, in the top left-corner; title and half-title on front and spine. On the front and back flap, a note on the work with a short bio-data on Spender.

Published by Harcourt, Brace and Company, New York, at $3.50 Printed in the United States of America. Copyright, 1948, 1949, 1951, by Stephen Spender. All rights reserved, including the right to reproduce this book or portions thereof in any form."

Introduction, pp. V-VII; Index, pp. 305-312; Poem: "Darkness and Light," p. [VIII].

Dedication: The same as the English edition.

Notes: On the back of the wrapper, selections from the author's preface describe the problem of autobiography: "Here I have tried to be as truthful as I can, within the limits of certain inevitable reticences, and to write of experiences from which I feel I have learned how to live."

First edition:

SHELLEY / *by* STEPHEN SPENDER / PUBLISHED FOR / THE BRIT-
ISH COUNCIL / and the NATIONAL BOOK LEAGUE / BY LONGMANS,
GREEN & CO. / LONDON, NEW YORK, TORONTO /

2 leaves, 5-56 pp., Frontispiece. 21.5 x 13.5 cm. Soft-bound in cream
paper, title printed on front in bold brown letters, the rest in black. On
back of the cover, a list of books published for the British Council and on
verso of the front, publisher's note on Spender.

Published by Longmans, Green & Co. Ltd., London, . . . in 1952 for the
British Council and the National Book League as Supplement to British
Book News: No. 29 of Bibliographical series whose General Editor was
T.O. Beachcroft. Original price, 2s., revised to 2s. 6d. net. Printed in Great
Britain by Benham and Company Limited, Colchester; on *verso* of half-title
a short note on Shelley. Select Bibliography, pp. 47-56. *Frontispiece*:
Portrait of Shelley from a painting of 1819 by Amelia Curran in the
National Portrait Gallery.

Notes: Publishers describe Spender as "one of the most distinguished
poets of his generation." ". . . His essay, with its long and valuable Select
Bibliography, is a notable contribution to the literature of the Romantics."

It may also be noted that Spender has been described as "the Shelley of
the twentieth century."

A28 LEARNING LAUGHTER 1952

a) *First edition:*

LEARNING / LAUGHTER / by / STEPHEN SPENDER / [Publisher's
emblem] / WEIDENFELD & NICOLSON LTD / 7 CORK STREET,
LONDON, W.1.

1 blank leaf, 3 leaves, V-VI, 1-201 [202] pp., end leaf. 22.5 x 14.5 cm.
Hard-bound in blue cloth with printing in silver on the spine. Dust-jacket
in white paper with author, title, and underneath a picture of a black and
white child in a field. Front flap has a note on the nature of the book;
the back of the wrapper and back flap: other publications of Weidenfeld
and Nicolson Ltd. Trimmed edges.

First published by Weidenfeld and Nicolson Ltd of London in November
1952 at 15s. Printed in Great Britain by Merritt and Hatcher Ltd. Illustrated with 17 photographs, some of which are by RIWKIN of Stockholm.
Introduction, pp. 1-4.

Dedication: To Vera Weizmann.

Contents: Introduction—I. The Artza Etcetera—II. Haifa—III. Arrival at

Jerusalem—IV. The Disturbed and the Disturbing—V. People, Conversations and Places—VI. The Phases of Youth Aliah—VII. Portrait of a Visionary—VIII. Mapam Kibbutz—IX. Modern Town and Old Village—X. The Italian Village—XI. Life in the Kibbutzim—XII. Jews of Cochin, Sephardim and Yemenites—XIII. A Middle East Pinnacle of Science—XIV. The Negev—XV. A Sum but not a Summing Up.

Notes: The book has been described as a travel book with a purpose: "The idea of a travel book with a theme appeals to me. Impressions inevitably superficial should . . . acquire proportion and direction, if they are related to a central subject."

Publisher's note: "Spender travelled on a 'children's boat' from Marseilles to Haifa. He toured Israel, visiting the settlements where live children and their parents, gathered from all over Europe and Asia . . ."

b) *American edition:*   [1953]

Learning / LAUGHTER / By / STEPHEN SPENDER / HARCOURT, BRACE AND COMPANY, INC / NEW YORK / [1953]

1 blank leaf, 3 leaves, V-VI, 1-201 pp., end leaf. Hard-boards in grey cloth with printing in black on the spine.

Published by Harcourt, Brace and Company of New York. Printed in Great Britain by Merritt and Hatcher Ltd. All rights reserved.

Dedication and Contents: The same as the English edition.

A29   THE CREATIVE ELEMENT   1953

First edition:

THE CREATIVE / ELEMENT / A Study of Vision, Despair and Orthodoxy / among some Modern Writers / [ornament] / by STEPHEN SPENDER / [Publisher's emblem] / HAMISH HAMILTON / LONDON

1 blank leaf, 4 leaves, [9] -199 pp., one blank leaf. 23 x 14 cm. Hardbound in red cloth, with title, author, and publisher's emblem printed in gold on the spine. Edges trimmed.

Dust-jacket in cream colored paper with front in decorative frame inside printed in black: THE / CREATIVE / ELEMENT / BY / STEPHEN / SPENDER / Author of / 'World Within World' / etc. / on the Spine, author and publisher in black type and title in red. Front flap carries a note on the book and on the back flap review of *European Witness*. Back of the wrapper has selected reviews of *World Within World*. Edges trimmed.

First published by Hamish Hamilton Ltd., 90 Great Russell Street, London W.C.1. Made and printed in Great Britain by William Clowes and Sons Limited, London and Beccles. Price tag from the wrapper removed. Introduction, pp. [9] -15.

Dedicated to Allen Tate.

Contents: Introduction—I. The Visionary Individualists—II. The Necessity of Being Absolutely Modern—III. Rilke and the Angels, Eliot and the Shrines—IV. Personal Relations and Public Powers—V. Pioneering the Instinctive Life—VI. Hammered Gold and Gold Enameling of Humanity—VII. Anti-Vision and Despair—VIII. The Theme of Political Orthodoxy in the Thirties—IX. The World of Evelyn Waugh—X. The New Orthodoxies.

Notes: This book may be regarded as a companion volume to *The Destructive Element*: "The creative element is the individual vision of the writer who realizes in his work the decline of modern values while isolating his own individual values from the context of society. He never forgets the modern context, in fact he is always stating it, but he does so only to create the more forcibly the visions of his own isolation."—From the introduciton to the book.

A30   SIRMIONE PENINSULA   1954

First edition:

SIRMIONE PENINSULA / by / STEPHEN SPENDER / illustrated by / LYNTON LAMB / [Pen drawing of a girl] / Faber and Faber / 24 Russell Square / London WC1

[4] pp., 21.5 x 14 cm. Soft-cover in pale pink paper. On top of the front: Ariel Poem, at bottom FABER AND FABER; in the center title in large black type: SIRMIONE PENINSULA, in smaller type author's and illustrator's name. Decorative design. Edges trimmed. Sewn with white thread.

First published by Faber and Faber in 1954 at 2s. net in the new series: "Ariel Poems." Printed in Great Britain by Jesse Broad & Co. Ltd., Manchester. All rights reserved. *Illustrated*: two pictures in black and white and one in color by Lynton Lamb.

Contents: A poem of thirty lines, beginning with: "Places I shared with her things that she touched"; *last line*: "Lips parted as though to greet the flght of a bird."

A31   THREE VERSIONS FROM THE GERMAN   1955

a)   *First edition:*

THREE VERSIONS / FROM THE GERMAN / by / STEPHEN SPENDER / [star] / CHRISTMAS / 1955 / [Ornamental Design]

4 pp., 16 x 11.5 cm. Bound in gold glazed art paper with red label 5.5 x 8.5 cm. glued on front with decorative outline framing title, author and date of publication in dark blue. Stitched with white thread. Printed on

ivory yellow paper.

Colophon on *verso* of last leaf: "100 copies of *Three Versions From the German* have been printed for their friends by Stephen and Natasha Spender."

Contents: The Disciple: After Stefan George—The Gardner (from *Das Kleine Wellttheater*): After Hugo von Hofmannsthal—Mein Kind Kam Heim: After Stefan George.

Notes: Presentation copy number 51 was examined; is signed: "To John with Christmas Wishes from Stephen and Natasha,"

"Mein Kind Kam Heim," published also in *The Generous Days*.

A32   COLLECTED POEMS   1955

a)   *First edition:*

COLLECTED POEMS / 1928-1953 / BY STEPHEN SPENDER / FABER AND FABER / 24 Russell Square / London

2 blank leaves, 3 leaves, 7-211 [212] pp., 2 end leaves. 21 x 13.5 cm. Hard-bound in red cloth with title, author, and publisher on the spine in black. Cream-colored wrapper, printed in red on front and spine with title, author, and publisher in cream on front decorated with stars and a line at bottom. Large letters: SPENDER down the spine in the center in cream with "Collected Poems by Stephen Spender" on top and "Faber and Faber" at bottom. On front flap trade-blurb in red and price; on back flap, other works by Spender. The back of the jacket poetry publications by Faber.

First published in 1955 by Faber and Faber Limited at 15s. net. Printed in Great Britain by Latimer Trend & Co. Ltd., Plymouth. All rights reserved.

Introduction, pp. 13-15; Index of first lines, pp. 209-211, dated May 30, 1954.

Dedication: General dedication of the book to Natasha *Part One*: to Christopher Isherwood; *Part Two*: to Isaiah Berlin; *Part Six*: to the Memory of Gully Mason, Michael Jones, Timothy Corsellis, W.J..Sipprell, Michael Spender; *Part Seven*: to Cecil Day Lewis; *Part Eight*: to Margaret Spender, who died on Christmas Day, 1945; *Part Ten*: to Edith Sitwell; and *Part Eleven*: to W.H. Auden who first saw these.

Contents: PART ONE (1930-1933): PRELUDES: 1. He Will Watch the Hawk with an Indifferent Eye—2. Rolled Over on Europe: The Sharp Dew Frozen to Stars—3. Marston, Dropping It in the Grate, Broke His Pipe —4. Not to You I Sighed. No, Not a Word—5. Acts Passed Beyond the Boundary of Mere Wishing—6. At the End of Two Months' Holiday There Came a Night—7. Different Living Is Not Living in Different Places—8. An 'I' Can Never be Great Man—9. Beethoven's Death Mask—10. Never Being,

Notes: From the *Introduction*:

"To collect and select these poems, I copied them into a large note-book, then typed them out and tried to consider how each poem would best take its place in a single volume. In this way, I have spent several months reconsidering and even re-experiencing poems I have written over the past twenty-five years . . . my aim has been to retrieve as many past mistakes, and to make as many improvements, as possible without 'cheating' . . . Poetry is a game played with the reader according to rules, but it is also a truth game in which the truth is outside the rules."

Presentation copy to Edith Sitwell signed 'Stephen,' Jan 1955 has this note hand-written in red ink:

Dearest Edith

The dedication to you is on p. 195. The poem I originally wrote which was dedicated to you is omitted as I did not think it good enough for you, or by me. I thought of putting the dedication

To Edith Sitwell
Poet friend of poets

and then thought the dedication to a poet from a poet already said all this.

With my great love and admiration

Stephen
Jan 1955.

b)   *Second impression:*   1959

The same as the first impression, except selections of reviews on the front flap of the wrapper:

The Times describes it as the poetic accompaniment to an autobiography and praises, among other things, his fine craftsmanship. G.S. Fraser, in the *New Statesman*, finds it deeply moving but is alo attracted by "the slow patience of the craftsman" in Spender.

A33   I SIT AT THE WINDOW   n.d.

STEPHEN SPENDER / I Sit at the Window / [Broadside] [n.d.] /

Broadsheet. Linden Broadsheet No. 5. Printed on one side of a decorated sheet of art-paper measuring 29 x 21.5 cm; edges untrimmed.

Artist: Honor Frost; Typographer: Shelley Fauset.

"This edition is limited to 175 copies and have been autographed."

Contents: A poem: "I sit at the window"

Notes: Copy No. 45 was examined. It was placed in a paper folder of The Brick Row Book Shop, Austin, Texas.

First edition:

THE / MAKING / of a / POEM / by / STEPHEN SPENDER / [Publisher's emblem[/HAMISH HAMILTON / LONDON /

1 blank leaf, 4 leaves, [9] -192 pp., end-leaf. 22 x 14.5 cm. Hard-bound in red cloth, with title, author, and publisher's emblem on the spine in silver. Dust-jacket made of white paper, blue front, decorated frame with title and author printed in black, except "making" and "Poem" in white. Back of the jacket has reviews of *World Within World*. Front flap carries a note on the author and the back flap, some works by Spender with selections from reviews and price. Trimmed edges.

First published in Great Britain by Hamish Hamilton, Ltd., 90 Great Russell Street, London, W.C.1, in 1955 at 15s. net. Printed in Great Britain by Western Printing Services Ltd., Bristol. *Introduction*, pp. [9] -12, dated 22 February 1955.

Dedicated to William Plomer.

Contents: The book is divided into *three* parts: *Part one*: CONTEMPORARIES: Inside the Cage: Reflections on Conditioned and Unconditioned Imagination—Greatness of Aim—The Making of a Poem—Confessions and Autobiography Two Landscapes of the Novel. *Part Two*: ROMANTICS: The Romantic Gold Standard—Goethe and the English Mind—The Painter as Poet. *Part Three*: SITUATIONS: Georgian Poetry—The Essential Housman—American Diction—Situation of the American Writer.

Notes: "Greatness of Aim" and "Georgian Poetry" were published in *The Times Literary Supplement*. A sketch of "Two Landscapes of the Novel" appeared in *Penguin New Writing*. Earlier version of "The Romantic Gold Standard" appeared as introduction to *A Choice of English Romantic Poetry* (Dial Press, New York). Notes used for his autobiography were developed into "Confessions and Autobiography," also a radio-broadcast. "American Diction vs American Poetry" and "Inside the Cage" appeared in *Encounter*. "The Essential Housman" and "The Situation of the American Writer," in *Horizon*, "The Painter as Poet" in *Art News*. Strong reaction by James Thurber to "The Situation of the American Writer" receives interesting comment by Spender in the introduction.

Spender "disclaims the title of criticism" for his essays. He calls them notes of a writer on writing. "Each essay is an aspect of that which gives the title to the collection—*The Making of a Poem*."

a)   *First edition:*

ENGAGED IN WRITING / AND / THE FOOL AND THE PRINCESS / by / STEPHEN SPENDER / [Publisher's Emblem] / HAMISH HAMIL-TON / LONDON /

1 blank leaf, 4 leaves, 9-239 [240] pp., end-leaf. 20.5 x 13.5 cm. Hard-bound in grey cloth with gold print down the spine: ENGAGED / IN / WRITING [Device] STEPHEN SPENDER / [Emblem]. Dust-jacket of pale-green paper, front decoratively designed by Leonard Rosoman, author and title on the left bottom printed in brown. On the wrapper spine title, author, and emblem in brown. The back of the wrapper carries reviews of *World Within World*, back flap, other works of Spender, with reviews and price; and the front flap, information about the stories in the book.

First published in Great Britain, in 1958, by Hamish Hamilton Ltd., 90 Great Russell Street, London, W.C.1. Copyright © 1958 by Stephen Spender. Printed in Great Britain by Western Printing Services Ltd., Bristol, Jacket design by Leonard Rosoman. Price: 15 s. net.

Dedication: To Hansi Lambert

Contents: "Engaged in Writing (1956 & 1957)," pp. 9-155; "The Fool and the Princess (1946 & 1957)," pp. 159-239.

Notes: "Engaged in Writing" is dedicated to Nicolas Nabokov and "The Fool and the Princess" to Christopher Isherwood. The two stories provide satirical sketches of post-war Europe.

Uncorrected proof copy examined: Probable publication date is given as January 1958.

b)   *American edition*:   1958

ENGAGED IN WRITING / AND / THE FOOL AND THE PRINCESS / by / STEPHEN SPENDER / FARRAR, STRAUS AND CUDHAY, INC. / NEW YORK /

1 blank leaf, 4 leaves, 9-239 [240] pp., end leaf. 21 x 14 cm. Hard-bound in grey cloth with printing in silver down the spine. Dust-jacket designed by Leonard Rosoman, the same as on the English edition. Title on the spine and on the front and back flap, a note on the book, and on the back cover, selections of English reviews.

Published by Farrar, Straus and Cudhay, 101 Fifth Avenue, New York 3, N.Y. Manufactured in the United States of America. Copyright © 1958 by Stephen Spender, Library of Congress Catalog number 58-10544.

Dedication and Contents the same as the English edition.

First edition:

4 pp., 21 x 14 cm., paper-cover, highly decorated in black & white designed by Richard Beer. Front with title and author printed in long hand. Back, information about the book.

Colophon: 'Inscriptions' by Stephen Spender is the first of a series of holograph poems to be published by the Poetry Book Society Limited, 4 St. James's Square, London, SW1. The cover was designed by Richard Beer. The booklet was printed by the Westerham Press and published in October 1958 in an edition of 1,100 copies, of which 1,000 are for sale to members of the Poetry Book Service and to the public. Price one shilling.

Contents: Three short poems—all on one page: Temple—Stele (*Athens Museum*)—Hiroshima Rebuilt.

Notes: The entire book is holographic.

A VOICE IN A SKULL / BY / STEPHEN SPENDER

A poem in holograph for the Deutsch-Englische Gessellschaft. Christmas 1960. Bound in grey paper.

Broadsheet: Poem: "Art Student."

Printed on a large white art-paper. 38.5 x 28 cm. Framed in black line; black large type.

Broadsheet: Poem: I Think Continually of Those Who Were Truly Great."

No title, first line in red, printed on mould-made Nideggen paper. 47.5 x 28 cm. Calligraphy by Fridolf Johnson.

For The Limited Editions Club with These Words 'at the bottom of the page: "To the flowering of Your Spirit During the coming Year."

A40   THE IMAGINATION IN THE MODERN WORLD   1962

First edition:

The Imagination / in the / Modern World / By STEPHEN SPENDER / Threee Lectures Presented Under the / Auspices of the Gertrude Clark Whittall / Poetry and Literature Fund / [Library of Congress Emblem] / REFERENCE DEPARTMENT / THE LIBRARY OF CONGRESS / WASHINGTON: 1962 /

Three leaves, 1-40 pp., end leaf. 23 x 15 cm. Paper-cover, half grey, half blue with ornamental line separating the two. On the front the grey half: The Imagination / in the / Modern World / By Stephen Spender; The blue half: THREE LECTURES . . . . Stapled.

Published by the Reference Department of the Library of Congress, Washington in 1962 for Sale by the Superintendent of Documents, U.S. Government Printing Office, Washington 25, D.C. Price: 25 cents. L.C. Card No. 62-64964.

Contents: The Imagination as Verb, 1-15; The Organic the Orchidaceous, The Intellectualized, 16-28; Imagination Means Individuation, 29-40. P. iii: A note on The Gertrude Clarke Whittall Poetry and Literature Fund.

Notes: "These three lectures, which were delivered on February 26, 27 and 28, 1962, are published by the Library to reach a wider audience and as a contribution to literary history and criticism."

A41   THE STRUGGLE OF THE MODERN   1963

a)   *First edition:*

The Struggle of the / Modern / [device] / by / STEPHEN SPENDER / [Publisher's emblem] / HAMISH HAMILTON / LONDON /

2 blank leaves, 3 leaves, VII-XIII [XIV], [1-3] 4-266 pp., 4 blank leaves. 22.5 x 14 cm. Hard-bound in blue cloth, with title, author, and publisher's emblem in gold on the spine. Dust-jacket in white paper, front and spine painted in spotted blue. Jacket design by Patricia Davey. Title and author printed in white on the front with a rose-colored band between them, running across the wrapper. Spine printing also in white. Back of the wrapper has reviews of *World Within World*; front flap describes the book and gives price; back flap has selections of reviews of *The Making of a Poem*. Edges trimmed.

First published in Great Britain in 1963 by Hamish Hamilton Ltd., 90 Great Russell Street, London W.C.1. Printed in Great Britain by Western Printing Services Ltd., Bristol. Copyright © 1963 by Stephen Spender. Price: 25s net.

Introduction, pp. [ix] -xiii.

Dedication: To Natasha at Berkeley

Contents:The book is divided into *four* parts: *Part One*: THE MODERN IMAGINATION: I. The Romantic Imagination—II. The Organic, The Orchidaceous, The Intellectualized—III. Imagination Is Personal. *Part Two*: THE OBSESSIVE SITUATION: I. Moderns and Contemporaries—II. The Modern as Vision of The Whole—III. The Modern Necessity—IV. The Seminal Image—V. Poetic Moderns and Prose Contemporaries—VI. A Short History of The Pers. Pron. 1st Sing. Nom.—VII. The World of Mechanical Metamorphosis. *Part Three*: NON-RECOGNIZERS, RECOGNIZERS, AND OVER-RECOGNIZERS: I. Non-Recognizers—II. The Recognizers—III. Dialogue With a Recognizer. *Part Four*: THE REVERSAL OF THE MODERN: I. Tradition-Bound Literature and Traditionless Painting—II. Hatred and Nostalgia in Death's Dream Kingdom—III. The Neo-Traditionalists—IV. The Nostalgic Fallacy—V. Poet-Critics and Critic-Poets—VI. The Modern and the Now.

Notes: Part One of the book is based on the three lectures Spender gave in 1961 at the Library of Congress under the auspices of the Gertrude Clarke Whittall Poetry and Literature Fund, published separately by the Library of Congress . Parts Two, Three, and Four are offered as a substitute for the series of Beckman Lectures he gave at Berkeley in 1959.

Spender describes this volume as a book of personal reflections on modern life, art, and literature.

b)   *American edition:*

The Struggle of the / Modern / [Device] / by / STEPHEN SPENDER / University of California Press / Berkeley and Los Angeles / 1963 /

2 blank leaves, 3 leaves, vii-xiii, [xiv] , [1-3] 4-266 pp., 4 blank leaves. 22 x 14 cm. Hard-boards in blue cloth, with printing in gold on the spine. Dust-jacket not available.

Published by the University of California Press, Berkeley and Los Angeles. California, in 1963. Printed in Great Britain. Copyright: © Stephen Spender.

Contents, dedication: The same as the English edition.

Also available in paperback edition.

A42   CHAOS AND CONTROL IN POETRY   1966

First edition:

Choas / and Control / in Poetry/ A LECTURE DELIVERED AT THE LIBRARY OF CONGRESS / October 11, 1965 / by STEPHEN SPENDER / Consultant in Poetry in English at the Library of Congress, 1965-66 / REFERENCE DEPARTMENT: THE LIBRARY OF CONGRESS / WASH-

1 leaf, 1-14 pp. 23.5 x 15 cm. Soft-bound in black paper, on front white cross bands and scattered strips across the page with title in three lines in white and author in smaller type, right bottom corner. Back: Library of Congress emblem and on *verso*, a list of other publications on literature issued by the Library of Congress.

Published by the Reference Department of the Library of Congress in 1966, priced at 15 cents. Printed by U.S. Government Printing Office, Washington, D.C., 10402 and for sale by the Superintendent of Documents. L.C. Card: 66-60054.

A43   THE YEAR OF THE YOUNG REBELS   1969

First edition:

The Year of / The Young Rebels / Stephen Spender / Weidenfeld & Nicolson / 5 Winsley Street London W1

3 leaves, [1-2] 3-182 pp. 22 x 14 cm. Soft-bound in thin orange paper, design of finger-pointing hands in white lines all over front, back and spine. In the centre on front framed within black outlines publisher, title, and author in black print. Title and author on spine. White glazy paper wrapper: Front: author's name in black in two lines and a separating band of black line; then the title. The Year / of the / in two lines in white; Young / Rebels / two lines in red and a red band across the page. Title, author, publisher downward the spine. Back of the wrapper: other books by Stephen Spender and right hand bottom corner: SBN 297-178350. Front flap: back-ground description of the book. Jacket design by John Curtis, and price (in U.K. only) 36 s. net. Backflap: Portrait of Spender from Universal Pictorial Press with brief biographical sketch.

First published in England by Weidenfeld and Nicolson at 36 s. net. Printed in Great Britain by C. Tinling & Co., Ltd., Liverpool, London and Prescot. Copyright: (1969) by Stephen Spender. Photograph of Stephen Spender from Universal Pictorial Press on back flap.

Contents: 1. The Columbia Happenings—2. Notes on the Sorbonne Revolution- -3. Czechoslovakia and Western Students—4. The Berlin Youth Model—5. Politics of the Non-Political—6. The Situation of Young Rebels —7. The University as Agora.

Notes: In the 'Sixties western universities burst into open rebellion. Spender here reports on "his search into the underlying causes of this outburst of student rebellion across the western world."

b)   *American editon:*   1969

Stephen Spender / The Year / of the / Young Rebels /. [publisher's emblem] / Vintage Books / A Division of Random House / New York /

1 blank leaf, 4 leaves, [1,2] 3-186 pp., 1 leaf, one end leaf. 18.5 x 11 cm. Soft-bound in orange with a design of a purple fist protruding from the open top of a building and title and publisher in black and author in white on front, and title and publisher on the spine. Back of the cover describes the background of events which motivated Spender in writing the book. Cover design by Bob Korn.

Published in the United States by Random House, Inc., New York, and distributed in Canada by Random House of Canada Ltd., Toronto. First Vintage Books edition, May 1969. Copyright © 1968, 1969 by Stephen Spender, Library of Congress Catalog Card Number: 78-78801. Manufactured in the United States. Price of the Vinatge Book (V-222): $1.95.

Contents: The same as the English edition.

Note: Also available in a hardcover edition from Random House.

A44   THE GENEROUS DAYS   1969

a)   *First edition:*

THE / GENEROUS / DAYS / [BY] / STEPHEN / SPENDER / TO MATTHEW / AND MARO / SPENDER, / CON AMORE / PUBLISHED BY DAVID R. GODINE / BOSTON / MCMLXIX

1 blank leaf, 3 leaves, 1-20 [21-22] pp., end leaf. 22 x 14 cm. Hard-board covered with paper of wall-paper design, spine in cloth, (some copies) in leatherette. No dust-jacket. Printed on art paper; edges trimmed.

Published by David R. Godine, Boston, in 1969; printed at the Press of David Godine in an edition of two hundred fifty copies. Fifty copies, bound by hand and signed by the author, are numbered I-L. Copyright © 1969 by Stephen Spender. Library of Congress Catalog card number: 78-104910. Errors corrected by hand on page 1 and 16, on some copies.

Contents: If It Were Not—Lost Days—To W.H. Auden, on His Sixtieth Birthday—The Generous Days—Voice from a Skull—Fifteen Line Sonnet in Four Parts—Four Sketches for Herbert Read—Fragments of *A Birthday Cantata*—Eleven Bagatelles—One More New Botched Beginning.

b)   *Second edition:*   1971

THE GENEROUS DAYS / STEPHEN SPENDER / FABER & FABER /

2 blank leaves, 4 leaves. 11-47 [48] pp., end-leaf. Hard-bound in yellow cloth, printing in blue on the spine. Dust-jacket in paper half-blue, half yellow separated by a white band. The blue-half has title and the yellow-

half, author's name in black both on the front and the spine. Front flap contains a note on Spender and the back-flap, other works of Spender. The back of the wrapper has a list of Faber poets.

First published in 1971 by Faber and Faber, 3 Queen Square, London WC1 at 20s. net. Printed in Great Britain by Ebenezer Baylis & Son Ltd., at The Trinity Press, Worcester and London. ISBN 0571 098479. All rights reserved © 1971 by Stephen Spender. Acknowledgements and Note, p. 47.

Dedicated: To Matthew, Maro and Saskia *con amore* (with love).

Contents: If It Were Not—Lost Days—The Chalk Blue Butterfly—Boy, Cat, Canary—A Father in Time of War—Child Falling Asleep in Time of War—Almond Tree By a Bombed Church—V.W. (1941)—Mein Kind Kam Heim
Sleepless—The Generous Days—On the Photograph of a Friend, Dead—Voice from a Skull—Fifteen Line Sonnet in Four Parts—What Love Poems Say—Four Sketches For Herbert Read: Innocence, Young Officer. Conferencier, Anarchist—To W.H. Auden On His Sixtieth Birthday—One More New Botched Beginning—Matter of Identity—To Become a Dumb Thing—Bagatelles: I. After the Inscription on a Greek Stele of a Woman Holding Her Grandchild on Her Knees; II. M.J. (1940); III. For Humphrey House; IV. Sentenced; V. Descartes, VI. Mosquito; VII. Moon; VIII. Present Absence; IX. After Tibullus; X. A Political Generation; XI. To My Japanese Translator (shozo); XII. Renaissance Hero—Central Heating System—Art Student.

Notes: Earlier edition printed and published by Mr. David Godine had only ten of these poems. This is a considerably enlarged edition of 47 recent poems.

This publication comes after more than twenty years of waiting by his admirers. These poems have been noted for their reflectiveness and acceptance which add "a new dimension to Mr. Spender's poetry."

c)   *American edition:*   1971

THE / GENEROUS / DAYS / [Device] / STEPHEN SPENDER /

1 blank leaf, 5 leaves, 11-44 [45-48] pp., end leaf. 22 x 14 cm. Hardbound in grey cloth, printing on the spine in silver. Grey paper wrapper with title in white and author's name in golden brown on front and spine. Decorative design on front between title and author. Stephen Spender's portrait on the back of the wrapper. Front flap: a note on the book and back flap: a note on Spender.

Published by Random House, New York. Manufactured in the United States of America. Described as First American Edition. Copyright © 1971 by Stephen Spender. All rights reserved under International and Pan-American Copyright conventions. Published simultaneously in Canada by Random House of Canada Limited, Toronto. Originally published in The

United Kindgom by Faber and Faber Limited, London. Copyright © 1971 by Stephen Spender. ISBN: 0-394-45606-8; Library of Congress Catalog Card Number: 71-159377. Jacket designed by Edith Dreikurs. Portrait of Stephen Spender is a photo by Camilla McGrath.

Dedication: The same as the British edition.

Contents: The same as the British edition.

Notes: Biographical note on the back flap mentions Spender's present position as "Professor of English at University College, London." Indicates that he "helped to forge a new consciousness and style in English poetry."

"These forty seven poems represent the mature work of one of the major English poets of the twentieth century."

A45   DESCARTES   1970

DESCARTES by STEPHEN SPENDER / [Broadsheet] /

Broadsheet No. 2. Designed and printed by Ralph Steadman on Swedish paper at Steam Press, Kensington Church Walk, London W8.

Edition limited to 50 copies only, numbered and signed by the author.

Contents: Poem: "Descartes" opening with the line: "Lightning, enlightening, turns." Has 9 lines.

Note: Examined signed copy No. 45.

A46   LOVE–HATE RELATIONS   1974

a)   *First edition:*

STEPHEN SPENDER / LOVE–HATE RELATIONS / A STUDY OF / ANGLO-AMERICAN SENSIBILITIES / [Device] / HAMISH HAMILTON / LONDON

One blank leaf, 4 leaves, [xi] -xviii, [1-3] 4-246 pp., end-leaf. 22.5 x 14 cm. Hard-boards in blue cloth, with printing in silver on the spine. Jacket designed by Jeanne Ross in deep blue paper; on front: STEPHEN / SPENDER in white, Love– / Hate / Relations, in red; A Study of / Anglo-American / Sensibilities, in purple. Front flap carries a note on the book and back flap, on Spender.

First published in Great Britain by Hamish Hamilton Ltd., 90 Great Russell Street, London W.C.1, in 1974 at £ 3.95 net. Printed in Great Britain by Western Printing Services Ltd., Bristol. Copyright © 1974 by Stephen Spender. SBN 241 02100 6 (cased); SBN 241 89052 7 (Paper). Introduction by Spender, pp. [xi] -xviii, dated 3 May 1973.

Dedication: To Christopher Isherwood and Don Bachardy.

Contents: THE IMMENSE ADVANTAGE: I. American Thoughts and English Thoughts—II. The American Ambivalence—III. Thinking American Through Being American—IV. Subjective America, Objective Europe. THE SPECTER OF AMERICANIZATION: I; Americanizing—II. European Attitudes—III. Past and Nowness—IV. American Solutions—V. American Materialism—VI. Americanization as Europeanization. HENRY JAMES AS CENTER OF THE ENGLISH-AMERICAN LANGUAGE: I. The Critic as center of His Own Fiction—II. The Refusal to be Provincial—III. The Aims of Fiction—IV. The Sexual Subject—V. The Choice of London—VI. America, 1904—VII. Baudelaire and Whitman—VIII. American Womanhood and English Language—IX. American Redemption. EBB TIDE IN ENGLAND: I. Georgians—II. The American Visitors—III. The Persona of Bridges—IV. Frost and Edward Thomas—V. English Poets and the War—VI. The Divergence of The Twain. ENGLISH THRENODY, AMERICAN TRAGEDY: I. Novelists of Poetry and of Saturation—II. Elegies for England: IV. Long-Term and Short-Term England—V. Post-Mortem Effects—VI. American Self-Improvement—VII. The American Advantage.

Notes: The idea for this book was contained in the Clark Lectures Spender gave in 1965 at Cambridge University. But "only five pages of the original lectures survive in this book." Therefore Spender calls it "a substitute for my never-to-be-published Clark Lectures."

The complex relationship between English and American literature, which Spender calls Love—Hate Relations is the subject of this book.

This is "Professor Spender's major literary Study, the result of a life-time's work and reflection . . . a landmark of literary criticism."

b)   *First American edition:*   1974

LOVE—HATE / RELATIONS / English and American Sensibilities / [ornament] / STEPHEN SPENDER / [ornament] / [Publisher's emblem] / Random House, New York

2 blank leaves, 5 leaves, [xi]] xiii [xiv], [1-3] 4-318 pp., 2 leaves, endleaf. 21.5 x 14.5 cm. Hard-boards bound in cream paper, spine in dark brown cloth with decorative design on front and author, device, title, publisher's name and emblem down the spine. Dust-jacket in ivory yellow paper; front: large blue letters for "Love—Hate Relations and Stephen Spender"; smaller type in black for "English and American Sensibilities; decorative red line above the author's name; spine: blue for title and author; smaller type in red for publisher and emblem. Back of the wrapper has Spender's portrait, a photograph by Jill Krementz. Front flap describes the book and its background; back flap has a note on Spender and on Random House.

Published by Random House, Inc., New York, N.Y. 10022 at $8.95. Manufactured and printed in U.S.A. Copyright © 1974 by Stephen Spender. All rights reserved under International and Pan-American Copyright

Conventions. *Library of Congress Cataloging Publication Data*: Stephen Spender, 1909—. Love hate relations. Based on the Clark Lectures given by the author at Cambridge University in 1965 . . . ISBN 0-394-49062-2. Portrait on the back of the wrapper. Introduction, pp. [xv] -xxviii, May 3, 1973.

Contents and Dedication: The same as the English edition.

Notes: "Mr Spender discusses the attitude of writers not because he has set out to write a book of literary criticism, but because at the level of consciousness at which imaginative literature evolves, the harmonies of love and hatred in these relations are at their most revealing." Publisher's note places this major publication next to D.H. Lawrence's *Studies in Classic American Literature*.

FORTHCOMING

A47   T.S. ELIOT (MODERN MASTERS SERIES),
       VIKING PRESS.

Date not set. Hardcover: ISBN: 0-670-29184-6, Priced at $10. Paper: ISBN: 0-670-01988-7, Priced at $3.95.

B

WORKS
EDITED, TRANSLATED,
OR
HAVING CONTRIBUTIONS
BY

STEPHEN SPENDER

POEMS / By / W.H. AUDEN / Privately printed by S.H.S. [STEPHEN HAROLD SPENDER] / 1928

Original edition not seen. A facsimile of the copy in the George Elliston Collection of Twentieth-Centry Poetry made in 1964 was examined.

2 blank leaves, 2 leaves, [1,2] 3-37 [38] pp., 1 blank leaf. 13 x 10 cm. Hard-bound in brown cloth with author and title printed in black on front, a long line separating the two.

Published by S.H.S. [Stephen Spender] in 1928. About 45 copies were made and numbered. Distributed free among friends and relations. Dedicated to Christopher Isherwood. Alterations, corrections, and deletions were made by hand on the printed copy. Copyright of the facsimile edition of 1964 rests with Elliston Poetry Foundation, University of Cincinnati, Cincinnati, Ohio.

Note: Foreword for the facsimile edition tells about "a very primitive printing press" which Spender had bought on which he printed his own *Nine Experiments* and this volume of Auden's *Poems*. ". . . After I had done the first half or so of the volume, the machine, the type, and my patience broke down . . ." The remaining portion of the book was printed and bound by Holywell Press, Oxford.

OXFORD POETRY / 1928 / Edited / With a Plea for Better Criticism / By Clere Parsons and B.B. / BASIL BLACKWELL / OXFORD / 1928

1 blank leaf, 2 leaves, v-xi [xii], 1-59 [60] pp., end-leaf. 19.5 x 13 cm. Hard-bound in black with yellow for spine. Front left-hand top corner has a white label with a black border pasted, 6.5 x 5 cm., with printing in black type: Oxford / Poetry / 1928 / Oxford / Basil Blackwell.

Published by Basil Blackwell, Oxford, in 1928. Made and Printed in Great Britain at the Kemp Hall Press in the City of Oxford.

Contents: A Plea for Better Criticism—Poems by: 1. G.C. Allen, 2 W.H. Auden, 3. Jocelyn Brooke, 4. Arthur Calder-Marshall, 5. Norman Cameron, 6. R.M.J. Campbell, 7. J.R.V. Collin, 8. Mary Crozier, 9. Jon Curling, 10, A.S.T. Fisher, 11. Phyllis Hartnoll, 12. Christopher Holme, 13. C.J. Pennethorne Hughes, 14. Louis MacNeice, 15. Clere Parsons, 16. W.M. Phillips. 17. Brian Roberts, 18. Frederick G. Roberts, 19. Nigel Maltby Robinson, 20. J.M. Ross, 21. E.J. Scovell, 22. W.M. Spackman, 23. Stephen Spender, 24. Anthony Thorne, 25. Geoffrey Tillotson, 26. Sholto Watt.

Notes: Included here are two poems by Spender: 1. "Quixote on Time," 2. "Voyage."

OXFORD POETRY / 1929 / Edited by / LOUIS MACNEICE and / STEPHEN SPENDER / BASIL BLACKWELL / OXFORD / 1929

1 blank leaf, 2 leaves, V-VII [VIII], 1-56 pp., end-leaf. 19.5 x 13 cm. Hardboards bound in black paper with yellow for spine. Front: white label with black border, 6.5 x 5 cm; Oxford / Poetry / 1929 / Oxford / Basil Blackwell, printed in black type. Edges untrimmed.

Published by Basil Blackwell of Oxford in 1929. Made and printed in Great Britain at The Kemp Hall Press in the City of Oxford.

Dedicated: Neither to 'Poesy'
             Nor to the 'Zeitgeist'

Contents: Poems by: 1. G.C. Allen (Trinity), 2, Phoebe Ashburner (Somerville), 3. Arthur Calder-Marshall (Hertford), 4. David Collin (Hertford), 5. H. Corbett-Palmer (New), 6. E.M. Crawford (Somerville), 7. R.H.S. Crossman (New), 8. Mary Crozier (Somerville), 9. John Hilton (Corpus), 10. H. Christopher Holme (Oriel), 11. Douglas Jay (New), 12. Louis MacNeice (Merton), 13. Clere Parsons (Christ Church), 14. Edouard Roditi (Balliol), 15. J.M. Ross (Wadham), 16. E.J. Scovell (Somerville), 17. Graham Shepard (Lincoln), 18. Phyllis Singleton (St. Hugh's), 19. W.M. Spackman (Balliol), 20. Bernard Spencer (Corpus), 21. Stephen Spender (University), 22. Roberta Teale Swartz (O.H.S.), 23. W.B.C. Watkins (Merton).

Notes: Spender's poems included here are: 1. "Marston, Dropping It in the Grate . . .," 2. "Lying Awake at Night," 3. "Hearing from Its Cage," 4. "Acts Thrust Beyond the Boundary of Mere Wishing."

OXFORD POETRY / 1930 / Edited by / STEPHEN SPENDER and / BERNARD SPENCER / BASIL BLACKWELL / OXFORD / 1930

1 blank leaf, 2 leaves, V-VI, 1-44 pp., 2 end-leaves. 19.5 x 13 cm. Hardbound in black paper with yellow for spine. On front left-hand top corner: white label, 6.5 x 5 cm.: Oxford / Poetry / 1930 / Oxford / Basil Blackwell, in black border. Edges untrimmed.

Published by Basil Blackwell of Oxford in 1930. Made and Printed in Great Britain by the Kemp Hall Press, Ltd., in the City of Oxford.

Contents: Poems by 1. George Allen (Trinity), 2. Phoebe Ashburner (Somerville), 3. Charles Brasch (St. Johns), 4. Peter Burra (Christ Church), 5. James Munro Cameron (Balliol), 6. Edwin Coope (Oriel), 7. David Collin (Hertford), 8. R.H.S. Crossman (New), 9. J. Dawson-Jackson (Christ Church), 10. Charles Drew (Lincoln), 11. Richard Goodman (New College), 12. Gilbert Highet (Balliol), 13. Christopher Holme (Oriel), 14. Humayun Kabir (Exeter), 15. Louis MacNeice (Merton), 16. Arthur Marshall (Hertford), 17. Dorothea Matthews (Somerville), 18. H.M. Phillips (Wadham), 19. Goronwy Rees (New College), 20. John Ross (Wadham), 21. W.M. Spackman (Balliol), 22. Bernard Spencer (Corpus), 23. Stephen Spender (University).

Notes: Spender's poems included with acknowledgements to *The Editor of The Criterion*: 1. "Souvenir de Londres," 2. "The Swan," 3. "The Faces of Living Friends I See on Water," 4. "Now You've No Work, Like a Rich Man," 5. "Because I Love You So."

B5   **NEW COUNTRY**   **1933**

First edition:

NEW COUNTRY / Prose and Poetry by the authors of / *New Signatures* / Edited by / MICHAEL ROBERTS / [Device] / PUBLISHED BY LEONARD AND VIRGINIA WOOLF / AT THE HOGARTH PRESS, 52 TAVISTOCK SQUARE / LONDON W.C. / 1933

One blank leaf, 3 leaves, 7-256 pp. end-leaf. 22 x 14. cm. Hard-boards in green cloth, printing on the spine in gold. Cream-colored dust jacket with decoratve lines in green. Front: NEW / COUNTRY / An anthology of Prose and Poetry / by / The Authors of "New Signatures" / Edited by Michael Roberts / [Publisher's emblem] / THE HOGARTH PRESS / 52 Tavistock Square, London, W.C. / printed in green, spine: [Green rules] / NEW / COUNTRY / By the Authors of / NEW / SIGNATURES / and others / edited by / Michael / ROBERTS / 7s. 6d. / net / THE HOGARTH / PRESS / [Green decorative lines] . Back of the wrapper carries a list of books recently published by The Hogarth Press. Front flap: A note on the anthology.

First published in 1933 by The Hogarth Press at 7s 6d. Made and printed in Great Britain by The Garden City Press, Ltd., Letchworth. Preface by Michael Roberts, pp. 9-21.

Contents: The book is divided into two parts: Prose, pp. 25-189; Poetry, 193-256. Contains Spender's prose piece: "Poetry and Revolution" and his poems: "The Morning Road . . . ," "After Success . . . ," "Alas, when he laughs . . ." and "At the end of two months' holiday . . ."

B6   PASTOR HALL AND BLIND MAN'S BUFF   [1939]

First edition:

[ornamental border—three blank lines] / Pastor Hall / By ERNST TOLLER / Translated from the German by Stephen Spender & Hugh Hunt / Blind Man's Buff / By ERNST TOLLER / AND / DENIS JOHNSTON / [Printer's emblem] / RANDOM HOUSE NEW YORK /

2 blank leaves, 3 leaves, [1-6] 7-172 pp., 3 blank leaves. 21.5 x 14.5 cm. Hard-boards in blue cloth, printing in gold on the spine: Pastor / Hall / By / ERNST / TOLLER / [dot] / Blind / Man's / Buff / By / ERNST TOL-LER / & / DENIS / JOHNSTON / [Publisher's emblem] RANDOM / HOUSE

Manufactured in the United States of America, First Printing. Copyright, 1938, 1939 by ERNST TOLLER. *Caution*: Professionals and amateurs are hereby warned that *Pastor Hall* and *Blind Man's Buff*, being fully protected under the copyright laws of the United States of America, the British Empire, including the Dominion of Canada, and all other countries of the copyright union, are subject to a royalty. All rights including professional, amateur, motion pictures, recitation, public reading, radio broadcasting are strictly reserved. In its present form this play is dedicated to the reading public only. All inquiries regarding this play should be addressed to Richard J. Madden Play Company, Paramount Building, New York City, N.Y.

The non-professional acting rights of *Pastor Hall* and the Dramatists' Play Service, 6 East 39th Street, New York City, without whose permission in writing no performance of these plays may be made.

DEDICATED TO THE DAY / WHEN THIS PLAY ME BE / PERFORMED IN GERMANY.

Contents: English translation of *Pastor Hall* and *Blind Man's Buff*.

B7   **DUINO ELEGIES**   **1939**

a)   *First edtion:*

RAINER MARIA RILKE / DUINO ELEGIES / THE GERMAN TEXT, WITH AN ENGLISH / TRANSLATION, INTRODUCTION AND / COMMENTARY BY / J.B. LEISHMAN / & / STEPHEN SPENDER / THE HOGARTH PRESS / 52 TAVISTOCK SQUARE / LONDON, W.C.1 / 1939

1 blank leaf, 2 leaves, 5-160 pp., end-leaf. 21.5 x 14 cm. Hard-boards in zinc orange cloth, with printing in gold on the spine. Dust jacket in ink blue paper with printing in black on front and spine. Front flap has a note on the translation and translators and back of the wrapper carries advertisement.

First published in England in 1939 by The Hogarth Press at 7s. 6d net. Printed in Great Britain by The Garden City Press Ltd., at Letchworth, Hertfordshire. Preface, p. 5; Introduction by Leishman, pp. 9-21; Commentary by Leishman, pp. 101-157; Appendix, pp; 158-160. Frontispiece: Picasso's *Les Saltimbanques.*

Dedication: THE PROPERTY OF PRINCESS MARIE VON THURN UND TAXIS-HOHENLOHE

Contents: Ten elegies in English translation with German text.

Notes: From the Preface: "In undertaking this most difficult piece of work, we have tried to devise a method which should achieve, above all, unity of style. Accordingly, J.B. Leishman prepared a draft of the whole work, on the basis of which Stephen Spender prepared a second version . . ."

b) *American edition:*   1939

Rainer Maria Rilke / DUINO / ELEGIES [in red] / THE GERMAN TEXT, WITH AN ENGLISH / TRANSLATION, INTRODUCTION, / AND COMMENTARY BY / J.B. LEISHMAN AND STEPHEN SPENDER / *NEW YORK* / W.W. NORTON & COMPANY, INC. / Publishers.

1 blank leaf, 3 leaves, frontispiece, vii-[viii], 9-130 pp., 1 leaf, end-leaf. 22 x 15 cm. Hard-boards in grey cloth, front decorated, rectangular purple blocks for DUINO ELEGIES and RAINER MARIA RILKE and between them a blue circle for a monogram: RMR. Blue and purple spine, gold printing: in top blue Rilke; center purple: Duino Elegies / bottom blue: Norton.

Published by Norton & Company; Printed in the United States / For the publishers by THE VAIL-BALLOU PRESS. Copyright, 1939, by W.W. Norton & Co., Inc., New York.

Contents: Preface—Introduction The First to The Tenth Elegies with German Text—Commentary and Appendices.

B8   **POEMS FOR SPAIN**   **1939**

First edition:

POEMS FOR SPAIN / Edited by / STEPHEN SPENDER & JOHN LEHMANN / with an introduction by / STEPHEN SPENDER / THE HOGARTH PRESS / 52 TAVISTOCK SQUARE / LONDON W.C.1 /1939

2 blank leaves, 2 leaves, 5-108 pp., 2 blank leaves. 22.5 x 14.5 cm. Hardbound in red cloth printed in yellow on front and spine. Yellow paper dust-jacket with title, editors, and publisher printed in black. Edges untrimmed.

First published in 1939 by the Hogarth Press at 6s. net. Printed in Great Britain by Western Printing Services Ltd., Bristol.

Contents: I. *Action*: Poem (John Cornford)—Hear This Voice (Miguel Hernandez)—The New Offensive (Margot Heinemann)—The Madrid Defenders (Richard Church)—Full Moon at Tierz (John Cornford)—Barcelona Nerves (T.R. Wintringham)—At Castellon (Stephen Spender)—Eves (Anonymous)—Retrospect (D.R. Marshall)—Battle (John Lepper)—Spain (H.B. Mallalieu). II. *Death*: The Winds of the People (Miguel Hernandez)—The

Heart Conscripted (Herbert Read)—Jarma Front (T.A.R. Hyndman)—Granien (T.R. Wintringham)—Bombing Casualties (Herbert Read)—The Ultimate Death (Manuel Altolaguirre)—Regum Ultima Ratio (Stephen Spender)—For R.J.C. (Margot Heinemann)—Grieve in a New Way (Margot Heinemann)—Poem (R.B. Fuller)—Arms in Spain (Rex Warner)—The Tolerance of Crows (Charles Donnelly)—III. *The Map*: Spain (Jack Lindsay)—From a painting by Picasso (Albert Brown)—The Tourist Looks at Spain (Rex Warner). IV. *Satire*: Almeria (Pablo Neruda)—To The Wife of Any Non-Intervention Statesman (E. Rickword)—For Those with Investments in Spain (Brian Howard)—Proud Motherhood (F.L. Lucas). V. *Romances*: In the Sweat of Thy Brow (Antonio Agray)—Bombers (C. Day Lewis)—The Victors (Redmayne Fitzgerald)—Guadalajara (J.Bronowski)—Fall of a City (Stephen Spender)—Waiting at Cerbere (Sylvia Townsend Warner)—Benicasim (Sylvia Townsend Warner)—My Brother Luis (Manuel Altolaguirre)—Against the Cold in the Mountains (Jose Petre)—Song for the Spanish Anarchists (Herbert Read)—Single Front (Pedro Garfias)—The Splint (T.R. Wintringham)—Poem for John Miro (Ruthven Todd)—Madrid (Manuel Altolaguirre)—Remembering Spain (Louis MacNeice). VI. *Lorca*: Lorca (Geoffrey Parsons)—The Death of Garcia Lorca (J. Bronowski)—Romancero a la Muerte de Garcia Lorca (Leopoldo Urrutia).

Notes: From Spender's Introduction: "...a document of our times... Poets and poetry have played a considerable part in the Spanish War, because to many people the struggle of the Republicans has seemed a struggle for the conditions without which the writing and reading of poetry are almost impossible in modern society."

"They (the poems) have the merits and defects of being extremely close to experience." Of the fighters here, John Cornford and Charles Donnelley were killed. Tom Wintringham was wounded.

Spender's poems included in the anthology:

1. "At Castellon," 2. "Regum Ultima Ratio," 3. "Fall of a City," 4. "Port Bou."

B9   DANTON'S DEATH   1939

First edition:

Translated by / Stephen Spender and / Goronwy Rees / a play in four acts / DANTON'S DEATH / by Georg Büchner / Faber & Faber Limited / 24 Russell Square / London

2 blank leaves, 2 leaves, 7-128 pp., 9 blank end-leaves. 22.5 x 14.5 cm. Hard-board in black cloth, printing in gold downward on the spine. Dust-jacket of yellow paper; front with a large claret-colored square: Title: Danton's Death printed in black on top in the yellow space and "published" on the left hand bottom corner; In the *claret* space; A play by / GEORG

BÜCHNER / Translated by / STEPHEN SPENDER / and / GORONWY REES / on the spine title, author, translators and publisher in black. On back flap a list of other plays published by Faber and Faber. On front flap, information about the play and on back flap, other books by Spender.

First published in March 1939 by Faber and Faber Limited at 7s. 6d. net. Printed in Great Britain by Western Printing Services Ltd., Bristol. All rights reserved. Introduction by Goronwy Rees, pp. 7-16.

Notes: This is a new translation of a famous German play *Dantons Tod*, a historical play based on the French Revolution, by Büchner (1813-1837). Notes on the Text indicate the the translators have used the text of *Dantons Tod* in the Insel-Bucherei, No. 88, Insel Verlag, Leipzig with a few variations chosen from another text.

Back flap: "This famous play about the French Revolution, written over a hundred years ago, is now presented in a new translation made by Stephen Spender and Goronwy Rees for production this year by the Group Theatre . . . The translators, apart from their reputations for their original work, are also well-known for work in translation, and their collaboration on this play has been extremely successful."

B10   POEMS: F. GARCIA LORCA   1939

First edition:

POEMS / F. GARCIA LORCA / With English translation by / STEPHEN SPENDER / and / J. L. GILI / Selection and introduction by / R.M. NADAL / [device] / THE DOLPHIN / 5 CECIL COURT / LONDON / 1939

3 blank leaves, 2 leaves, and one color plate, V-XXVIII, color plate facing xxii, [1] 2-143 [144] pp., 1 blank leaf. 22.5 x 14.5 cm. Hard-bound in purple cloth with Lorca Poems and publisher's emblem printed in gold on the spine. Dust-jacket in pale green paper printed in dark green letters on front and spine. The front flap contains information about Lorca, translation and introduction; the back flap has complete works of Lorca in Spanish.

Published by The Dolphin Press, London, in May 1939 at 7s. 6d. Printed in Great Britain by Stephen Austin and Sons Ltd., Hertford. Frontispiece has a black and white portrait of F. Garcia Lorca by Gregorio Prieto drawn in Madrid, June 1936. Facing p. xxii is a crayon drawing of "Our Lady of the Seven Dolours" (Paso) by F. Garcia Lorca reproduced by permission of Gregorio Prieto.

Introduction by R.M. Nadal, an intimate friend of Lorca, pp. vii-xxviii; notes, p. 141; acknowledgements, p. 143.

Contents: This is a bilingual edition, and the contents are given in Spanish: Ballad of the Little Square—Song—Hunter—Little Ballade of the Three Rivers—Village—*Paso*—The Guitar—Ballad of the Bullfight—Serenade—Song —Nocturnal Song of the Andalusian Sailors—Song of the Rider—Somnambule Ballad—The Faithless Wife—Death of Antoñito el Camborio—Thamar and Ammon—Song—NORM: I&II—Sonnet—Adam—Ode to the King of Harlem—Ode to Walt Whitman—Dialogue of the Manikin and the Young Man— Speech by a Raindrop—Monologue of the Moon—With a Kinfe—Yerma— Gazelle of the Morning Market—Casida of the Rose—Casida of the Branches —Casida of the Clear Death—Casida of Flight—Lament for Ignatio Sanchez Mejias—Rosa Mutabile—Wind of Love—Song of the Small Death—Song of the One Wounded by the Water—The Lament.

Notes: It is claimed that the translations here are not only accurate but retain "as much as possible the magic and beauty of the original."

B11   MANUEL ALTOLAGUIRRE   1939

First edition:

NUBE / TEMPORAL / POEMAS DE / MANUEL ALTOLAGUIRRE / EN LA COLLECCION / "el ciervo herido" / LA HABANA, 1939

1 blank leaf, 6 leaves, 15-73 [74] pp., 1 leaf, end-leaf 14.5 x 9 cm. Soft-bound in white with title and other details on front: NUBE (black) / TEMPORAL (green) / POEMAS DE (black) / MANUEL ALTOLAGUIR-RE (green) / in small type: Con un autografo de / Jules Supervielle / Y un poema de / STEPHEN SPENDER / EN LA COLLECCION / "el ciervo herido" (green) / LA HABANA, 1939 (black) /

Printed and published by the poet Manuel Altolaguirre on the 28th of September 1939 in La Veronica at La Habana.

Contains a poem in English by Stephen Spender' "To a Spanish Poet" (For Manuel Altolaguirre).

B12   AIR RAIDS   1943

First edition:

[Three lines] / AIR RAIDS / with / an Introduction by / STEPHEN SPENDER / 1943 / OXFORD UNIVERSITY PRESS'/ LONDON. NEW YORK TORONTO / [Double rule]

2 leaves, 5-62 pp., end-leaf. 19 x 12 cm. Soft-bound in cream colored paper. Front framed in black and red lines with "WAR PICTURES / by / BRITISH ARTISTS with in ornamental design followed by "Second Ser-

ies," a sketch and "AIR RAIDS." On the spine: Oxford. War Pictures by British Aritsts. No. IV. AIR RAIDS. Back cover has a list of artists contributing to the second series of drawings and printings and also other titles in the series.

Published by Oxford University Press in 1943 in the series entitled "War Pictures." Printed in Great Britain by Harrison & Sons, Ltd., Printers to His Majesty the King, 44-47, St. Martin's Lane, London, W.C.2. Price: £1.10.

Contents: 50 drawings and paintings for air raids reproduced. Introduction by Spender. Notes on pictures, pp. 59-62.

B13   **JIM BRAIDY**   **1943**

First edition:

[Thick black rule] / JIM BRAIDY / The Story of Britain's Firemen / [Within a square of black outlines] / Sketches of firemen's hats / By / WILLIAM RANSOM, JAMES GORDON, / STEPHEN SPENDER / [Black dot] / ILLUSTRATED BY THE WORK OF FIREMAN ARTISTS / LINDSAY DRUMMOND LTD., LONDON / [Thick black rule] / 1943

Softbound in art paper 25 x 18.5 cm., [1] -64 pp. FRONT: Framed in thick blue rule, JIM BRAIDY [in gold] / The story of Britain's Firemen [in gold] / [Sketch of a Fireman] Illsutrated with [in gold] PAINTINGS BY FIREMAN ARTISTS [gold rule] / TWO SHILLINGS AND SIXPENCE [in blue]. Back of the cover: advertisement for FIRE AND WATER: An N.F.S. Anthology. Back side: a note on The Firemen Artists.

Published in 1943 by Lindsay Drummond Ltd., London at two shillings and sixpence and printed by Merritt & Hatcher Ltd., London, S.E.10.

Contents: 1. The story of Jim Braidy [Mr. James Braidwood, 1800-1861] and of the Fire Brigade and of the brave firemen. 2. Paintings by firemen artists exhibited in London and America, with explanatory notes.

B14   **SELECTED POEMS OF**   **1943**
                 FREDERICO GARCIA LORCA

a)   *First edition:*

SELECTED POEMS OF / FREDERICO GARCIA / LORCA / Translated by / J.L. GILI and STEPHEN SPENDER / The New Hogarth Library / Vol. XI / THE HOGARTH PRESS / 37 MECKLENBURGH SQUARE / LONDON, W.C.1.

1 blank leaf, 2 leaves, 5-56 pp., 1 blank leaf. 18.5 x 12.5 cm. Hard-bound in crimson cloth with title and author's name printed in gold on the spine.

Tan colored dust-jacket with title, author's and translators' names printed in red. At bottom: The New Hogarth Library, also in red.

First published by the Hogarth Press in 1943 at 3s. 6d. as volume XI of their New Hogarth Library. On *verso* of title-leaf: Printed in Great Britain at the Leagrave Press by Gibbs, Bamforth (Luton) Ltd. and "Distributed in Canada by our exclusive agent, The Macmillan Company of Canada Limited, 70 Bond Street, Toronto."

Contents: Ballad of the Little Square—Hunter—Little Balade of the Three Rivers—Village—The Guitar—Song—Song of the Rider (1860)—Nocturnal Song of the Andalusan Sailors—Somnambule Ballad—The Faithless Wife—Thamar and Ammon—Song—Adam—The Dawn—Ode to Walt Whitman—Monologue of the Moon—With a Knife—Casida of the Rose—Yerma—Casida of the Clear Death—Lament for Ignacio Sanchez Mejias: (i) "Cogida" and Death, (ii) The Spilled Blood, (iii) The Laid out Body, (iv) Absent Soul—Song of the One Wounded by the Water—The Lament. Foreword by Gili and Spender, pp. 6-8.

Note: On front flap of the wrapper:

In 1938 Gili and Spender published a literal translation of some poems of Lorca. "In this new selection, they have not only made numerous improvements and corrections, but have attempted a more poetic rendering . . . They have also included a number of entirely new translations."

b) *Second impression:*   1946

c) *Second edition:*   1947

SELECTED POEMS OF / FREDERICO GARCIA / LORCA / *TRANS-LATED by* / J.L. GILI and STEPHEN SPENDER / 1947 / THE HOGARTH PRESS / 40-42 WILLIAM IV STREET / LONDON, W.C.2

1 blank leaf, 2 leaves, 5-56 pp., 1 blank leaf. Hard-bound in blue cloth with: FREDERICO GARCIA LORCA [star] SELECTED POEMS printed in red on the spine. The same kind of dust-jacket with the same print on the front with the addition of "Second Edition" beneath the translator's name.

Published in 1947 by The Hogarth Press. Price-tag cut off. On *verso* of title-leaf: First published in 1943, second impression 1946. Printed in England by The Replica Process by Lund Humphries, London and Bradford. Half-title: F. Garcia Lorca / Poems.

Contents: The same as in the first edition. Foreword by Gili and Spender, pp. 6-8.

d) *American edition:*   1947

The same as the English edition with the exception of the publisher: TRANSATLANTIC ARTS INC., NEW YORK named in addition to THE HOGARTH PRESS, LONDON

On *verso* of title-leaf: First American Edition 1947 and Printed in England by the Replica Process for Transatlantic Arts, Inc. by Lund Humphries . . .

Note: It still continues to be named Vol. XI of The New Hogarth Library. A list of the series is printed on the back flap of the dust-jacket of the English edition.

B15   ARAGON   [1945]

First edition:

ARAGON / Poet of the French Resistance / Edited by / Hannah Josephson / and / Malcolm Cowley / DUELL, SLOAN AND PEARCE. NEW YORK /

2 blank leaves, 2 leaves, vii-xii, [1-2] 3-167 pp., end-leaves. 20.5 x 12.5 cm. Hard-boards in grey cloth with gold printing on front and on spine with red band. Grey dust-jacket with title in white and editors' names in black separated by red decorative design. Front framed in red lines. Back of the cover has portrait of Louis Aragon. Front flap: introduction to the poet and the book. Back flap: publisher's advertisement of another book by Aragon.

Published by Duell, Sloan and Pearce, 270 Madison Ave., New York 16, N.Y. in 1945 at $2.00. Printed in the United States of America by American Book-Stratford Press, Inc., New York. Copyright, 1945, by Duell, Sloan & Pearce, Inc. All rights reserved, including the right to reproduce the book or portions thereof in any form. Introduction by Hannah Josephson, xi-xii.

Contents: Selections in English translations by various authors from the French original of Louis Aragon, led by an essay by Malcolm Cowley "Poet of this war."

Notes: Spender's translation of a poem "Paris" is included here.

B16   A CHOICE OF ENGLISH ROMANTIC POETRY   1947

First edition:

EDITED WITH AN INTRODUCTION By / STEPHEN SPENDER / [Ornamental rule] / A CHOICE OF / ENGLISH / ROMANTIC / POETRY / A PERMANENT LIBRARY BOOK / THE DIAL PRESS 1947 NEW YORK

1 blank leaf, 1 leaf, 3-384 pp., end-leaf. 22 x 14.5 cm. Nile-green cloth boards, front decorated with three brown line-border and printed in brown on the spine are editor, title, and publisher. Dust-jacket of white paper with front printed in three colors—middle portion is dark red with editor and title in white; border is made of red and grey with names of Romantic poets printed on it. Front corners are decorated with leaf-designs. The

spine of the wrapper has white and black letters and leaf design on top. On front and back flap is information about the anthology and the editor. Back of the jacket has a list of The Dial Press Publications in The Permanent Library Series.

Published by The Dial Press, Inc., New York. Manufactured in the United States of America; typography by Eugene M. Ettenberg; copyright, 1947 by the Dial Press. A Permanent library book. Preface, pp. 7-30; Index arranged alphabetically by title, first line, and poet, pp. 381-384.

Notes: Selected and edited with an intorduction by Stephen Spender who is "regarded by many as the sole faithful continuator of the English Romantic Tradition."

The publisher claims: "This is not the usual anthology. In our opinion it marks the beginning of a new epoch in the appreciation of the nineteenth century's achievement in literature . . . Mr. Spender's selections do more than make a point—they also fill in a new and more representative picture of the accomplishment of these poets, preparing the way for a revaluation of their work that will accord better with the modern temper and modern tastes."

B17   THE DEDICATED LIFE IN POETRY   1948

First edition:

PATRICE DE LA TOUR DU PIN / [ornamental] / THE DEDICATED LIFE / IN POETRY / AND / THE CORRESPONDENCE OF LAURENT DE CAYEUX / TRANSLATED BY / G.S. FRASER / WITH AN INTRODUCTION BY / STEPHEN SPENDER / [Ornamental design in red] / CHANGING WORLD SERIES / LONDON: THE HARVILL PRESS

1 blank leaf, 2 leaves, v-xix [xx], 1-63 [64] pp., 1 end-leaf. 19 x 12 cm. Green cloth board, gold print on the spine. Dust-jacket in cream paper; front has red rectangular boxes, top and bottom, with black line border for: "Changing World Series" and "The Harvill Press Ltd.," author and title and introduction by Stephen Spender in black, each item separated by red ornamental rule; down the spine, author and title in black. Back of the wrapper has a picture of Patrice de la Tour de Pin with a brief note on him. Front and back flap contain information about "Changing World Series."

Published in 1948 by The Harvill Press, London, for The Changing World Series at 7s 6d. Printed at the Curwen Press, Plaistow, London, E. 13. The French version of *The Dedicated Life in Poetry* appeared as part of *La Somme de Poesie* in 1947; English translation published by The Harvill Press in 1948. Introduction by Stephen Spender, pp. VII-XIX.

First edition:

THE PITMAN GALLERY / [Rule] / BOTTICELLI / (1444-1510) / with an introduction / and notes by / Stephen Spender [rule] PITMAN PUBLISHING CORPORATION / NEW YORK LONDON / MCMXLVIII

1 blank leaf, [1] -24 pp., end-leaf. 31 x 23 cm. Hardbound in blue cloth, spine printing in gold.

Published by Pitman Corporation, New York and London in 1948.

Contents: 10 plates of reproductions of the paintings of Botticelli with notes. Introduction by Stephen Spender, pp. 1-5, continued on page 24.

Note: Editor's note on p. 24: "We knew before we started that no reproduction could ever do justice to the countless colour subtleties in this part of Botticelli's masterpiece. But we resolved to have a shot at it. And we have, I think, captured something of the ecstatic quality that makes the original so moving and exciting [R.H.W.].

a)   *American edition:*

[Double decorative rule] / THE GOD / THAT FAILED / by ARTHUR KOESTLER IGNAZIO SILONE / RICHARD WRIGHT ANDRÉ GIDE / LOUIS FISCHER / STEPHEN SPENDER / RICHARD CROSSMAN, *Editor* / [Device] / HARPER & BROTHERS, PUBLISHERS, NEW YORK / [Decorative double rule]

One blank leaf, 2 leaves, V-[VIII], 1-273 [274] pp. 4 end-leaves. 21 x 14 cm. Hard-bound in grey cloth. Dust-jacket not seen.

Published in the United States by Harper and Brothers of New York. Printed in the United States of America. Copyright, 1949, by Richard Crossman, copyright, 1944, by Richard Wright; copyright, 1949, by Louis Fischer; copyright, 1949, by Ignazio Silone. All rights in this book are reserved. No part of the book may be reproduced in any manner whatsoever without written permission except in the case of brief quotations embodied in critical articles and reviews. For information address Harper & Brothers.

Contents: Introduction by Richard Crossman, M.P., PART I: The *Initiates:* Arthur Koestler, Ignazio Silone, Richard Wright—PART II: *Worshipers from Afar:* André Gide, *presented by* Dr. Enid Starkie, Louis Fischer, Stephen Spender.

Notes: Stephen Spender's essay, opening with a short biographical note, pp. 229-273.

/ [ornament of a rooster] / —line— BANTAM MATRIX EDITIONS / [rule] / THE GOD THAT FAILED / [dot] / by / André Gide / Richard Wright / Ignazio Silone / Stephen Spender / Arthur Koestler / Louis Fischer / [dot] / Richard Crossman, editor / Bantam Books / [rule] NEW YORK / TORONTO / LONDON /

3 leaves, 1-248 pp., 1 leaf, 18 x 10.5 cm. Soft-bound in pink front and spine, and white for back. Front has title in white and authors "describe their journeys into communism and their return" in gold [4 lines]. Fifth line in gold: Edited and with an introduction by Richard Crossman. Right hand top corner: Publisher's emblem in black. In center: hammer and sickle design. Spine: price, publisher's emblem and title all in black. Back cover: title; and quotation by Arthur Koestler "We ex-communists are the only people on your side who know what it's all about." Then a statement: "André Gide in France, Richard Wright in Chicago, Ignazio Silone in Italy, Stephen Spender in England, Arthur Koestler in Germany, and Louis Fischer--an American journalist in Russia, tell how their search for the betterment of humanity led them to Communism, and the personal agony and revulsion which caused them to reject it." Then a quotation by Arthur Schlesinger, Jr., "The story of the emotions which drew such men to communism and of the events which disillusioned them states concretely and compellingly the great issues of our time." Finally *New York Herald Tribune:* "An important contribution to our understanding of communism in its full dimensions and awful depths."

Contents the same as the first edition.

Note: 1st page. A quotation from Crossman's introduction and from *The Saturday Review:* "A BOOK OF GREAT POWER, FASCINATION AND SIGNIFICANCE." Back of the title page contains total printing history of the book.

A Bantam Book / published by arrangement with Harper & Row, Publishers. Numerous editions and impressions from 1950-1965.

B20   SELECTED POEMS OF WALT WHITMAN   1950

First edition:

[ornamental circular design] / SELECTED POEMS / WALT / WHITMAN / EDITED / AND INTRODUCED BY / STEPHEN SPENDER / [Publisher's emblem] / GREY WALLS / THE CROWN CLASSICS /

1 blank leaf, 1 leaf, 5-64 pp., end-leaf. 20 x 12.5 cm. Hard-bound in orange cloth with ornamental design on front and back, in the center white square with title and editor in black. Title and the publisher on the spine. Dust-jacket with the same color and design by Leslie Atkinson. Front flap carries a note on Whitman and Spender. Back-flap, titles of

crown classics.

First published in 1950 in the crown classics series by the Grey Walls Press Limited, 7 Crown Passage, Pall Mall, London S.W.1. Printed in Great Britain by Lee and Nightingale Limited, Liverpool. Also published in Australia, New Zealand, Canada, and South Africa. All rights reserved. Price: 3s. 6d. net.

Contents: Introduction—In Cabin'd Ships at Sea—I Hear America Singing—Selections from Song of Myself.—From Pent-up Aching Rivers—Native Moments—For You, O Democracy—Recorders Ages Hence—We Two Boys Together Clinging—Sometimes with One I Love—Full of Life Now—The Runner—A Farm Picture—The Dalliance of the Eagles—The Centenarian's Story—The Centenarian—By the Bivouc's Fitful Flame—A March in the Ranks of the Hard-Prest—A Sight in Camp—The Wound Dresser—Long, Two Long America—O Tan-Faced Prairie-Boy—Look Down Fair Moon—Reconciliation—As I Lay with My Head in Your Lap Camerado—Turn O Libertad—Memories of President Lincoln—Old Ireland—What Am I After all—Whispers of Heavenly Death—A Noiseless Patient Spider—The Last Invocation—To a Locomotove in Winter—By Broad Potomac's Shore—A Clear Midnight—Ashes of Soldiers—A Font of Type—Halcyon Days—Soon Shall the Winter's Foil Be Here.

Note: Spender concludes his introduction with: "To read Whitman is to experience one of the greatest and most powerful poetic sensibilities of the modern age."

B21   PAUL ELUARD   1950

LE DUR DÉSIR DE DURER by Paul Eluard. Translation in verse by Stephen Spender with the assistance of Frances Cornford. Illustrated by Marc Chagall.

Published in 1950 by Grey Falcon Press, Philadelphia.

B22   THE LIFE OF THE VIRGIN MARY   1951

First edition:

RAINER MARIA RILKE / [rule] / THE LIFE OF THE / VIRGIN MARY / [DAS MARIEN-LEBEN] / rule / The German text with an English / translation and introduction by / STEPHEN SPENDER / VISION

1 blank leaf, 3 leaves, 7-49 [50] pp., 2 end-leaves. 19 x 13 cm. Hardboards in blue [in some copies, black] cloth, title printed in gold on front and on the spine, author, title and publisher, also in gold. Dust-jacket in tan with author's and translator's name in black and title in red on front; on the spine, author, title, and publisher in black. Front flap contains a note on Rilke and his poem; back flap, a list of publications by Vision.

Published in *1951* by Vision Press Limited, Callard House, 74A Regent Street, London, W1, at 8s 6d. Made and printed in Great Britain by Thomasons Limited, Cedar Press, Hounslow, England. Introduction, pp. 7-10. Greek motto: "Stress within."

Notes: "Rilke's personal interpretation of the Christian Story." "This cycle has been strangely neglected even by Rilke's admirers, possibly because of the unorthodox manner in which the poet approaches his theme. ... At the present moment, when literature in its search for values tends to discover new meanings in old stories, Rilke's moving recreation of the most meaningful story of all offers us a deeply rewarding experience."

B23   THE YEAR'S WORK IN LITERATURE 1950   1951

First edition:

THE YEAR'S WORK / IN / LITERATURE / 1950 / Edited by / JOHN LEHMANN / Published for / THE BRITISH COUNCIL / By LONGMANS, GREEN AND CO. / LONDON NEW YORK TORONTO

1 leaf, portrait [frontispiece], 3 leaves, 9-90 pp., 1 end-leaf. 23.5 x 15.5 cm. Soft-bound in blue paper, front has title in white decorative square and has ornamental device below. White border with black line. Title and publisher in black on the spine. Back of the cover has price in white and information about cover "printed by Fosh and Cross Ltd., London."

Published in 1951 at Five Shillings net by Longmans, Green and Co. for the British Council, Printed in Great Britain at the Curwen Press Ltd., Plaistow, E. 13. Illustrated with 13 plates. Introduction by John Lehmann, pp. 9-11 (February 1951). Bibliography and Index, pp. 80-90.

Contents: An article: On 'The Cocktail Party' by Stephen Spender, pp. 17-23. Facing page 68, a portrait of Stephen Spender in black and white and a note on him as contributor, p. [7].

B24   EUROPE IN PHOTOGRAPHS   1952

First edition:

EUROPE / IN PHOTOGRAPHS / COMMENTARY / BY STEPHEN SPENDER / 248 PHOTOGRAVURE PLATES AND / HISTORICAL NOTES / [Device] / LONDON. THAMES AND HUDSON. NEW YORK

4 leaves, v-xiii [xiv], 1-280 pp., end-leaf. 30 x 21.5 cm. Hard-boards in grey cloth with gold device in front and printing down the spine.

Produced and published by Thames and Hudson Limited, New York and London and by Atlantis Verlag Zurich. Printed in Great Britain by Jarold and Sons Limited, Norwich 1952. Gravure plates printed by Gebr. Fretz A.G. Zurich.

Contents: Commentary by Spender, pp. V-XII; photographs, 1-248 pp.; historical notes, 250-277 pp.; photographic sources, p. 278; Index, 279-280 pp.

B25   **FIVE TRAGEDIES OF SEX**   **1952**

First edition:

FIVE TRAGEDIES / OF SEX / BY FRANK WEDEKIND / With an introduction by / Lion Feuchtwanger / translated by / Frances Fawcett and Stephen Spender / THEATRE ARTS BOOKS / NEW YORK

1 blank leaf, 3 leaves, 7-434 pp., end-leaf. 21 x 13.5 cm. Hard-bound.

Published by Theatre Arts Books, 124 East, 30th Street, New York 16. Made and printed in Great Britain by G.T. Wray Ltd. London. All rights reserved. Introduction by Lion Feuchtwanger, pp. 7-21.

Contents: I. Spring's Awakening—II. Earth-Spirit—III. Pandora's Box—IV. Death and Devil—V. Castle Wetterstein.

B26   **GEORGE BERNARD SHAW**   **1953**

First edition:

[double rule] / George Bernard SHAW: / A CRITICAL SURVEY. EDITED / By LOUIS KRONENBERGER / [Device] / Cleveland and New York / THE WORLD PUBLISHING COMPANY

1 blank leaf, 3 leaves, vii-xvii [xviii], [1-2] 3-262 pp., one leaf, one end-leaf. 24 x 16 cm. Hard-boards in brown cloth.

Published by The World Publishing Company in 1953. Manufactured in the United States. Typography by Joseph Trautwein. Copyright 1953 by The World Publishing Company. All rights reserved. Library of Congress Catalog Card number: 52-5197.

Contents: A short chronology—introduction-essays by various contributors —Index.

Note: Spender's essay: "The Riddle of Shaw," pp. 236-239. Reprinted from *The Nation*, April 30, 1949.

First edition:

The Arts at Mid-Century / Edited by Robert Richman / Horizon Press New York 1954.

4 blank leaves, ix-xi, [1-2] 3-306 pp., end-leaf. 24 x 15 cm. Hard-boards in black cloth with printing on the spine; edges rough trimmed.

Published by Horizon Press, New York in 1954. Manufactured in the United States by H. Wolff, New York. Designed by Marshall Lee. Copyright 1954 by Horizon Press, Inc. Library of Congress Catalog Card Number: 54-7896. Preface by Robert Richman, pp. ix-xi, Washington 1954.

Contents: Some General Essays: 1. The New Orthodoxies (Stephen Spender); 2. An Age of Criticism (John Crowe Ransom); 3. The Muses' Sterner Laws (Archibald MacLeish); 4. The Blur of Mediocrity (Francis Biddle); 5. Moral Action in Art (Allen Tate); 6. Symbolism: American Style (John Crowe Ransom); 7. Progress in Music (Robert Evett); 8. Primitive Art and Modern Man (Herbert Read); 9. The Masters of the Twentieth Century (Robert Richman). The *Arts in France:* 10. The French Novel at Mid-Century (Henri Peyre); 11. Mid-Century French Poetry (Wallace Fowlie); 12. The Challenge of Boimondau (Herbert Read); 13. An Existentialist in the Underworld (Joseph Frank); 14. Recent French Painting (Kermit Lansner); 15. Music in France (Norman Demuth); 16. French Theatre: The National Genius (William Becker); 17. The French Film (Parker Tyler). *The Arts in Italy:* 18. The Fiction of Giovanni Verga (Mark Shorer); 19. Silone the Faithful (Paolo Milano); 20. Ambiguities in Italian Literature (Nicola Chiaromonte); 21. Italian Painting (Kermit Lansner); 22. The Italian Theatre (Eric Bentley); 23. Italian Films (Parker Tyler). *The Arts in Germany;* 24. An Impenitent Prussian; 25. The German Novel at Mid-Century (Ray B. West, Jr.); 26. The "Double Life" of Gottfried Benn (Joseph Frank); 27. The Position of Bertolt Brecht (William Becker); 28. The German Film (Park Tyler). *The Arts in England;* 29. English Fiction at Mid-Century (Elizabeth Bowen); 30. English Poetry at Mid-Century (Kathleen Raine); 31. English Painting in the Fifties (Stephen Spender); 32. Music in England (Norman Demuth); 33. English Theatre: A Budding Traditionalism (William Becker); 34. The British Film: Phonetics, *Fumed Oak*, and Fun (Parker Tyler). *The Arts in the United States.* 35. American Novels since the war (Malcolm Cowley); 36. American Poetry in the Twentieth Century (Arthur Mizener); 37. Recent Literary Criticism (Delmore Schwartz); 38. The Younger Generation and Its Books (Kenneth Rexroth); 39. American Painting and Sculpture at Mid-Century (Robert Richman); 40. Give My regards to Broadway (Eric Bentley); 42 The American Film: Trends in (Parker Tyler). *The Fifties:* Notes on the Contributors.

Notes: Spender has contributed two essays: 1. The New Orthodoxies and 2. English Painting in the Fifties.

First edition:

LEDA AND THE SWAN / AND OTHER RECENT WORK / [by] SID-NEY NOLAN / 16 JUNE-16 JULY 1960 / THE MATTHIESEN GALLERY / 142 NEW BOND STREET, LONDON, W.1. /

Cat. No. 1. LEDA AND SWAN, 1958, has Spender's introduction to the art of Sidney Nolan, an Australian painter, who had one-man shows in Paris, London, New York and in Australian capital cities.

First edition:

(ornament) / GREAT WRITINGS OF / GOETHE / Edited and / with an Introduction by / STEPHEN SPENDER / (Publisher's emblem) / A MENTOR BOOK / Published by THE NEW AMERICAN LIBRARY

3 leaves, vii-xix [xx], 21-278 [279-280] pp., 18 x 11 cm. Bound in glazed paper; front in gold, white, and blue strips: title printed in the golden part on top and "A Mentor Book" at bottom; the blue strip in the middle has Goethe's picture and a description of the book; in the white strip: "edited with an introduction" in red and in the second line, "Stephen Spender" in large bold black type. Price and Mentor numbers listed on left hand corner on top. On the spine, the title, editor, and Mentor number of the book in black. Back of the cover is in gold and blue strips separated by a white band, carrying a quotation from Thomas Mann and a description of the works included in the book and a bust of Goethe. The bottom strip has publisher's name. Edges trimmed and stained red. The first leaf has a list of Mentor Publications of their philosophers' series. On *verso*, a brief note on Goethe and Spender. The last leaf has a list of Mentor Books.

Published in 1958 by the New American Library of World Literature, Inc., 501 Madison Avenue, New York 22, New York, as a Mentor Book number 235. First printing, August 1958, in the United States of America. All rights reserved. © 1958 by Stephen Spender. Priced at 75c. Introduction by Stephen Spender, pp. vii-xix.

Contents: I. From conversations of Goethe with Ekermann and Soret (translated by John Oxenford)–II. Letters from Goethe–III. Poems–IV. First Love and Coronation–V. Faust (Part One)–VI. Travels in Italy–VII. Poems with classical Themes–VIII. Elective Affinities–IX. Novelle–X. Poems: Middle and Late–XI. Reflections and Maxims–XII. Two Poems.

Notes: Letters of Goethe, translated by M. von Herzfeld and C. Melvil

Sym; Part I of *Faust*, translated by Louis MacNeice ("Elective Affinities" from *Novels and Tales*, translated by James Anthony Froude and R. Dillon Boylan; "First Love and the Coronation," translated by Eithne Wilkins and Ernst Kaiser.)

From Spender's introduction: "I have emphasized the autobiographical elements in this selection, because autobiography is the clue to Goethe."

B30   MEMOIRS OF A PUBLIC BABY   1958

a)   *First edition:*

MEMOIRS OF / A PUBLIC BABY / by / PHILIP O'CONNOR / With an Introduction / by / STEPHEN SPENDER / FABER AND FABER / 24 Russell Square / London

2 blank leaves, 3 leaves, 9-231 [232] pp., end-leaf. 20.5 x 14 cm. Hardboards in beige cloth, and printing on the spine. Yellow dust-jacket, front with title in black and author's name boxed in red decorative frame. Spine printing of author and title in black and "introduction by Stephen Spender" in red letters. Back of the wrapper has a list of publications by Faber; front flap, a note on the nature of O'Connors's autobiography; and back flap, other books by Spender.

First published in 1958 by Faber and Faber Limited at 18s. net. Printed in Great Britain by Wyman and Sons Ltd., Fakenham. All rights reserved: © Phillip O'Connor. Introduction by Stephen Spender, pp. 13-18.

Dedication: For Anna Wing.

Notes: P. [11] has a quotation from Montaigne.

b)   *First American edition:*

The same as the British edition, except the publisher who is "British Book Center, New York." Dust-jacket is more fanciful and the front and back flaps have selections from reviews and Spender's introduction. Back of the wrapper has Portrait of Philip O'Connor by Elliott & Fry Ltd. American edition priced at $4.00.

B31   SCHILLER'S MARY STUART   1959

First edition:

Schiller's / MARY STUART / freely translated / and adapted / by / STEPHEN SPENDER / with a preface / by / PETER WOOD / FABER AND FABER / 24 Russell Square / London / [1959]

2 blank leaves, 2 leaves, 7-101 [102] pp., end-leaves. Blue cloth boards, printing on the spine in gold. Dust-jacket in sky-color, printed in red and black on front, and on spine, title framed with red border. Front flap con-

tains information about the German original and its English translations published by Faber and back flap, other books of Spender.

First published in 1959 by Faber and Faber Limited at 15s. net. Printed in Great Britain by Latimer Trend & Co. Ltd., Plymouth. All rights reserved: © Stephen Spender 1959 *"Mary Stuart* is fully protected by copyright. Applications for all performing rights in the play should be addressed to the author's agent, Peters & Ramsey, 14A Goodwin's Court, London, W.C.2. No performance may take place unless a license has been obtained." Preface by Peter Wood, pp. 7-9; introduction by Stephen Spender, pp. 11-14.

Notes: From the front flap: a classic of the German theatre, but until now existed in English only in the translation made by Charles Mellish in 1802. "In making this version, which was commissioned by the Old Vic for the Edinburgh Festival of 1958, Stephen Spender set himself the task of inventing from Schiller's text a play in modern English idiom. To do this he translated very freely . . . where it seemed a poetic necessity, Mr. Spender endeavored to observe close fidelity to Schiller's poetry."

The introduction by Spender describes the methods and principles he used in translating this play.

The first performance in Great Britain of Schiller's *Mary Stuart*, translated by Stephen Spender and adapted by Peter Wood, was given at the Church of Scotland Assembly Hall, Edinburgh, on 2nd September 1958 by the Old Vic Company. It was directed by Peter Wood, the costumes and decor were by Leslie Hurry and the music was composed by John Hotchkiss. Mary's role was played by Irene Worth.

B32   **GREAT GERMAN STORIES**   **1960**

First edition:

Great German / Short Stories / Edited and introduced by / Stephen Spender / LAUREL / [device] / EDITION

4 leaves, [9] -284 pp., 2 leaves. 16.5 x 10.5 cm. Soft-bound in green paper; on front: left hand top corner: DELL / LAUREL / EDITION / LC 148; right hand top: 50¢. Center: "Great German / short stories," in yellow; "Edited and introduced by / Stephen Spender," in white; [ornamental design] ; names of authors in white. On the spine the title in yellow and the publisher in blue. On the back cover a list of stories with their authors in the anthology.

Published by DELL PUBLISHING CO. INC., 750 Third Ave., New York 17, N.Y. First printing, May 1960; designed and produced by Western Printing and Lithographing Company. Copyright, © 1960, by Stephen Spender, Laurel ® T.M. Dell Publishing Company, Priced at 50c.

Contents: Introduction by Stephen Spender—Georg Büchner: "Lenz"—Adalbert Stifter: "Brigitta::—Heinrich von Kleist: "The Earthquake in Chile"—Gottfried Keller: "A Little Legend of the Dance"—Hugo Von Hofmannsthal: "A Tale of the Cavalry"—George Heym: "The Autopsy"—Rainer Maria Rilke: "In the Penal Colony"—Robert Walser: "A Village Table"—Gottfried Benn: "The Conquest." *The Living Authors*: Ilse Aichinger: "The Bound Man"—Henrich Böll: "The Man With the Knives"—Heinz Huber: "The New Apartment"—Hans Erich Nossack: "The Meeting in the Hallway"—Gerd Gaiser: "The Game of Murder—Wolfgang Hildesheimer: "A World Ends."

Notes: This is part of the Laurel Literature series. Edited and introduced by Spender, and stories translated by many hands.

B33   THE WRITER'S DILEMMA   1961

First edition:

THE / WRITER'S DILEMMA / ESSAYS FIRST PUBLISHED IN / THE TIMES LITERARY SUPPLEMENT / UNDER THE HEADING / "LIMITS OF CONTROL" / WITH / an introduction by / STEPHEN SPENDER / LONDON / OXFORD UNIVERSITY PRESS / NEW YORK TORONTO / 1961

1 blank leaf, 3 leaves, vii-xxi [xxii], 11-88 pp., 1 leaf, end-leaf. 20 x 13.5 cm. Hard-boards in black cloth, gold printing on the spine. Paper wrapper in white with blue for front and spine. Title in white and authors of essays and introduction in black. Title in white on the spine and publisher in black. Back of the jacket has a list of Oxford books and front flap, information about the book. Trimmed edges.

Published by Oxford University Press, Amen House, London E.C.4, at $2.50. Printed in Great Britain by The Bowering Press, Plymouth. Copyright for ten essays and 'Limits of Control': © The Times Publishing Company Ltd., 1960; for Introduction by Stephen Spender: © Oxford University Press 1961. All rights reserved.

Contents: Introduction: "The Sector of Communication," by Stephen Spender, pp., vii-xix. Ten essays by various writers.

Notes: On the front flap of the dust-jacket:

"What are the limits beyond his own control that threaten the modern writer? The Editor of *The Times Literary Supplement* put this question to ten representative authors, and invited them to consider the position of the writer in an age which places greater value on the progress of technology than on the state of the individual. . . . Stephen Spender introduces the essays.

First edition:

The Concise Encyclopedia of / ENGLISH AND AMERICAN / Poets and
Poetry / Edited by / STEPHEN SPENDER and / DONALD HALL / HAW-
THORN BOOKS INC., *PUBLISHERS*, NEW YORK / 1963

2 blank leaves, 3 leaves, 7-415 [416] pp., 2 end-leaves. 25 x 19 cm. Hard-
boards in blue cloth with printing in gold on the spine.

First published in 1963 by Hawthorn Books, Inc., 70 Fifth Avenue, New
York City. Designed and produced by George Rainbird Ltd., London.
Printed and bound by The Garden City Press Ltd., Letchworth, England.
The blocks for the monochrome plates were made by Austin Miles Ltd.,
London. The end papers and the jacket were printed by Garrod and Loft-
house Ltd., London. Published simultaneously in Canada by McClelland &
Stewart Ltd., 25 Hollinger Road, Toronto 16. Library of Congress Catalog
No. 63-8015. Priced at $17.95. *Illustrated.*

Contents: List of contributors—List of general articles—List of plates—In-
troduction, by the editors—Publisher's note—The Concise Encyclopedia—
For further reading—Key to initials and notes on the contributors—Ac-
knowledgements—Index of poets quoted—General index. General articles:
American Poetry—Anglo-Saxon Poetry—Australian Poetry—Canadian Poet-
ry—Classic and Romantic—Criticism and Poetry—English Poetry in Africa—
"Everyman and the miracle Plays—Foreign Influences on English Poetry—
Fugitive Group—Hymns, songs and carols—Imagery—Imagism—Indian
Poetry in English—Metaphor—Middle English Lyric—Music and Poetry—
Myth and Poetry—New Criticism—New Directions in Metrics—New Zea-
land Poetry—Poetry and Publishing: Britain—Poetry and Publishing:
United States—Popular Poetry—Prosody, Forms of Verse, and Some
Usages—Religion and Poetry—Satire—Science and Poetry—Society and the
Poet—South African Poetry in English—Symbolism—Translation.

Illustrated with nearly 100 pictures of poets.

Contributors: 78.

Notes: The editors claim: "We have tried to collect information necessary
to the student of poetry and to represent the best contemporary critical
opinion."

B35   EROTIC POETRY   1963

First edition:

[On *verso* of half title] Erotic Poetry / DECORATIONS BY WARREN
CHAPPELL [smaller type in blue] / [on *recto*] [Device] The Lyrics, Bal-
lads, Idyls / and Epics of Love — / Edited by WILLIAM COLE / Fore-

word by Stephen Spender / [Publisher's emblem] / [rule] / RANDOM HOUSE / 1963 /

1 blank leaf, 3 leaves, vii-liv, [1-4] 5-501 [502] pp., one leaf, 24.5 x 16.5 cm. Hard-boards in green cloth, with front title in gold and sketch of eros and woman in red, ornamented spine and printing in gold: [ornament] / Erotic / Poetry / [dot] / William / Cole / [ornament] / [publisher's emblem] / Random House. Dust-jacket in yellow and red, front: sketch of man, woman and cupid / Title / subtitle / edited by William Cole / Foreword by Stephen Spender / Followed by a list of poets included in the volume. Spine in red with yellow box for title, subtitle, sketch of cupid, editor's name and publisher. Front flap: description of the book, back flap: picture of the editor with a biographical note. Back of the dust-jacket gives contents of the book.

Published by Random House, New York, simultaneously in Toronto, Canada, by Random House of Canada, Limited. Manufactured in the United States of America. Copyright, 1963, by William Cole. Designed and illustrated by Warren Chappell. Priced at $8.95.

Contents: Foreword by Stephen Spender, pp. [xxiii] -xxvii—Introduction by William Cole—I. Of Women—II. Incitement and Desire—III. Importunities and Advice—IV. Celebrations and Delights—V. Womanizers and Seducers—VI. The World and The Flesh—VII. By-Paths and Oddities.

Notes: Included is a poem by Spender: "O Night, O Trembling Night," p. 276.

B36   **ENCOUNTERS**   **1963**

First edition:

ENCOUNTERS / An Anthology from the First Ten Years / of *Encounter* Magazine / Editors: / STEPHEN SPENDER, IRVING KRISTOL, MELVIN J. LASKY / BASIC BOOKS, INC., PUBLISHERS / NEW YORK /

1 blank leaf, 2 leaves v-xiii [xiv], [1-2] 3-561 [562] pp., end-leaf. 24.5 x 16 cm. Hard-boards in red cloth, printing on the spine in gold and blue with thick decorative rules. Dust-jacket in ornament design by Lawrence Ratzkin, with title in big, bold type in white and half-title in red with names on the spine. Front and back flap carries information about the anthology. Edges trimmed.

Published by Basic Books, Inc. of New York in 1963 at $8.50. Manufactured in the United States of America. © 1953-1963 by *Encounter* Magazine. Library of Congress Catalog Number: 63-21691. Acknowledgments, pp. ix-x; Preface by M.J. Lasky, pp. xi-xiii (London, April 1963). Notes on Authors, pp. 557-[562].

Contents: I. Persons & Places—II. Problems & Polemics—III. Arts & Letters —IV. Men & Ideas—V. Stories—VI. Poems.

Spender's article, "European Notebook," pp. 240-255. His poem, "Subject: Object: Sentence," p. 541 (April 1958).

Notes: A note on Spender in "Notes on Authors" appears on p. 558.

B37   GHIKA   1964

First edition:

GHIKA / Paintings, Drawings, Sculpture / Introduction by Christian Zervos / Texts by Stephen Spender and Patrick Leigh Fermor / Lund Humphries 12 Bedford Square London WC1

1 blank leaf, 4 leaves, 1-69 [70] pp., end-leaf. 32 x 24.5 cm. Hard-boards in white with "GHIKA" on front and title and publisher on the spine. Frontispiece in black and white: Ghika in Paris, 1954.

Published in the autumn of 1964 by Lund Humphries. Made and printed in Great Britain by Percy Lund, Humphries & Co. Ltd., London and Bradford.

Contents: Ghika and his art by Christian Zervos—Ghika by Stephen Spender—The background of Niko Ghika by Patrick Leigh Fermor—List of plates—Plates—Reflections by Ghika—Appreciations—Biographical Notes with a Bibliography.

B38   SHELLEY (in French)   1964

First edition:

ÉCRIVAINS / d'Hier et / d'AUJOURD' HUI / 17 / SHELLEY / Un tableau synoptique de la vie et des oeuvres de P.B. Shelley et des / evenements artistiques, littéraires et historiques de son époque. / Une suite iconographique accompagnée d'un commentaire sur / P.B. Shelley et son temps. / une étude sur l'écrivain par STEPHEN SPENDER / un choix de judgements / Un choix de texts de P.B. Shelley. / Une bibliographie / P.S. Editions Pierre Seghers /

Paperback in blue with a portrait of Shelley on the front, pp. 1-191. Copyright © 1952 British Council, London. 1954 by Editions Seghers, Paris.

B39   OPINIONS AND PERSPECTIVES   1964

First edition:

OPINIONS / AND PERSPECTIVES / from / The New York Times Book Review / Edited and with an introduction / By Francis Brown / [Publisher's emblem] / HOUGHTON MIFFLIN COMPANY BOSTON / The Riverside Press Cambridge [in decorative type] / 1964.

1 blank leaf, 2 leaves [v] -xiii [xiv], [1-3] 4-441 [442] pp., dark green cloth with gold printing on front and the spine.

Published by Houghton Mifflin Co. Boston in 1964. Printed by the Riverside Press, Cambridge. Copyright © 1955, 56, 58, 59, 60, 61, 62, 63, 64 by The New York Times Company . . . All rights reserved. Library of Congress Card Catalog No. 64-24018.

Contents: Introduction—Part I. Consider the Contemporary—Part II. American Classics—Part III. Reviews and Reappraisals—Part IV. Points of View—Part V. Somewhat Personal—Part VI, The Author's Experience—Part VII. Men and Measures—Index.

Notes: Spender has contributed two essays: 1. "Is There no More Need to Experiment," pp. 34-40; 2. "Literary London: A Tight Little Isle," pp. 284-291.

B40   UNDER THE VOLCANO   1965

First edition:

UNDER / [ornamental design] / THE / VOLCANO / MALCOLM LOWRY / With an Introduction by / Stephen Spender / J.B. LIPPINCOTT COMPANY / PHILADELPHIA AND NEW YORK / 1965

2 blank leaves, 3 leaves, vii-xxvi, [1-2] 3-375 [376-377], end-leaves. 21 x 14 cm. Hard-bound in grey paper, spine in brown cloth. Title, author, publisher on the spine in black type. Dust-jacket designed by David Lunn. Author and title in black on the front in black, in the center a sketch in red and green, "introduction by Stephen Spender" in red letters. Printing on the spine. Selections from reviews on front and back flap. On the back cover a note on the author and the book.

Introduction by Stephen Spender, pp. vii-xxvi.

B41   THE MAGIC FLUTE   1966

First edition:

THE MAGIC FLUTE / RETOLD BY / STEPHEN SPENDER / PICTURES BY BENI MONTRESOR / G.P. PUTNAM'S SONS / NEW YORK / [Large Colored Sketch]

One blank leaf, no pagination, 3 leaves. [1-42] pp., end-leaf. 24 x 26 cm. Hard-boards in dark orange with printing on the spine. Illustrations.

Published by Putnam's Sons, New York and printed in the United States of America. Published simultaneously in Canada by Longmans Canada Limited. Toronto. Library of Congress Catalog Card Number: AC66-10258.

Story retold by Stephen Spender with illustrations by Beni Montressor.

Notes: For children of the age of 7 and up. The story was set by Mozart and presented some 175 years ago in a small Viennese Theatre. The paintings in the book are based on the production of the Magic Flute for the New York City Opera. Spender recreates faithfully the fairy tale atmosphere and provides new lyrics for Mozart's Characters.

B42   THE POEMS OF P.B. SHELLEY   1971

First edition:

THE POEMS OF / PERCY BYSSHE SHELLEY / Selected, edited, and introduced by / STEPHEN SPENDER / [ornamental device] / *Illustrated with wood engravings by* / RICHARD SHIRLEY SMITH / Printed for the members of THE LIMITED EDITIONS CLUB / at the University Printing House / Cambridge: 1971

One blank leaf, 2 leaves, v-[xxviii], [1-2] 3-312 [313-316] pp., end-leaf. 28 x 17 cm. Hard-boards in brown cloth with Shelley's bust printed on front; spine bound in chocolate leather with the title imprinted in gold on black.

Colophon: Of this edition of THE POEMS OF SHELLEY fifteen hundred copies have been made for the members of The Limited Editions Club. It has been designed by John Dreyfus and printed at the University Printing House in Cambridge by Brooke Crutchley, Printer to the University. . .

Contents: PART ONE: The Confessional Poet—PART TWO: Love—PART THREE: Nature, Imagination, Joy, and Grief—PART FOUR: Politics—PART FIVE: The Invitation—PART SIX: The Triumph of Life—PART SEVEN: Mutability—PART EIGHT: Translations—Appendix—Index of First Lines—Index to Titles.

Notes: 1. Introduction by Spender, pp. ix-xxvii, STORRS, Connecticut, May, 1970. 2. Copy examined: No. 262 and is signed by the illustrator, R.S. Smith.

B43   A CHOICE OF SHELLEY'S VERSE   1971

First edition:

A CHOICE OF / SHELLEY'S VERSE / Selected / with an introduction by / STEPHEN SPENDER / FABER AND FABER / 3 Queen Square / London

1 blank leaf, 2 leaves, 5-92 pp., end-leaf. 21 x 13.5 cm. Hard-boards in blue cloth, title, author and publisher printed in gold on the spine. White dust-jacket, on the front: A CHOICE OF / in green letters, Shelley's / verse / in black, and Selected with an Introduction by / STEPHEN SPENDER in black. A portrait of Shelley in green on the front. On the spine

title, author, and publisher printed in black. Back of the wrapper has a list of books in the series with prices. Front flap has a note on Spender and back flap, advertisement for Faber books.

First published in 1971 by Faber and Faber Limited and printed in Great Britain by Latimer Trend and Co. Ltd., Plymouth. All rights reserved. Hard-bound and paper-bound editions published simultaneously. ISBN (hard-bound edition): 0 571 08789 2 and ISBN (paper-bound edition): 0 571 08790 6. Copyright of the introduction © Stephen Spender 1971 and of this selection © Faber and Faber 1971. Introduction, pp. 7-15; Index of First Lines, pp. 91-92.

Contents: 35 poems with some selections from longer poems.

B44   **THE LULU PLAYS AND**   **1972**
                OTHER SEX TRAGEDIES

First edition:

GERMAN EXPRESSIONISM / THE LULU PLAYS / & OTHER SEX TRAGEDIES / Earth Spirit / Pandora's Box / Death and Devil / Castle Wetterstein / FRANK WEDEKIND / Translated from the German by / Stephen Spender / CALDER AND BOYARS, LONDON

One blank leaf, 4 leaves, 9-281 [282] pp., 2 leaves, 2 end-leaves. 21 x 13.5 cm. Hardboards in orange paper, printing in gold on the spine.

First published in 1972 by Calder Boyars Ltd., 18 Brewer Street, London. Printed in Great Britain by Latimer Trend & Co. Ltd., Whitstable. All rights including performing rights strictly reserved. Copyright © These Translations Stephen Spender 1952, 1972. Application for performances should be made to C & B (Theatre) Ltd., 18 Brewer Street, London W1.

Contents: Translations of the follwoing plays: 1. Earth Spirit; 2. Pandora's Box; 3. Death and Devil; 4. Castle Wetterstein.

Note: Last pages give a list of C and B Playscripts and price.

B45   **PENGUIN MODERN POETS -23**   **1973**

Penguin Modern Poets / -23- / GEOFFREY GRIGSON / EDWIN MUIR / ADRIAN STOKES / [short rule] / *Guest Editor*: STEPHEN SPENDER / [Emblem of a Penguin] / Penguin Books /

2 leaves, 5-160 pp., 17 x 10.5 cm. Soft-cover, front decorative design by Alan Spain, and on the left top corner in white: Penguin Modern Poets-23 / Geoffrey Grigson / Edwin Muir / Adrian Stokes. On back of the cover description of the purpose of this publication and prices in U.K. Australia, New Zealand, and Canada.

First published in 1973 by Penguin Books Ltd., for 35 p. in U.K., $1.00 in Australia, $1.00 in New Zealand, and $1.50 in Canada. Made and printed in Great Britain by © Nicholls and Company Ltd. Set in monotype. Copyright: The poems by Grigson © Geoffrey Grigson, 1963, 1969, 1971, 1973; The poems by Edwin Muir are copyright © Willa Muir, 1960; and the poems are copyright © Adrian Stokes, 1973.

Contents: I. Biographical notes on the poets included on p. 1. II. Poems by Grigson, Muir and Stokes.

B46   **D.H. LAWRENCE**   **1973**

First edition:

D.H. LAWRENCE / Novelist, Poet, Prophet / *Edited by* / Stephen Spender / HARPER & ROW, PUBLISHERS / NEW YORK, EVANSTON, SAN FRANCISCO, LONDON

1 blank leaf, 3 leaves, 1-250 pp., end-leaf. 25.5 x 19 cm. Hard-boards in red cloth, white printing down the Spine: D.H. LAWRENCE / Novelist, Poet, Prophet / sideways and in the center: Spender; at bottom: Harper & Row. Dust-jacket in white. Front has portrait of D.H. LAWRENCE with the name on top and subtitle in black, the words: Edited by / Stephen Spender in red, and names of contributors in small black type. On the spine the title in red and editor's name in black. Front flap has a note on Lawrence followed by one on Spender. Back of the cover has a quotation by Diana Trilling and back flap, contents of the book.

First U.S. edition published by Harper & Row, Publishers, Inc., 10 East 53rd Street, New York, N.Y. 10022. Printed in Great Britain. Copyright © George Weidenfeld and Nicolson Ltd., 1973. All rights reserved . . . copyright © 1958. A. Alvarez, "The Single State of Man" from *The Shaping Spirit* by A. Alvarez is reprinted with the permission of Charles Scribner's Sons . . . Standard Book Number: 06-013956-0. Library of Congress Catalog Number: 73-2000. Price at $12.95. Illustrated.

Contents: Diana Trilling: D.H. Lawrence and the Movements of Modern Culture—Barbara Weekley Barr: Memoir of D.H. Lawrence—David Garnett: Frieda and Lawrence—Alan Silitoe: D.H. Lawrence and His District—Stephen Spender: D.H. Lawrence, England, and the War—Frank Kermode: The Novels of D.H. Lawrence—Barbara Hardy: Women in D.H. Lawrence's Works—John Carey: D.H. Lawrence's Doctrine—Jeffrey Meyers: D.H. Lawrence and Homosexuality—Clive James: D.H. Lawrence in Transit—Tony Tanner: D.H. Lawrence and America—Denis Donoghue: 'Till the Fight Is Finished,' D.H. Lawrence in His Letters—A. Alvarez: Lawrence's Poetry, The Single State of Man—Edward Lucie Smith: The Poetry of D.H. Lawrence, with a glance at Shelley—John Russell: D.H. Lawrence and Painting—Notes—Index—Sources of Illustrations.

/ [double rule / W.H. AUDEN / a tribute / [double rule] / edited by Stephen Spender / WEIDENFELD AND NICOLSON LONDON

1 blank leaf, 2 leaves, [5] -255 [256] pp., end-leaf. 15.5 x 18 cm. Hardboards in gold cloth, with a line drawing of Auden on right hand bottom corner and printing on the spine: title in large bold type in black; in small type in black: A tribute edited by / Stephen Spender and publisher, at bottom. Dust-jacket in black and white art paper with a large portrait of Auden on front with W.H. Auden on top in large white letters and in smaller type in red below: A tribute edited by / Stephen Spender. On the spine, title in black and half-title in red and publisher in small black type. Back of the wrapper carries a list of contributors and front flap, a note on Auden, Spender, and the book. Back flap has a photograph of Spender by Mark Gerson with a brief biographical note.

Published by Weidenfeld and Nicolson of London at £ 4.50 (in U.K. only). Printed Offset Litho in Great Britain by Cox & Wyman Ltd., London, Fakenham and Reading. Edited with introduction by Stephen Spender. Illustrated.

Introduction, pp. [7] -8; illustrations: 64 pages of photographs; index. pp. [253] -255. Copyright owners: The Estate of W.H. Auden, Faber & Faber, and George Weidenfeld & Nicolson Ltd., (1974-75).

Contents: Apart from the introduction by Spender, there is a poem by him on page [242] : "Auden at Milwaukee," which is "a note from my diary written on my sixty-first birthday, 28 February 1970, after dining with Auden in New York; and a "Valediction" on pp. 244-248: It is "The address Spender gave on 27 October 1973 at Auden's memorial service in Christ Church.

BN

ANTHOLOGIES AND COLLECTIONS

OF
PROSE AND POETRY
CONTAINING
POEMS AND ESSAYS
BY
STEPHEN SPENDER

BN1

MODERN BRITISH POETRY: A Critical Anthology, edited by Louis Untermeyer (New York: Harcourt, Brace and Company, 1931).

Contains: 1. "Farewell in a Dream" (p. 767); 2. "Statistics," p. 768; 3. "Old Wives in March," p. 768; 4. "Winter Landscape," p. 769; 5. "A Whim of Time," p. 770; 6. "Exile," p. 771; 7. "Epilogue," p. 771.

BN2

NEW COUNTRY (LONDON: The Hogarth Press, 1933).

Contains: "Poetry and Revolution," pp. 62-71.

BN3

RECENT Poetry: 1923-1933, edited with an introduction by Alida Monro (London: Gerald Howe Ltd and The Poetry Bookshop, 1933).

Contains: "The Express," "After They Have Tired," "He Will Watch The Hawk," pp. 179-183.

BN4

MODERN POETRY: 1922-1934, AN ANTHOLOGY, selected and edited by Maurice Wollman, Senior English Master, Barking Abbey School (London: Macmillan and Co. Ltd., 1935), in the Scholar's Library Series.

Contains: "I Hear The Cries of Evening," p.37.

Note: The editor proclaims that the poems included in this anthology have been judged solely on their merits.

BN5

POEMS OF TOMORROW, An Anthology of Contemporary Verse, chosen from *The Listener*, edited by Smith (London: Chatto & Windus, 1935).

Contains: 1. "I Think of Those Who Were Truly Great," 2. "After They Have Tired," 3. "Misfortunes Cannot Fall," 4. "From All These Events," 5. "The Shapes of Death."

BN6

THE POET'S TONGUE, AN ANTHOLOGY CHOSEN BY W.H. AUDEN AND JOHN GARRETT (LONDON: G. Bell & Sons Ltd., 1935).

Contains two poems of Spender: 1. "From All These Events, From the Slump, From the War, From the Boom," p. 23; 2. "The Secret of These Hills Was Stone, and Cottages," p. 155.

Note: Introduction by Auden and Garrett.

BN7

THE OXFORD BOOK OF MODERN VERSE: 1892-1935, chosen by W.B. Yeats (Oxford: Clarendon Press, 1936).

Contains two poems: "The Shapes of Death," pp. 432-33; "An 'I' Can Never Be Great Man," p. 433.

BN8

THE NEW REPUBLIC ANTHOLOGY: 1915-1935. Edited by Groff Conklin (New York: Dodge Publishing Company, 1936).

Contains: "Poem" by Spender: "Even whilst I watch him I am remembering," p. 468. Reprinted with permission of Random House.

BN9

THE FABER BOOK OF MODERN VERSE, edited by Michael Roberts (London: Faber and Faber, 1936; second edition, 1951; Third edition, 1965; many impressions).

Contains: 1. "The Prisoners," p. 308; 2. "In Railway Halls," p. 309; 3. "After They Have Tired," p. 310; 4. "The North," p. 311; 5. "An Elementary School Classroom," p. 312-13; 6. "Poor Girl," p. 314; 7. "Already," p. 315; 8. "Ice" p. 316; 9. "Anno Santo," p. 317.

BN10

FROM ANNE TO VICTORIA, essays by Various Hands, edited by, B. Dobrée (New York: Charles Scribner's Sons, 1937).

Contains: "Keats and Shelley," an essay by Spender, pp. 574-87.

BN11

A NEW ANTHOLOGY OF MODERN POETRY, edited with an introduction by Selden Rodman (New York: The Modern Library, 1938, 1946 . . .)

Contains: "The Express," pp. 278-79; "I Think Continually of Those Who Were Truly Great," p. 280; "The Funeral," p. 281; "Oh Young Men Oh Young Comrades," p. 282; "Spiritual Exercises," pp. 283-87.

BN12

FROM BEOWULF TO MODERN BRITISH WRITERS. AN ANTHOLOGY, edited by John Ball, based on Robert Shafer's FROM BEOWULF TO THOMAS HARDY (New York: The Odyssey Press, Inc., 1939, 40, 59).

Contains: 1. "Acts Passed Beyond the Boundary of Mere Wishing"; 2. "I Hear the Cries of Evening"; 3. "Different Living Is Not Living in Different Places"; 4. "An 'I' Can Never Be Great Man"; 5. "My Parents Kept Me from Children Who Were Rough"; 7. "I Think Continually of Those Who Were Truly Great"; 8. "The Express"; 9. "The Landscape Near an Aerodrome"; 10. "The Pylons"; 11. "The Double Shame"; 12. "Seascape."

BN13

THIS GENERATION: A Selection of British and American Literature from 1914 to the Present with Historical and Critical Essays, by George K. Anderson and Eda Lou Walton (New York: Scott, Foresman and Company, 1939).

Contains: Selections from Spender's *Poems* (New York: Random House): Nos. i, xii, xiii, xvi, xxv.

BN14

NEW VERSE, an anthology compiled by Geoffrey Grigson (London: Faber and Faber, 1939).

Contains: "Orpheus Eurydice Hermes," "The Uncreating Chaos," "Poem: If it were not too late!"

This is an anthology of poems which have appeared in the first thirty numbers of "New Verse." It includes photographs and short biographies of poets chosen for the anthology.

BN15

BEST POEMS OF 1941 (London: Jonathan Cape, 1941)
Contains: "The War God," pp. 26-27.

BN16

A LITTLE BOOK OF MODERN VERSE, chosen by Anne Ridler, with a preface by T.S. Eliot (London: Faber and Faber, 1941).
Contains: 1. "In 1929," p. 125; 2. "The Room Above the Square," p. 126; 3. "Two Armies," p. 127; 4. "Ultima Ratio Regum," p. 128.

BN17

NEW POEMS: 1940, an anthology of British and American Verse, edited by Oscar Williams, A Living Age Book (New York: The Yardstick Press, 1941).
Contains: "To Poets and Airmen," "Air Raid," "Dusk" "At Night" "The Double Shame" pp. 191-199.

BN18

NEW POEMS: 1942, an Anthology of British and American Verse, edited by Oscar Williams (Mount Vernon, N.Y.: Peter Pauper Press, 1942).
Contains: "Daybreak," "Ultima Ratio Regum," "The Fates," "Napoleon in 1814," "In Memoriam," pp. 207-210.

BN19

POETS' CHOICE: A programme anthology of poems read by their authors at the poetry reading at Wigmore Hall, September 14, 1943 (London: Arts and Letters Committee, National Council of Women, 1943).
Contains: "Lines for Edith Sitwell" and "I Think Continually . . .," pp. 44-45.

BN20

NEW POEMS: 1943, an Anthology of British and American verse, edited by Oscar Williams (New York: Howell, Soskin, Publishers, 1943).
Contains: "Winter and Summer," "A Stopwatch and an Ordnance Map," "Houses at Edge of Railway Lines," pp. 222-225.

BN21

THE FABER BOOK OF TWENTIETH CENTURY VERSE: An Anthology of Verse in Britain 1900-1950, edited by John Heath-Stubbs and David Wright (London: Faber and Faber, 1943, 1955).

Contains: 1. "Marston," p. 313; 2. "A Footnote," p. 313; 3. "Your Body Is Stars," p. 314; 4. "Song," p. 315; 5. "Word," p. 317.

BN22

NEW POEMS: 1944, an Anthology of American and British Verse, with a Selection of Poems from The Armed Forces, Edited by Oscar Williams (New York: Howell, Soskin, Publishers, 1944).

Contains: "Epilogue to a Human Drama," "Spiritual Exercises," "Lines for Edith Sitwell," "To Natasha," "Statue of Apollo," pp. 135-144.

BN23

INTRODUCING MODERN POETRY, an anthology compiled by W.G. Bebbington (London: Faber and Faber, 1944).

Contains: 1. "My Parents Kept Me from Children Who Were Rough," p. 67; 2. "In Railway Halls, on Pavements Near the Traffic," p. 67; 3. "The Living Values," p. 68; 4. "Thoughts During an Air-Raid," p. 69; 5. "Two Armies," p. 70; 6. "Port Bou," p. 71; 7. "Air-Raid Across the Bay at Plymouth," p. 73; 8. "The Barn," p. 75; 9. "Sirmione Peninsula," p. 76.

BN24

QUESTION OF HENRY JAMES, a collection of critical essays, edited by F.W. Dupee (New York: Henry Holt and Company, 1945).

Contains: "The Golden Bowl," excerpt from *The Destructive Element*, pp. 236-245.

BN25

THE WAR POETS: An Anthology of The War Poetry of the 20th Century, edited with an introduction by Oscar Williams (New York: The John Day Company, 1945).

Contains: 1. "Not Palaces, an Era's Crown," p. 415; 2. "I Think Continually of Those Who Were Truly Great," p. 416; 3. "Ultima Ratio Regum," p. 416; 4. "To Poets and Airmen," p. 417; 5. "Two Armies," p. 418.

BN26

SOLDIERS' VERSE, verses chosen by Patric Dickinson, with original lithographs by William Scott (London: Fredrich Muller, 1945).

Contains: "Ultima Ratio Regum," p. 52-53.

BN27

THE PARTISAN READER: Ten Years of *Partisan Review*, 1934-1944, an anthology edited by Williams Phillips and Philip Rahv, introduction by Lionel Trilling (New York: The Dial Press, 1946).

Contains: Poem: "Rejoice in the Abyss," pp. 284-85. Prose: "September Journal: André Gide," pp. 354-362.

BN28

LITTLE REVIEWS ANTHOLOGY: 1946, edited by Denys Val Baker (London: Eyre and Spottiswoode, 1946).

Contains: an essay: "Writers in the World of Necessity," pp. 103-111.

BN29

A LITTLE TREASURY OF MODERN POETRY: (English and American), edited with an introduction by Oscar Williams (New York: Charles Scribner's Sons, First Published in 1946).

Contains: 1. "Ultima Ratio Regum," p. 479; 2. "Not Palaces, an Era's Crown," p. 480; 3. "After They Have Tired," p. 481; 4. "I Think Continually of Those Who Were Truly Great," p. 482; 5. "The Landscape Near an Aerodrome," p. 483. 6. "The Express," p. 484; 7. "The Double Shame." p. 484.

BN30

MODERN BRITISH WRITING, edited by Denys Val Baker (Vanguard, 1947).

Contains: "Writers in the World of Necessity," pp. 137-48.

BN31

BRITISH THOUGHT 1947, Essays by Various Authors, Introduction by Ivory Brown (Woking, Great Britain: Gresham Press, 1947).

Contains: "Poetry for Poetry's Sake and Poetry Beyond Poetry," pp. 351-68.

BN32

CRITICISM: FOUNDATIONS OF MODERN LITERARY JUDGMENT, edited by M. Schorer, Miles, and McKenzie (New York: Harcourt, Brace & World, Inc., 1948).

Contains: "The Making of a Poem," pp. 187-95.

BN33

T.S. ELIOT: A SELECTED CRITIQUE, edited by L. Unger (New York: Holt, Rinehart & Winston, 1948).

Contains: an excerpt from *The Destructive Element*.

BN34

CELEBRATION FOR EDITH SITWELL, edited by Jose Garcia Villa (New Directions, 1948).

Contains: "Images in the Poetic World of Edith Sitwell." p. 11-19.

BN35

NEW BRITISH POETS: AN ANTHOLOGY, edited by Kenneth Rexroth (A New Directions Book, 1949).

Contains: 1. "A Childhood," pp. 229-230; 2. "On the Pilots Who Destroyed Germany in the Spring of 1945," pp. 230-31; 3. "The Labourer in the Vineyard," pp. 231-32; 4. "On the Third Day," pp. 232-33; 5. "O Night O Trembling Night." p. 234.

BN36

POETRY OF THE PRESENT: An anthology of the Thirties and After, compiled and introduced by Geoffrey Grigson (London: Phoenix House, 1949).

Contains: "The Prisoners," "From All These Events," "Beethoven's Death Mask," "Never Being," "I Think Continually of Those," "Orpheus Eurydice Hermes," pp. 192-198.

BN37

THE PENGUIN BOOK OF CONTEMPORARY VERSE, selected with an introduction and notes of Kenneth Allot (Harmondsworth: Middlesex: Penguin Books, 1950).

Contains: "The Landscape Near an Aerodrome," "Fall of a City," "The Double Shame," "Elegy for Margaret, IV, pp. 183-89.

BN38

PERMANENCE OF YEATS, SELECTED CRITICISM, edited by F. Hall and M. Steinmann (Macmillan and Company, 1950).

Contains: "Yeats as a Realist," an excerpt from *The Destructive Element*, pp. 179-92.

BN39

LOVE POEMS OF SIX CENTURIES, edited by Helen Husted (New York: Coward-McCann, Inc., 1950).

Contains: "Two Kisses" from "Ruins and Visions" in *The Still Centre*, p. 33.

BN40

GOETHE AND THE MODERN AGE, edited by A. Bergstraesser, the international convocation at Aspen, Colorado, 1949 (Chicago: Henry Regnery Company, 1950).

Contains: "Goethe and the English Mind," pp. 113-34.

BN41

ESSAYS IN TEACHING, edited by Harold Taylor (New York: Harper & Row, Publishers, 1959).

Contains: "On Teaching Modern Poetry," pp. 96-110.

BN42

AMERICA AND THE MIND OF EUROPE, essays by various writers, selected from *The Saturday Review of Literature* with an introduction by Raymond Aron (New York: Library Publications and London: Hamish Hamilton, 1952).

Contains: "Britain: Culture in Official Channels: Does the English Writer Have a Chance?" pp. 61-69.

BN43

THE CREATIVE PROCESS: A Symposium, edited by B. Ghiselin (Berkeley: University of California Press, 1952).

Contains: An excerpt from *The Making of a Poem*.

BN44

NEW POEMS (London: Michael Joseph, 1952).

Contains: "In Attica" and "After Reading Arthur Waley's Li-Po," pp. 145-146.

BN45

THE NEW PARTISAN READER, 1945-1953, edited by William Phillips and Philip Rahv (New York: Harcourt, Brace & Company, 1953).

Contains: "The Making of a Poem," pp. 193-297. Dated 1946 and included in the section: Interpretations.

BN46

GEORGE BERNARD SHAW: A CRITICAL SURVEY, edited by L. Kronnenberger (Cleveland, Ohio: The World Publishing Company, 1953).

Contains: "Riddle of Shaw," pp. 236-39.

BN47

THE GOLDEN HORIZON, edited together with an introduction by Cyril Connolly (London: Weidenfeld & Nicolson Limited, 1953).

Contains: in section: 1939, "From September Journal," pp. 2-14; in section: 1941, "Air Raid (Poem)," pp. 25-26; in section: 1945, "From 'Rhineland Journal,' " pp. 120-130; in section: "Personal Anthology": "O Night O Trembling Night (Poem)," p. 432.

BN48

SPECTATOR HARVEST, with a foreword by Wilson Harris (British Book Centre, 1953).

Contains: "W.H. Auden," pp. 51-55.

BN49

FORM AND THOUGHT IN PROSE, edited by W.H. Stone and Hoopes (New York: The Ronald Press Company, 1954).

Contains: An excerpt from *World Within World*, pp. 728-38.

BN50

ARTS AT MID-CENTURY, edited by R. Richman (New York: Horizon Press, 1954).

Contains: 1. "New Orthodoxies," pp. 3-23; 2. "English Painting in the Fifties," pp. 221-26.

BN51

ENGLISH LITERATURE: A Period Anthology, edited by Albert C. Baugh and George McClelland (New York: Appleton-Century-Crofts, Inc., 1954).

Contains: 1. "I Think Continually of Those Who Were Truly Great," 2. "The Express," 3. "The Landscape Near an Aerodrome," 4. "The Pylons," 5. "In Railway Halls," 6. "Sonnet: You Were Born; Must Die . . .," 7. "Epilogue to a Human Drama."

BN52

CRITIQUES AND ESSAYS IN CRITICISM: 1920-1948, representing the achievement of modern British and American Critics, with a foreword by Cleanth Brooks, selected and edited by R.W. Stallman (New York: The Ronald Press Co., 1954).

Contains: "The Making of a Poem," pp. 17-29.

BN53

NEW POEMS: A P.E.N. Anthology (London: Michael Joseph, 1954).

Contains: "Missing My Daughter," p. 19.

BN54

EXPLORING POETRY, edited by M.L. Rosenthal and A.J.M. Smith (New York: The Macmillan Company, 1955).

Contains: 1. "I Think Continually of Those Who Were Truly Great," p. 628; 2. "The Express," p. 535.

BN55

EXPLORATIONS: Reading, Thinking, Discussion, Writing (Prentice-Hall English Composition and Introduction to Literature Series), edited by Thomas Clark Pollock and Others (Englewood Cliffs, N.J.: Prentice-Hall, Inc., 1956).

Contains: "The Making of a Poem," pp. 155-68.

BN56

THE PENGUIN BOOK OF ENGLISH VERSE, edited by John Hayward (Penguin Books, 1956).

Contains: 1. "I Think Continually of Those Who Were Truly Great," 2. "Elegy for Margaret, VI, pp. 458-459.

BN57

AN OXFORD ANTHOLOGY OF ENGLISH POETRY, chosen and edited by Howard Foster Lowry and Willard Thorp (New York: Oxford University Press, 1956).

Contains: 1. "My Parents Kept Me from Children Who Were Rough," p. 1309; 2. "What I Expected," p. 1310; 3. "I Think Continually of Those Who Were Truly Great," p. 1310; 4. "The Landscape Near An Aerodrome," p. 1311; 5. "An Elementary School Classroom in a Slum," p. 1311; 6. "To a Spanish Poet," p. 1312.

BN58

NEW POEMS, edited by Stephen Spender, Elizabeth Jennings and Dannie Abse (London: Michael Joseph, 1956).

Contains: "My Child Came Home" and "Remembering the Thirties," pp. 45-46.

Note: Poems were selected from about 10,000 manuscripts, from periodicals and by writing to established writers for new material.

BN59

POEMS OF THE MID-CENTURY, edited by John Holloway (London: George G. Harrap & Co., 1957).

Contains: "Seascape," pp. 151-52.

BN60

THE MODERN POETS' WORLD, edited with an introduction and commentary by James Reeves (London: Heinemann, 1957).

Contains: 1. "My Parents Kept Me from Children," p. 88; 2. "Shapes of Death Haunt Life," p. 89.

BN61

MODERN VERSE IN ENGLISH: 1900-1950, edited by David Cecil and Allen Tate, with critical introduction on British and American Poetry and biographical notes on poets included (New York: The Macmillan Company, 1958).

Contains: "The Express," p. 539; "The Landscape Near an Aerodrome," pp. 539-40.

BN62

LITERATURE FOR OUR TIME, an anthology for college students, edited by Harlow O. Waite and Benjamin P. Atkinson (New York: Books for Libraries Press, 1958, reprinted 1970).

Contains: 1. Excerpt from Foreword to *The Still Centre*, 2. "The Express," 3. "Not Palaces, an Era's Crown," 4. "The Landscape Near an Aerodrome," 5. "Ultima Ratio Regum," 6. From "Spiritual Explorations," 7. "I Think Continually of Those Who Were Truly Great."

BN63

THE POEM: A CRITICAL ANTHOLOGY, edited by Josephine Miles (Englewood Cliffs, N.J., Prentice-Hall, Inc., 1959).

Contains: "Responsibility: The Pilots Who Destroyed Germany in the Spring of 1945," pp. 266-267.

BN64

THE GUINNESS BOOK OF POETRY: 1957/58 (LONDON: Putnam, 42 Great Russell Street, 1959).

Contains: "Instructions," p.115.

BN65

THE CHERRY TREE: A Collection of Poems, chosen by Geoffrey Grigson (New York: The Vanguard Press, Inc. 1959).

Contains: "I Think Continually of Those Who Were Truly Great," p. 377.

BN66

A SCHILLER SYMPOSIUM, in observance of the bicentenary of Schiller's birth, essays by Harold Jantz [and others], edited with an introduction by A. Leslie Willson, Dept. of Germanic languages. University of Texas (Austin: University of Texas Press, 1960).

Contains: "Schiller, Shakespeare, and the Theme of Power," pp. 51-61.

BN67

THE INTELLECTUALS: A CONTROVERSIAL PORTRAIT, edited with an introduction and overviews by George Bernard de Huszar (New York: The Free Press of Glencoe, Inc. 1960).

Contains: "The English Intellectuals and The World of Today," pp. 470-76.

BN68

WRITING POETRY, by J. Holmes (Boston, Mass. The Writer, Inc., 1960).

Contains: "Can't We Do Without the Poets?" pp. 104-110.

BN69

NEW POEMS, edited by Anthony Cronin, Jon Silkin, and Terrence Tiller, with a preface by Alan Pryce-Jones, the President of the P.E.N. (London: Hutchinson & Co., Publishers Ltd., 1960).

Contains: "Orpheus, Adam, Christ," p. 108.

Note: P.E.N. Anthology.

BN70

THE PENGUIN BOOK OF CONTEMPORARY VERSE, selected with an inroduction and notes by Kenneth Allott (Penguin Books, 1950-1960).

Contains: 1. "The Landscape Near an Aerodrome," p. 185; 2. "Fall of a City," p. 186; 3. "The Double Shame," p. 187; 4. "Poor Girl, Inhabitant of a Strange Land" (Elegy for Margaret, IV), p. 188.

BN71

THE POCKET BOOK OF MODERN VERSE, edited by Oscar Williams: English and American Poetry of the last 100 years from Walt Whitman to Dylan Thomas (A Washington Square Press Book, 1960).

Contains: 1. "Ultima Ratio Regum," p. 503; 2. "Not Palaces, an Era's Crown," p. 504; 3. "I Think Continually of Those Who Were Truly Great," p. 505.

BN72

CHIEF MODERN POETS OF ENGLAND AND AMERICA, selected and edited by Gerald De Witt Sanders and John Herbert Nelson (New York: The Macmillan Company, 1960).

Contains: 1. "He Will Watch the Hawk," p.436; 2. "Rolled Over on Europe," p.436; 3. "Never Being but Always at the Edge of Being," p.436; 4. "Your Body Is Stars," p. 437; 5. "Without That Once Clear Aim," p. 437; 6. "I Think Continually of Those Who Were Truly Great," p. 438; 7. "The Funeral," p. 439; 8. "The Pylons," p. 439; 9. "In Railway Halls," p.440; 10. "Not Palaces, an Era's Crown," p. 441; 11. "The Room Above the Square," p. 442; 12. The Bombed Happiness," p. 442, 13. "Two Kisses," p. 443; 14. "To a Spanish Poet," p. 443.

Note: The first edition of this anthology was published in 1929. This is the third edition.

BN73

ADVENTURES OF THE MIND (Second Series), edited by Richard Thruelsen and John Kobler (New York: Alfred A. Knopf, Inc., 1961).

Contains: "The Connecting Imagination," pp. 21-33.

BN74

THE HUMANISTIC FRAME, edited by Sir J.S. Huxley (New York: Harper & Row, Publishers, 1961).

Contains: "Social Purpose and the Integrity of the Aritst," pp. 221-32.

BN75

WORD, MEANING, POEM, edited by Morse Pekham and Seymour Chatman (New York: Thomas Y. Crowell Company, 1961).

Contains: "Polar Exploration," pp. 651-52.

BN76

THE QUEST FOR TRUTH, compiled by M.T. Boaz (Metuchen, N.J.: Scarecrow, 1961).

Contains: "Tendencies in Modern Poetry," pp. 21-38.

BN77

AN ANTHOLOGY OF MODERN VERSE, chosen and with an introduction by Elizabeth Jennings (London: Methuen & Co., Ltd., 1961).

Contains: "The Double Shame," "Song," "Spiritual Explorations," "Elegy for Margaret," pp. 246-51.

BN78

THE RIDDLE OF SHAKESPEARE'S SONNETS, with interpretive essays by Edward Hubler [and others], including the full text of Oscar Wilde's "The Portrait of Mr. W.H." [and the text of the sonnets]. (New York: Basic Books, Inc., Publishers, 1962).

Contains: "The Alike and the Other," pp. 91-128.

BN79

THE CRITICAL READER: Poems, Stories, Essays, Compiled and edited by Wallace Douglas, Roy Lamson and Hallett Smith (New York: W.W. Norton and Company, 1962).

Contains: 1, "I Think Continually of Those Who Were Truly Great," pp. 132-33; 2. "The Express," pp. 133-34; A critical analysis of "The Express," pp. 134-36.

BN80

THE PARTISAN REVIEW ANTHOLOGY, edited by William Phillips and Philip Rahv (New York: Holt Rinehart & Winston, Inc., 1962).

Contains: "Anglo-Saxon Attitudes," pp. 478-83.

BN81

ENCOUNTERS, an anthology from the first ten years of *Encounter Magazine*, edited by Stephen Spender and Others (New York: Basic Books, Inc., Publishers, 1963).

Contains: "European Notebook," pp. 240-55.

BN82

HENRY JAMES: A COLLECTION OF CRITICAL ESSAYS, edited by Leon Edel. A Spectrum Book: Twentieth Century Views (Englewood Cliffs, N.J.: Prentice-Hall, Inc., 1963).

Contains: "The Contemporary Subject," excerpt from *The Destructive Element* (Chapter: "Henry James and The Contemporary Subject"). pp. 102-110.

BN83

AUDEN, a collection of critical essays (A Spectrum Book: Twentieth Century Views), edited by M.K. Spears (Englewood Cliffs, N.J.: Prentice-Hall, Inc., 1964).

Contains: "W.H. Auden and His Poetry," pp. 26-38.

BN84

THE CONTEMPORARY POET AS ARTIST AND CRITIC, eight symposia by Leonie Adams and Others, edited by A.J. Ostroff (Boston, Mass.: Little, Brown & Company, 1964).

Contains: "On W.H. Auden's 'A Change of Air,' " pp. 178-82.

BN85

OPINIONS AND PERSPECTIVES, from The New York Times Book Review, edited with an introduction by Francis Brown (Boston, Mass.: Houghton Mifflin Company, 1964).

Contains: 1. "Is There No Need to Experiment?", pp. 34-40; 2. "Literary London: A Tight Little Isle," pp. 284-91.

BN86

NEW POEMS, 1963: A British P.E.N. Anthology, edited by Lawrence Durrell (New York: Harcourt, Brace & World, Inc., 1964).

Contains: "The Generous Days (Aetat 18)," pp. 105-106.

BN87

THE GOLDEN TREASURY OF THE BEST SONGS & LYRICAL POEMS IN THE ENGLISH LANGUAGE, selected and arranged by Francis Turner Palgrave with a FIFTH BOOK, selected by John Press (London: Oxford University Press, Fifth edition, 1964).

Contains: "Ice" and "Missing My Daughter," pp. 520-21.

BN88

CIVIL LIBERTIES AND THE ARTS, selections from *Twice a Year* 1938-48, edited with an introduction by William Wasserstrom (Syracuse, N.Y.: Syracuse University Press, 1964).

Contains: "The Spiritual Future of Europe," pp. 273-82.

BN89

THE GREAT IDEAS TODAY (1965), edited by Robert M. Hutchins and J.A. Mortimer (Chicago: Encyclopedia Britannica, Inc., 1965).

Contains: "Literature" with sketches of writers, bibliography and a note to the reader. Has Spender's portrait at the top of the article, pp. 166-211.

BN90

ONE HUNDRED YEARS OF THE NATION: A CENTENNIAL AN-THOLOGY, edited by Henry M. Christman and Abraham Feldman (New York: Macmillan Company, 1965).

Contains: "Writers in America," pp. 269-73.

BN91

TO THE YOUNG WRITER: HOPWOOD LECTURES, (Second Series), edited by A.L. Bader (Ann Arbor, Mich.: University of Michigan Press, 1965).

Contains: "To the Young Writer, Present, Past, and Future," pp. 1-16.

BN92

T.S. ELIOT: THE MAN AND HIS WORK, a critical evaluation by twenty-six distinguished writers: A Seymour Lawrence Book (New York: Delacorte Press Books, 1966).

Contains: "Remembering Eliot," pp. 38-64.

BN93

THE TERRIBLE RAIN: The War Poets: An anthology selected and arranged, with an introduction and notes by Brian Gardner. (London: Methuen & Co. Ltd., 1966).

Contains: 1. "Air Raid Across the Bay at Plymouth" p.50; 2. "Memento," p.182.

BN94

THE IDEA OF THE MODERN IN LITERATURE AND THE ARTS, edited with an introduction by Irving Howe (New York: Horizon Press, 1968).

Contains: "The Modern as Vision of the Whole," excerpt from *The Struggle of the Modern*, pp. 43-49.

BN95

PERSPECTIVES IN CONTEMPORARY CRITICISM, a collection of recent essays by American, English, and European Literary critics, edited by S.N. Grebstein (New York: Harper, & Row, Publishers, 1968).

Contains: "The Visionary Individualists," excerpt from *The Creative Element*, pp. 188-201.

BN96

THE GREAT IDEAS TODAY, 1968 (Encyclopedia Britannica).

Contains: "The Vital Self and Secondary Means," pp. 98-107.

BN97

THE NEW YORKER BOOK OF POEMS, selected by the editors of the New Yorker (New York: The Viking Press, 1969).

Contains: 1. "Awaking" (1948); 2. "The Empty House" (1948); 3. "One More New Botched Beginning" (1964); 4. "Word," (1949); originally published in *The New Yorker*. Later editions of this anthology, including the 1974 edition, contain Spender's poems.

BN98

THE ART OF SYLVIA PLATH: A SYMPOSIUM, selected criticism, with a complete bibliography, checklist of criticsm, and an appendix of uncollected and unpublished work, edited by C.H. Newman (Bloomington: Indiana University Press, 1970).

Contains: "Warnings from the Grave," pp. 199-203.

BN99

THE OXFORD BOOK OF 20TH CENTURY VERSE, chosen by Philip Larkin (Oxford: Clarendon Press, 1973).

Contains: 1. "Acts Passed Beyond the Boundary of Mere Wishing," p. 440; 2. "Beethoven's Death Mask," p. 440; 3. "I Think Continually of Those Who Were Truly Great," p. 441; 4. "The Landscape Near an Aerodrome," p. 442; 5. "Two Armies," p. 443-44.

BN100

PRE-RAPHAELITISM, a collection of critical essays, edited with an introduction by J, Sambrook (Chicago: University of Chicago Press, 1974).

Contains: "The Pre-Raphaelite Painters," pp. 118-125.

C

CONTRIBUTION BY
STEPHEN SPENDER
TO
PERIODICALS

1929

C1 "Problems of the Poet and Public," *Spectator* 143 (August 3, 1929), 152-53.

Expressing the younger point of view regarding the lack of sympathy which exists between poets and the general public.

1930

C2 Four Poems (For W.H. Auden): 1. The Port, 2. The Swan, 3. Lines written when Walking Down the Rhine, 4. "Not to you I sighed," *Criterion*, X: 38(Oct. 1930), 32-34.

1931

C3 Poem: "What I Expected," *New Statesman*, 36 (February 21, 1931), 586.

C4 Review: "The Notebook of Malte Laurids Brigge," *Criterion*, X: 41 (July 1931), 744-45.

Review of the notebook by Rainer Maria Rilke (Hogarth Press, 7s.6d.).

C5 Three Poems: 1. "Moving Through the Silent Crowd," 2. Your Body Is Stars Whose Million Glitter Here," 3. "The Prisoners," *Criterion*, XI: 42(Oct. 1931), 47-49.

1932

C6 Story: "The Burning Cactus," *Hound and Horn*, 7 (Jan.-March 1932), 218-318.

C7 Article: "Portraits by Desmond MacCarthy," *Criterion*, XI: 44(April 1932), 554-57.

Review of *Portraits* (Putnam, 7s.6d.)

C8 Article: "Lost Lectures, or The Fruits of Experience," *Criterion*, XI: 45(July 1932), 747-49.

Review of the book by Maurice Baring published by Davies at 10s.6d.

C9 Article: "This Age in Poetry," *Bookman* (London), 83 (October 1932), 10.

Our poets should stop worrying about poetry, science, and above all, about themselves; perhaps then they would have time to reflect that we are living in one of the most remarkable ages it has ever been people's fortune or misfortune to live in.

1933

C10 Article: "The Enemy to the Stars," *Criterion*, XII: 47(Jan. 1933), 313-15.

Review of the book by Wyndham Lewis (Harmsworth, 10s. 6d.).

C11 Article: "The Common Reader," *Criterion*, XII: 48(April 1933), 522-24.

Review of Virginia Woolf's Part Two of the book.

C12 Poem: "Bird," *New Statesman and Nation*, 5 (May 27, 1933), 684.

C13 Article: "Collected Poems of Harold Munro," *Criterion*, XII: 49 (July 1933), 680-83.

Review of the Poems, edited by Alida Monro, with a biographical sketch by F.S. Flint and a critical note by T.S. Eliot (Cobden Sanderson, 8s.6d.).

C14 Article: "De la Mare," *New Verse*, 4(July 1933).

Review of The *Fleeting and Other Poems* by Walter de la Mare (constable).

C15 Poem: "Autumn Day," by Rainer Maria Rilke, translated by Spender, *Spectator* (July 28, 1933), 125.

C16 Poem: "Orpheus Eurydice Hermes," *New Verse*, 5(Oct. 1933), 2-4.

R.M. Rilke, translation by Spender.

C17 Article: "Germany After the War," *Criterion*, XIII: 50 (Oct. 1933), 156-58.

Review of 1. *Germany Under The Treaty* by W.H. Dawson, 2. *Spotlight on Germany* by Erich Roll.

C18 Poem: "Van der Lubbe," *Spectator*, 151 (Sept. 29, 1933), 400.

C19 Poem: "Van der Lubbe," *Living Age*, 345 (Nov. 1933), 197.

From *The Spectator*, London.

C20 Article: "Murry on Blake," *New Verse*, 6(Dec. 1933), 22-24.

Review of Middleton Murry's book on Blake.

C21 Article: "Politics and Literature in 1933," *BOOKMAN*, 85 (Dec. 1933), 147-148.

What is most important to writers today is their freedom. The enemy of that freedom is Fascism.

1934

C22 Article: "The School of Experience in the Early Novels of Henry James," *Hound and Horn*, VII: 3(April/May 1934), 417-433.

Later incorporated into *The Destructive Element.*

C23 Poem: Shapes of Death Haunt Life . . . ," *Hound & Horn*, VII: 4(July-Sept. 34), 609-610.

1935

C24 Article: "Modern Satire and Tradition," *London Mercury*, 31 (Jan. 1935), 293-94.

Review of *Fisbo* by Robert Nichols.

C25 Poems: "My Parents Kept Me from Children . . ." and "What I Expected . . .", *Scholastic*, 26(April 6, 1935), 10.

C26 Poems: "Elementary School Classroom," "At Night," and "Exiles," *London Mercury*, 32(May 1935), 8-11.

C27 Article: "An English Woman in Austria," *London Mercury*, 32 (May 1935), 81.

Review of *Modern Austria* by Cicely Hamilton.

C28 Poem: "An 'I' Can Never Be a Great Man," *Saturday Review of Literature*, 12 (June 8, 1935), 13.

C29 Story: "Strange Death," *London Mercury*, 32 (Aug. 1935), 332-44.

A story about Austria before the assassination of Chancellor Dollfuss.

C30   Poem: "The North," *New Republic*, 84(Sept. 11, 1935), 127.

C31   Article: "Mary Stuart—A German Portrait," *London Mercury*, 32 (Sept. 1935), 505.

Review of *Maria Stuart* by Stefan Zweig.

C32   Article: "Romance and Sensibility," *London Mercury*, 32(Oct. 1935), 601.

Review of *Janus* by George Barker.

C33   Poem: "The Uncreating Chaos," *New Verse*, 17 (Oct-Nov. 1935), 11-14.

C34   Poem: "Easter Monday," *New Verse*, 17(Oct-Nov. 1935), 16.

C35   Review: "Mr. MacNeice's Poems," review of *Poems* of Louis Mac-Neice (Faber), *New Verse*, 17(Oct-Nov. 1935), 17-19.

C36   Story: "The Strange Death," *Living Age*, 349(Dec. 1935), 328-38.

From *The London Mercury*, London Literary Monthly.

1936

C37   "Freud and Marx," *New Republic*, 86(April 8, 1936), 251-52.

C38   Poem: "Town Shore at Barcelona," *New Statesman and Nation*, 11 (April 11, 1936), 566.

C39   Poem: "The Sad Standards," *New Writing*, 5:1 (Spring 1936), 113.

C40   Poem: "The Half of Life," translated from the German of Hoelder-lin, *New Writing*, 5:1 (Spring 1936), 114.

C41   Poems: "The Short Poems," "Buonaparte," translated from the German of Hoelderlin, *New Writing*, 5:1 (Spring 1936), 115-117.

C42   An open letter to Aldous Huxley on his "Case for Constructive Peace," *Left Review*, 2:11 (Aug. 1936), 539-541.

C43   Poem: "If It Were Not Too Late," *New Verse*, 22 (Aug/Sept. 1936), 3-4.

C44 Article: "Liberal Individualism," *New Masses*, 21(Nov. 10, 1936), 3-5.

Analyses the position of those friends of liberty who declare that the arena of politics is not for them.

C45 Article: "Fable and Reportage," *Left Review*, 2:14 (Nov. 1936), [779]-782.

Review of *The Ascent of F6* by W.H. Auden & Christopher Isherwood, *Look, Stranger!* by W.H. Auden, and *New Writing 2*, edited by John Lehmann.

C46 Article: "Music and Decay," *Left Review*, 2:15 (Dec. 1936), 834:36.

Review of *Ulysses* by James Joyce.

1937

C47 Poem: "Speech" by the brother of Pietzruch, a Communist Polish Jew murdered by Nazis in January 1933, *Poetry*, English number edited by W.H. Auden and Michael Roberts, 49:4(Jan. 1937), 184-85.

C48 Article: "D.H. Lawrence: Phoenix," *Left Review*, 2:16(Jan. 1937), 902-904.

C49 Article: "The Sheltered Muse," *London Mercury*, 36(Jan. 1937), 334-36.

Review of *Bridges: Collected Essays*, XXVII, XXVIII, XXIX, XXX (Oxford University Press).

C50 "Mr. Leavis's Essays," *Criterion*, XVI:63(Jan. 1937), 350-53.

Review of *Revaluation, Tradition and Development in English Poetry* by F.R. Leavis (Chatto & Windus, 7s.6d.).

C51 Article: "Admirable Artificiality," *New Statesman and Nation*, 13 (Feb. 6, 1937), 208.

Review of *Collected Poems*, by Sacheverell Sitwell, with a long introductory essay by Edith Sitwell (Duckworth, 15s.).

C52 Poem: "Two Speeches from a Play," *New Writing*, 3 (Spring 1937), 9-10.

I. "Civilization which was sweet," II. "In the eye heroic."

C53 Article: "Heroes in Spain," *New Statesman and Nation*, 13(May 1, 1937), 714-15.

Account of the Civil War in Spain.

C54 Poem: "Two Armies," *New Statesman and Nation*, 13(May 8, 1937), 770.

C55 Poem: "Regum Ultima Ratio," *New Statesman and Nation*, 13 (May 15, 1937), 811.

C56 Poem: "War Photograph," *New Statesman and Nation*, 13(June 5, 1937), 922.

C57 Article: "New Poetry," *Left Review*, 3:6(July 1937), [358]-361.

Review of *Calamiterror* by George Barker, *Poems* by Rex Warner, *The Disappearing Castle*, by Charles Madge, *Spain* by W.H. Auden, and *The Fifth Decad of Cantos* by Ezra Pound.

C58 Article: "Pictures in Spain," *Spectator*, 159(July 30, 1937), 199.

How art works were scrupulously preserved even during civil war.

C59 Article: "International Writers' Congress," *London Mercury*, 36 (Aug 1937), 373.

C60 Poem: "The Moment Transfixes the Space Which Divides," *New Statesman and Nation*, 14(Aug 21, 1937), 280.

C61 Article: "A Communication," *London Mercury*, 36(Aug. 1937), 373.

A note on the second International Writers' Congress held in Valencia-Madrid, deploring the absence of the English Writers to represent and champion the causes of democracy and freedom.

C62 Poem: "Two Armies," *Living Age*, 353(Sept. 1937), 17.

From *The New Statesman and Nation*, London.

C63 Article: "Spain Invites the World's Writers." *New Writing*, (Autumn 1937), 245-51.

Notes on the International Congress, Summer 1937.

C64 Poem: "Ultimate Death," from the Spanish of Manuel Altolaguirre, *New Statesman and Nation*, 14(Oct. 9, 1937), 531.

C65 Article: "Art Treasures and the Spanish War, The Loyalists Guard Their Inheritance," *New Republic*, 92(Oct 13, 1937), 265-66.

How people fighting for their lives carry a vision of the future in their hearts and protect their heritage of art.

C66 Article: "Oxford to Communism," *New Verse* 26-27(Nov. 1937), 9-10.

Auden double number: A note on Auden by Spender.

C67 Poem: "My Brother Luis," translated from the Spanish of Manuel Altolaguirre, *New Statesman and Nation*, 14(Oct. 30, 1937), 681.

C68 Poem: "Landscape," *New Statesman and Nation*, 14(Dec. 4, 1937), 929.

C69 Article: "The Spanish Mind," *London Mercury*, 37(Dec. 1937), 203-204.

Review of *Invertebrate Spain* by Jose Ortega Y Gasset and *Wars of Ideas in Spain* by Jose Castillejo.

1938

C70 Poem: "I Demand the Ultimate Death," from the Spanish of Manuel Altolaguirre, translated, *New Statesman and Nation*, 15(Jan. 8, 1938), 39.

C71 Article: "Heine in English," *London Mercury*, 39(Jan. 1939), 355-56.

Review of *The Poems of Heinrich Heine*, translated by Louis Untermeyer.

C72 Article: "The Power and the Hazard," *Poetry*, 71 (March 1938), 314-18.

Review of the 4th book of published poetry *Trial of a Poet* by Karl Shapiro: Shapiro is a difficult poet to estimate, for he combines in his work elements of technical accomplishment with crudeness and insensitivity.

C73 Poem: "Hampstead Autumn," *New Statesman and Nation*, 15 (March 12, 1938), 409.

C74   Article: "Poetry and Expressionism," *New Statesman and Nation*, 15(March 12, 1938), 407-409.

The serious play is very close to poetry as poetry is to drama.

C75   Poem: "Sonnet," *New Verse*, 29(March 1938), 9.

"The world wears your image on the surface."

C76   Article: "Mr. Yeats' Vision," *Criterion*, XVII: 68(April 1938), 536-37.

Review of *A Vision* by W.B. Yeats (MacMillan, 15s.).

C77   Article: "Concerning the Label Emigrant," translated from the German of Bertolt Brecht, *New Writing*, V(Spring 1938), 42.

Explains how the word "emigrant" is misused.

C78   Translated Poem: "Hear This Voice" by Miguel Hernandez, translated from the Spanish by Inez and Stephen Spender: "Nations of the earth, fatherlands of the sea, brothers," *New Writing*, V(Spring 1938), 56-58.

C79   Article: "Poetry and Mass Observation," *New Statesman and Nation*, 15(March 19, 1938), 477.

I symphathise with the aims of Mass Observers, but it seems they are somewhat restricted in space and time.

C80   Article: "Salzburg Nazified," *London Mercury*, 38(May 1938), 39-41.

Germany's loss is our gain. The exile of the Busches has meant Glyndebourne to us, and now with the exile of Austrian musicians, Glyndebourne will be further strengthened.

C81   Poem: "Thoughts During an Air Raid," *New Republic*, 95(May 18, 1938), 42.

C82   Poem: "Three Days," *New Statesman and Nation*, 15(May 28, 1938), 907.

C83   Poem: "Madrid," from the Spanish of Manuel Altolaguirre, *New Statesman and Nation*, 16(July 9, 1938), 73.

C84   Article: "A Forerunner," *New Statesman and Nation*, 16(July 9, 1938), 88-89.

Review of *T.E. Hulme* by Michael Roberts (Faber, 10s.6d.).

C85   Article: "Shelley Plain," *New Statesman and Nation*, 16(July 16, 1938), 122.

Review of *On Shelley* by Edmund Blunden, Gavin de Beer, and Sylva Norman (Oxford University Press, 5s.).

C86   Poem: "The Word Dead and the Music Mad," *Spectator*, 161(July 29, 1938), 204.

C87   Poem: "Fall of a City," *New Statesman and Nation*, 16(Aug. 6, 1938), 219.

C88   Article: "Grocer's Wine," *New Statesman and Nation*, 16(Aug. 13, 1938), 255-56.

Reviews of 1. *Poems* by Ruthven Todd & others, 2. *Hoelderlin's Madness* by David Gascoyne, 3. *Memoir, 1887-1937* by G.R. Hamilton, 4. *Sonnets and Verse* by Hilaire Belloc, 5. *The Bones of My Hand* by Edward James.

C89   Article: "In Ironic Vein," *London Mercury*, 38 (Aug 1938), 380.

Review of *Power and Glory* by Karel Kapek, a drama in three acts, translated by Paul Selver and Ralph Neale.

C90   Article: "The Poetic Dramas of W.H. Auden and Christopher Isherwood," *New Writing: New Series*, I(Autumn 1938), 102-108.

C91   Article: "Rainer Maria Rilke," *London Mercury*, 38(Aug. 1938), 328-32.

An appreciation of Rilke's *Later Poems*.

C92   Poem: "At Castellon," *New Writing*, New Series, I(Autumn 1938), 25.

C93   Poem: "The Word Dead and the Music Mad," *Living Age*, 355(Sept. 1938), 74.

C94   Poem: "Regum Ultima Ratio," *New Republic*, 96(Sept. 7, 1938), 124.

C95   Poems: "Port Bou-Firing Practice," "Till Death Completes Their Arc," *New Writing*: New Series, I(Autumn 1938), 25-27.

C96   Article: "The Left Wing Orthodoxy," *New Verse*, 31-32(Autumn 1938): Commitments: A Double Number, 12-16.

The orthodoxy which unites the writers of the left should be a new

Realism, a new realisation of the structure of society today, the relation of the society to the individual, an examination of the assumptions on which democracies rest.

C97   Article: "Fall of a Dictator," *New Statesman and Nation*, 16(Oct. 1, 1938), 498-500.

Comments on The Memoirs of Caulaincourt, Duke of Vicenza, Master of the Horse, Vol. II, 1814 (Cassell, 21s.).

C98   Article: "Picasso's Guernica," *New Statesman and Nation*, 16(Oct. 15, 1938), 567-68.

Comments on the painting at the New Burlington Gallery.

C99   Poem: "The Human Condition," *Poetry*, 53 (October 1938), 8-11.

C100   Article: "The Will to Live," *New Statesman and Nation*, 16(Nov. 12, 1938), 772.

Review of *John Cornford: A Memoir*, edited by Pat Sloan.

C101   Article: "Innocence and Guilt," *London Mercury*, 39:229(Nov. 1938), 92-94.

Review of Franz Kafka's *America*, translated from the German by Edwin and Willa Muir (Routledge).

C102   Poem: "Express," *Scholastic*, 33(Dec. 10, 1938), 20E.

1939

C103   Article: "Dante in English," *New Statesman and Nation*, 17:1(Jan. 14, 1939), 56-68.

Review of *Dante's Purgatorio*, The Italian text with a translation into English Triple Rhyme by Laurence Binyon (Macmillan, 7s.6d.).

C104   Poem: "The Bombed Happiness," *New Statesman and Nation*, 17 (Feb. 4, 1939), 167.

C105   Poem: "Midlands Express," *Spectator*, 162(Feb. 17, 1939), 259.

C106   Article: "Hoelderlin," *New Statesman and Nation*, 17:1(Feb. 11, 1939), 216-18.

Review of *Hoelderlin* by Ronald Peacock (Methuen, 10s.6d.).

C107 Story: "Deus *ex* Machina," *Living Age*, 355(Feb. 1939), 545-548.

From the *Listener*, Weekly Organ of the British Broadcasting Corporation. About a man who for one dark moment saw himself with the powers of a god.

C108 Article: "The Talking Bronco," *New Statesman and Nation*, 17:1 (March 11, 1939), 370.

Reivew of *Flowering Rifle* by Roy Campbell (Longmans, 6s.).

C109 Article: "The Other Side of the Nazi Medal," *London Mercury*, 39 March 1939), 549.

Review of Experssionism in German Life, Literature and the Theatre, 1900-1924, by Richard Samuel and R. Hinton Thomas.

C110 Poem: "Mask," *Saturday Reivew of Lieterature*, 19(April 22, 1939), 8.

C111 Four Poems: 1. "The Houses Fronting the Railway Lines," 2. "Poem," 3. "The Marginal Field," 4. "A Footnote to Marx's Chapter, 'The Working Day'," *Poetry*, 54:1(April 1939), 1-6.

C112 Article: "The Importance of W.H. Auden," *London Mercury*, 39:234(April 1939), 613-618.

Auden's poetry is a phenomenon, the most remarkable in English verse of this decade.

C113 Article: "The Jews We Deserve," *New Statesman and Nation*, 17:2 (May 6, 1939), 690-92.

Review of *The Jews, Are They Human?* by Wyndham Lewis (Allen and Unwin, 3s.6d.).

C114 Article: "Pomp and Circumstance," *New Statesman and Nation*, 17:2 (June 17, 1939), 940.

Reivew of *Man's Unconquerable Mind* by Professor R.W. Chambers (Cape, 15s.).

C115 Article: "Pictures in Switzerland," *New Statesman and Nation*, 17 (June 24, 1939), 972-73.

Switzerland is now a storehouse of some of the greatest masterpieces of art, past and present.

C116 Article: "Translation and the Classics," *New Statesman and Nation*, 18:1(July 22, 1939), 152-53.

Review of *The Collected Works of R.C. Trevelyan*, Vol. I—Poems (Longmans, 15s.) and Dante: The Divine Comedy, Vol. II—Inferno, with translation and comment by John D. Sinclair (John Lane, 10s.6d.).

C117 Article: "The American in France," *New Statesman and Nation*, 18:1(Aug. 12, 1939), 252-54.

Review of *A Diary of the French Revolution* by Governeur Morris (Harrap, 2 vols., 42s.).

C118 Article: "Explaining Modern Poetry," *New Statesman and Nation*, 18:1 (Sept. 9, 1939), 378-80.

Reivew of *A Dialogue on Modern Poetry* by Ruth Bailey (Oxford University Press, 5s.).

C119 Article: "Where Dons Delight," *New Statesman and Nation*, 18:1 September 30, 1939), 464.

Review of *Orion Marches* by Michael Roberts, *The Turning Path* by Ronald Bottral, *Sonnets. In Exitu Israel. Peace: an Ode* by E.H.W. Meyerstein, *Huntsman, What Quarry?* by Edna St. Vincent Millay, *I Have Seen Monsters and Angels* by Eugene Jolas and *The Road Is Wider Than Long* by Ronald Penrose.

C120 Article: "The Greeks in the Black-Out," *New Statesman and Nation*, 18:2 (Oct. 14, 1939), 528.

Review of *Aeschylus: Prometheus Unbound*, translated by R.C. Trevelyan (Cambridge, 2s.6d.); *Euripides: Medea*, translated by Trevelyan (Cambridge); *A Greek Garland* a Selection from the Palatine Anthology, translated by F.L. Lucas (Cambridge, 2s.6d.).

C121 Article: "Honey-Bubblings of the Boilers," *New Statesman and Nation*, 18:2 (Nov. 11, 1939), 686-87.

Review of *On the Boiler* by W.B. Yeats (Dublin, 3s.6d) and *The Arrow*: W.B. Yeats Commemoration Number (Dublin, 1s.).

C122 Poem: "Letters from the G.O.M.," *New Statesman and Nation*, 18 (Nov. 25, 1939), 755.

C123 Article: "Old Wine in New Bottles," *New Statesman and Nation*, 18:2(Dec. 9, 1939), 832-34.

Review of *Poets of Tomorrow*. First Selection (Hogarth, 6s.), *Poems* by Christopher Caudwell (Lane, 6s.), *The Spirit Watches* by Ruth Pitter (Cresset, 3s.6d.), *Collected Poems of Robert Frost*.

C124 Poem: "The Vase of Tears," *New Writing*: New Series, III(Christmas, 1939), 55-57.

Facing page is a picture of Spender in the company of Auden & Isherwood.

C125 Poem: "The Ambitious Son," *New Writing*: New Series III(Christmas, 1939), 55-57.

1940

C126 Article: "A Catholic on the Jews," *New Statesman and Nation*, 19 (Jan. 13, 1940), 49-50.

Review of *Anti-Semitism* by Jacques Maritain (Geoffrey Bles, 3s.6d.).

C127 Article: "How Shall We Be Saved?", *Horizon*, 1:1(Jan. 1940), 51-56.

Reivew of four books by Heard, Aldous Huxley, T.S. Eliot, and H.G. Wells: ". . . the fact that these four books should have been written contemporaneously offers a faint hope that if politics descend to a new level of force and cynicism, men may withdraw their support from their leaders."

C128 Article: "September Journal," *Horizon*, 1:2 (Feb. 1940), 102-121.

To be continued.

C129 Article: "September Journal," *Horizon*, 1:3(March 1940), 211-224.

To be concluded.

C130 Article: "A Morality Play with No Morals," *New Statesman and Nation*, 19(March 16, 1940), 363.

Review of Sean O'Casey's *The Star Turns Red* where characters exist only as symbols.

C131 Article: "The Essential Housman," *Horizon*, 1:4(April, 1940), 295-301.

Review of *The Collected Poems* of A.E. Housman (Cape, 7/6).

C132 Article: "Absent Intellectuals," *Spectator*, 164(April 26, 1940), 596.

Letter to the editor regarding Mr. Nicolson's remarks about Auden, Isherwood and others leaving for U.S.A. Spender has every intention of remaining in England . . .

C133 Poem: "The Double Shame, *Folios of New Writing*, I(Spring 1940), 116-117.

C134 Article: "September Journal," *Horizon*, 1:5(May 1940), 356-66. Concluded.

C135 Poem: "Near the Snow," *Horn Book*, 16(May 1940), 173.

C136 Article: "Bards," *New Statesman and Nation*, 19(May 11, 1940), 620-22.

Reivew of *The Sober War* by Rostrevor, *The Last Ditch* by Louis MacNeice, and several other books.

C137 Article: "Rilke's Letters to This War," *New Statesman and Nation*, 20(June 20, 1940), 10-11.

Rilke's belief in war as a disaster but also an opportunity for man to change his ways of life.

C138 Article: "Being Alive," *New Statesman and Nation*, (June 22, 1940), 777-78.

Review of *The Story and The Fable* by Edwin Muir and several other books.

C139 Poem: "The Drowned," *Horizon*, 1:7(July 1940), 530-531.

C140 Poem: "At Night," *New Statesman and Nation*, 20(July 20, 1940), 62.

C141 Article: "The Change of Heart," *New Statesman and Nation*, 20 (July 27, 1940), 94-96.

Review of *Passion and Society* by Denis de Rougemont (Faber, 12s.6d.), and *The Integration of the Personality* by Carl C. Jung (Kegan Paul, 15s.).

C142 Article: "Wise Man and Fool" *New Statesman and Nation*, 20 (August 31, 1940), 214-15.

Review of *Scattering Branches*: Tributes to the Memory of W.B. Yeats, edited by Stephen Gwynn (Macmillan, 8s.6d.).

C143 Poem: "At Night," *Living Age*, 359 (Sept. 1940), 26.

C144 Poem: "The Air Raid Across the Bay," *Horizon*, 2:9(Sept. 1940), 27.

C145 Article: "A Look at the Worst," *Horizon*, 2:9 (Sept. 1940), 103-117.

About war as a conflict between Democracy and Fascism.

C146 Article: "Graves Supérieur," *New Statesman and Nation*, 20 (September 21, 1940), 286-88.

Review of *No More Ghosts, Selected Poems*, by Robert Graves (Faber, 2s6d.).

C147 Article: "The Creative Imagination in the World Today," *Folios of New Writing* (Autumn 1940), 145-60.

Poets are faced with the problem of transforming into the comprehensible terms of the imagination the chaos of this politically obssessed world.

C148 Article: "Forerunner of a Future Poetry," *Dublin Review*, 209 (Oct. 1941), 183-88.

C149 Letter to a Colleague in America," *New Statesman and Nation*, 20 (November 16, 1940), 490.

Dissociates himself from those writers who have accused their English colleagues in America of running away.

C150 Poem: "The Air Raid Across the Bay," *Living Age*, under poems of the month selected by Oscar Williams, 359:449(Nov. 1940), 285.

C151 Two Poems: 1. "Doing Anything and Everything Is a Drug," 2. "As I Sit Staring Out of My Window," *Poetry*, prize award number, 57:2(Nov. 1940), 122-124.

C152 Poem: "June 1940," *Decision*, 2:5-6(Nov-Dec. 1941), 22-24.

C153 Article: "Poets of Two Wars," *New Statesman and Nation*, 20(Dec. 7, 1940), 570-72.

Review of *Rhymed Ruminations*, Poems by Siegfried Sassoon (Faber, 5s.) and *The Trumpet and Other Poems* by Edward Thomas (Faber, 2s.6d.).

C154 Poem: "To Poets and Airmen," *New Statesman and Nation*, 20 (Dec. 21, 1940), 651.

C155 Article: "The Case of Herbert Read," *New Statesman and Nation*, 21(Jan. 18, 1941), 67-68.

Review of *Annals of Innocence and Experience* by Herbert Read Faber, 10s.6d.).

C156 Poem: "Escapists Live on Borrowed Time," *Living Age*, 359(Jan. 1941), 415-418.

C157 Article: "Books and the War-I," *Penguin New Writing*, 2(Jan. 1941), 126-39.

C158 Poem: "Separation," *New Statesman and Nation*, 21(Feb. 15, 1941), 159.

C159 Letter to Arthur Calder-Marshall, *New Statesman and Nation*, 21 (Feb. 22, 1941), 182-83.

Reply to Marshall's criticism of the socalled left-wing writers of the 'thirties.

C160 Article: "Poetry in 1941," *Horizon*, 5:26(February 1942), 96-111.

Review of the year's poetry publications. Has a short bibliography of poetry published recently.

C161 Poem: "Song" "Stranger, You Who Hide My Love," *New Statesman and Nation*, 21(March 22, 1941), 297.

C162 Poem: "Speech from a Play," *Penguin New Writing*, 6(May 1941), 14-15.

C163 Article: "New Poems and Reprints," *New Statesman and Nation*, 22(July 12, 1941), 40.

Review of *Selected Poems of Robert Bridges, The Ship of Death* by D.H. Lawrence, *Make Bright the Arrows* by Edna St. Vincent Millay and several other books of poetry.

C164 Poem: "The War God," *The Listener*, (August 14, 1941).

C165 Article: "The Youngest Poets," *New Statesman and Nation*, 22 (August 23, 1941), 186-88.

Review of *The White Horseman*, edited by Hendry and Treece, *Poems* by Terence Tiller, and *A Book for Priscilla: Poems* by Nicholas Moore.

C166 Poem: "Tod und das Mädchen," *Horizon*, 4:20(August 1941), 84.

C167 Poem: "Song: Stranger, You Who Hide My Love," *Decision*, 2:3 (Sept. 1941), 64-65.

C168 Article: "Being Definite," *New Statesman and Nation*, 22(Sept. 20, 1941), 290-92.

Review of *Ideals and Illusions* by Susan Stebbing (Watts, 8s.6d.).

C169 Poem: "Winter and Summer," *Horizon*, 4:21(September 1941), 165.

C170 Four Poems: "A Wild Race," "No Orpheus, No Eurydice," "June 1940," "In Memoriam," *Folios of New Writing* (Autumn 1941), 28-35.

C171 Article: "Selected Notices," *Horizon*, 4:23(November 1941), 365-66.

Reivew of *Awake, and Other Poems* by W.R. Rodgers.

C172 Article: "Books and The War—X": The Poets in Revolt," *Penguin New Writing*, XI(Nov. 1941), 117-127.

All modern poets are engaged in a common task of analysing the universal human situation in terms of contemporary life.

C173 Article: "Women Poets," *New Statesman and Nation*, 22(Dec. 27, 1941), 528.

Review of *Tomorrow is a Revealing* by Lilian Bowes-Lyon, *Selected Poems* by V. Sackville-West, *A Dream Observed* by Anne Ridler.

C174 Poems: "Air Raid" and "Dusk," *Horizon*, 3:14(1941), 93-96.

C175 Article: "The Year's Poetry," *Horizon*, 3:14(1941), 138-148.
A survey.

C176 "To Be Truly Free" (essay) and "Oliveiro Decides" (an episode from a play), *Daylight*, 1(1941), 11-16; 96-110.

1942

C177 Article: "Highbrow Fireman," *New Statesman and Nation*, 23(Jan. 3, 1942), 12-13.

Review of *London's Burning* by Maurice Richardson (Hale, 5s.).

C178 Poem: "In Memoriam," *Decision*, 3:1-2(Jan/Feb. 1942), 53.

C179 Article: "From England: War and the Writer," *Partisan Review*, 9:1 (Jan/Feb. 1942), 63-66.

A letter dated Oct. 25, 1941 was written for publication in *Common Sense*. It has been passed on to this *Reivew* for 1942.

C180 Poem: "The Fates," *Poetry*, 59:6(March 1942), 309-14.

C181 Poem: "Winter and Summer," *Nation*, 154(April 11, 1942), 426-27.

C182 Article: "Books and the War—XI": Victorian Poetry," *Penguin New Writing*, 12(April 1942), 131-142.

Comments on The Oxford Book of Victorian Verse compiled by Sir Arthur Quiller Couch.

C183 Poem: "Daybreak," *New Republic*, 106(April 13, 1942), 504.

C184 Poem: "The Journey: Upon what confident iron rails," *Penguin New Writing*, 12(April 1942).

C185 Article: "Walt Whitman and Democracy," *Penguin New Writing*, 13 (April/June 1942), 116-26.

Whitman's great work is like Moby Dick—the rarest and the strangest, and in some way the purest of monsters—stranded upon the shores of literature without any one knowing quite what to think of it.

C186 Article: "Morale and Short Term Education," *Fortnightly*: 157 (June 1942), 436-42.

Plea for increasing war-effort by unifying the country by pulling down class barriers.

C187 Article: "Disinterestedness of War Workers," *New Statesman and Nation*, 23(June 13, 1942), 382.

About starting a mass education movement to make people believe in what they are fighting for.

C188 Article: "Modern Poets and Reviewers," *Horizon*, 5:30(June 1942), 431-38.

With the best will in the world, it is difficult to think that much of value can be said by critics at the present stage.

C189 Article: "The Creative Spirit—I," *New Writing and Daylight* (Summer 1942), 24-33.

Discusses elements of the modern with illustrations from Baudelaire.

C190 Article: "Walter de la Mare," *New Statesman and Nation*, 24(July 18, 1942), 45-46.

Review of *Collected Poems* by Walter de la Mare (Faber, 12s.6d.).

C191 Article: "The Novel and Narrative Poetry," *Penguin New Writing*, 14(July/Sept. 1942), 123-32.

About the future of narrative poetry: Should the novel be factual in its foundations or use poetic method? Answer: both.

C192 Article: "Books in General," *New Statesman and Nation*, 24(August 15, 1942), 110.

Review of *Phoenix* by H.G. Wells (Secker and Warburg, 8s.).

C193 Article: "The P.E.N. Shelter," *New Statesman and Nation*, 24 (October 3, 1942), 225-26.

Reivew of *Thomas Hardy* by Nevinson, *Magic Casements* by Farjeon, and several others.

C194 Article: "Literature and Public Events," *Penguin New Writing*, 15 (Oct/Dec. 1942), 127-37.

The most impressive fact of our time is that many creative artists, including writers, have declared their support for the cause of freedom.

C195 Article: "Citizenship and C.D.," *Spectator*, 169(Dcc. 18, 1942), 571.

Civil Defence offers an enormous opportunity to democracy. C.D. Workers should become the leaders of morale in towns.

C196 Poem: "On the Executions in Poland," *New Statesman and Nation*, 24(Dec. 19, 1942), 407.

C197 Article: "The Creative Spirit in New Writing-II," *New Writing and Daylight* (Winter 1942-43), 78-85.

The struggle of the contemporary writer against the forces of evil, like Milton in his time.

1943

C198 Article: "Sensuousness in Modern Poetry," *Penguin New Writing*, 16(Jan/March 1943), 118-126.

Plea for establishment of standards by which poetry can be judged apart from the literary, political, philosophical or theological programme which the poet sets for himself. Suggests *sensousness* as the complete fusion of the world of ideas, experience etc. through the medium of his own sensibility. It is more than an appeal to the eye. It works through all the senses and has a muscular, kinetic quality which suggests the movement of life itself.

C199 Article: "Man the Master," *Horizon*, 7:40(April 1943), 277-82.

Review of *God and Evil* by C.E.M. Joad and *Man the Master* by Gerald Heard.

C200 Article: "The Poet's Maturity," *New Statesman and Nation*, 25 (April 17, 1943), 260-61.

Review of *Selected Poems* by John Hall, *Forty Poems* by John Lehmann and other books.

C201 Poem: "June 1940," *Penguin New Writing*, 17(April/June 1943), 112-13.

C202 Poem: "Lines for Edith Sitwell," *Horizon*, 8:43(July 1943), 6.

C203 Three Poems: "A Trance," "The Statue of Apollo," "Bridle of the Sun," *Penguin New Writing*, 18(July/Sept. 1943), 49-50.

C204 Poem: "Prague Dressed in Light," *New Writing and Daylight* (Summer 1943), translated from Czech by Stephen Spender and Jiri Mucha.

C205 Article: "Hoelderlin, Goethe and Germany," *Horizon*, 8:46(Oct. 1943), 273-280.

Germans could be re-educated through their great artists.

C206 Article: "Flux," *New Statesman and Nation*, 26(October 2, 1943), 220.

Review of *A Private Country* by Lawrence Durrell, *Under the Cliff* by Geoffrey Grigson, and other books.

C207 Article: "The Crisis of Symbols," *New Writing and Daylight*, 19 (Oct/Dec. 1943), 129-135.

The task of the modern poet is not the invention of new poetic symbols, but the interpretation of the confused symbolic language of the modern industrialized world in terms of the past and the future.

C208 Poem: "Spiritual Exercises," 45-48; article: "Lorca in English, 125-133; *New Writing and Daylight* (Winter 1943-44).

Why Lorca's poetry makes itself felt through the medium of translation and why his English imitators fail.

C209 Poem: "No Orpheus, No Eurydice," *Penguin New Writing*, 17 (1943), 112-113.

1944

C210 Poem: "Abyss," *New Statesman and Nation*, 27(March 11, 1944), 171.

C211 Article: "Lessons of Poetry 1943," *Horizon*, 9:51(March 1944), 207-216.

Review of the year's poetry: "Intelligence, sensitivity, imagination, perception and enormous quantity of good intentions flow into the stream of contemporary poetry . . ."

C212 Poems: "Man and Woman," "The Child," *Horizon*, 9:54(June 1944), 367-368.

C213 Article: "A Czech Poet," *New Statesman and Nation*, 27(June 10, 1944), 392.

Review of *The Wounds of the Apostles*: Poems by Fred Marnau, translated by Ernst Sigler (Grey Walls Press, 7s.6d.).

C214 Poem: "Perfection," *Horizon*, 9:54(June 1944), 368.

C215 Poem: "Rejoice in the Abyss," *Partisan Review*, 11:3(Summer 1944), 283-84.

C216 Article: "Selected Notices: Recent Poetry," *Horizon*, 10:58(Oct. 1944), 280-87.

Review of several books of recent poetry publications.

C217 Poem: "Ocean," *New Writing and Daylight* (Autumn 1944), 75-76.

C218 Poem: "Almond Blossom in War-Time," *New Writing and Daylight* *(Autumn 1944), 75-76.*

C219 Article: "Books in General," *New Statesman and Nation*, 27(Nov. 25, 1944), 355.

Review of *The Athenians*, being correspondence between Thomas Jefferson Hogg and his friends, Thomas Love Peacock, Leigh Hunt, Percy Bysshe Shelley and Others; and *Harriet and Mary*, being the Relations between the Shelleys and Hogg.

C220 Poem: "Lines for Edith Sitwell," *Atlantic Monthly*, 174:6(Dec. 1944), 91.

C221 Poem" Four Eyes," *New Road* (1944), 168.

C222 "A Christmas Anthology," compiled by Stephen Spender, *Horizon*, 10:60(December 1944), 370-381.

Contains poems by several poets.

C223 Article: "The International Patriot," *Transformation*, II(1944), 95-101.

C224 Poem: "The Conscript," *New Road* (1944), 168.

C225 Article: "Writers in the World of Necessity," *Polemic* (1944), 20-25.

C226 Poem: "The Conscript," *Maryland Quarterly*, I(1944), 1.

C227 Article: "The Sensuous World of Keats," *New Writing and Daylight*, 20(1944), 142-50.

Keats' touchstone of poetry: "Sensuousness" which is, "indeed, the poet's only certain reality and guide."

C228 "Oliveiro Decides (An Episode from a Play)," *New Writing and Daylight*, 22(1944), 95-105.

1945

C229 Article: "Four Poets," *New Statesman and Nation*, 29(Jan. 13, 1945), 29-30.

Review of books of poetry by Edmund Blunden, Herbert Read, G.S. Fraser, and Francis Brett Young.

C230 Article: "A Poetic Tribute," *New Statesman and Nation*, 29(Jan. 27, 1945), 62-63.

Review of *Robert Bridges* (1844-1930) by Edward Thompson (Oxford University Press, 7s.6d.).

C231 Article: "Healing Dreams?" *New Statesman and Nation*, 29(March 31, 1945), 213.

Review of *The Lady of the Hare, a Study in the Healing Power of Dreams*, by John Layard (Faber, 12s.6d.).

C232 Poem: "The Child," *Contemporary Poetry*, 5:1(Spring 1945), 4.

C233 Article: "Impressions of French Poetry in Wartime," *Horizon*, 11:65(May 1945), 339-347.

French poetry possesses deep unity with the agony of humanity in Europe . . . Contains a short bibliography.

C234 Poems: "Seascape," *Atlantic Monthly*, 175:6(June 1945), 74.

C235 Poem: "Almond Blossoms in War Time," *Atlantic Monthly*, 175:6 (June 1945), 74.

C236 Article: "Modern Writers in the World of Necessity," *Partisan Review*, 12:3(Summer 1945), 352-60.

The curse of Fascism on every aspect of life in the world which the modern writer has to face. Defines freedom as the acceptance of necessity.

C237 Article: Review of *For the Time Being* by W.H. Auden, *Poetry Quarterly*, 7:1(Spring 1945), 22-26.

C238 Article: "Comment," *Horizon*, 12:67(July 1945), 5-10.

Comment as editor.

C239 Poem: "Summer," *Horizon*, 12:67(July 1945), 11.

C240 Article: War and Peace—II—"Rhineland Journal,", *Horizon*, 12:72 (December 1945), 394-413.

C241 Article: "The Pre-Raphaelite Literary Painters," *New Writing and Daylight*, (Sept. 1945), 123-21.

C242 Article: "Selected Notices," *Horizon*, 10:57(Sept. 1945), 216-18.

Review of *Other Men's Flowers*, Selected and annotated by A.P. Wavell (Cape).

C243 Article: "Moods and Reactions," *Poetry*, 67(Nov. 1945), 88-95.

A brief review of modern poetry, attempting to place poets of our time in the background of various movements and tendencies.

C244 Article: "The Realist Novel and Poetic Imagination," *Penguin New Writing*, 23(1945), 112-116.

The task of the novelist is to discover significance in everything and transform contemporary life into an important image; It is not reportage nor propaganda. It is the liberation of ideas within events, personalities and appearances.

C245 Article: "Prescriptions for a Modern Masterpiece," Specially written for this issue, *New Writing and Daylight*, 24(1945), 147-156.

The spirit of the present time is least congenial for creativity, yet it may be its greatest significance.

C246 Article: "Two Landscapes of Novel," Specially written for this issue, *New Writing and Daylight*, 25(1945).

One landscape is the Nineteenth Century, the other, the twentieth century.

C247 Article: "The Pre-Raphaelite Literary Painters," *New Writing and Daylight* VI(1945), 123-31.

The inspiration of Pre-Raphaelitism was verbal, literary, poetic, rather than of painting.

1946

C248 Article: "Have English Writers Marked Time?", *Saturday Review of Literature*, 29(Jan. 5, 1946), 5.

C249 Article: "Germany in Europe," *Fortnightly*: New Series, No. 954 (June 1946), 401-407.

Germany should be Europeanized and integrated with the rest of Europe.

C250 Article: "The Influence of Hoelderlin on English Poetry," *The Listener*, 36:918(15 Aug. 1946), 216-17.

C251 Article: "The Making of a Poem," *Partisan Review*, 13:3(Summer 1946), 294-308.

Perhaps, literature becomes a humble exercise of faith in being all that one can be in one's art, of being more than oneself.

C252 Article: Review of *This Way to The Tomb*, by Ronald Duncan, *Poetry Quarterly*, 8:2(Summer 1946), 115-117.

C253 Article: "Questionnaire: The Cost of Letters," *Horizon* 14:81 (Sept. 1946), 171-73.

Spender answers questions on how much a writer needs to live on, should he have second occupation, and the like.

C254 Article: "German Impressions and Conversations," *Partisan Review*, 13(Winter 1946), 6-24.

Excerpts from a Journal.

C255 Poem: "Meeting," *New Writing and Daylight*, 27(1946), 82-84.

1947

C256 Article: "Intellectuals and Europe's Future," *Commentary*, 3(Jan. 1947), 7-12.

C257 Article: "Can Unesco Succeed?" *Fortnightly*, New Series, No. 963(March 1947), 185-190.

Discusses various conditions required for Unesco to succeed.

C258 Article: "Horatio Hits Back," *New Statesman and Nation*, 33(April 26, 1947), 295.

Review of *Illusion and Reality*, a Study of the Sources of Poetry by Christopher Caudwell (Lawrence and Wishart, 12s.6d.).

C259 Letter: "Chief Glory," *New Statesman and Nation*, 33(April 26, 1947), 295.

Suggestions regarding the Government's reduction of paper quota for publishers.

C260 Article: "United Nations: Cultural Division," *Commentary*, 3(April 1947), 336-40.

C261 Poem: "O Night O Trembling Night," *Horizon*, 16:90(July 1947), [3]

C262 Poem: "On the Pilots Who Destroyed Germany in the Spring of 1945," *Nation*, 165(Oct. 18, 1947), 414.

C263 Poem: "The Labourer in the Vineyards," *Yale Poetry Review*, 6 (1947), 30.

C264 Poem: "The Almond Tree in a Burned City," *Yale Poetry Review*, 6(1947), 30-31.

1948

C265 Article: "U.S. Cultural Influence in Europe," *New York Times* (Jan. 26, 1948), 22-24.

C266 Article: "The Power and the Hazard," *Poetry*, 71(March 1948), 314-318.

Review of *Trial of a Poet* by Karl Shapiro (Reynal & Hitchcock, $2.00).

C267 Open Letter to *Pravda, Nation*, 166(March 20, 1948).

Art should not be dictated by politics. Spender calls upon intellectuals of the world to speak out in behalf of the oppressed humanity against the political forces of the world which have been playing the role of the oppressor.

C268 Article: "We Can Win the Battle for the Mind of Europe," *New York Times Magazine* (April 25, 1948), 15.

The Europeans, even those behind the Iron Curtain can still be swung to Western culture. (Carries the picture of Soviet propaganda outpost—propaganda center in Prague.)

C269 Poem: "Awaking," *New Yorker*, 24(May 15, 1948). 36.

C270 Article: "A Note On Seriousness in Poetry," *Poetry*, 72 (May 1948), 92-98.

Poetry provides significant insights into human experience and should not be treated as a game like that of chess. On p. [88] ; a picture of Spender and his wife Natasha.

C271 Poem: "Madonna," *Partisan Review*, 15:6(June 1948), 672.

C272 Letter: "Message to Wroclaw," *Nation*, 167(Sept. 18, 1948), 326.

Message sent to the cultural congress for peace, held in Wroclaw, which Spender could not attend. The letter is dated Sept. 2.

C273 Poem: "Empty House," *New Yorker*, 24(Sept. 25, 1948), 32.

C274 Poem: "Tom's A-Cold," *Poetry*, 73:1(October 1948), 1-6.

C275 Poem: "Faust's Song," *Wake*, the creative magazine edited by Seymour Lawrence, José Garcia Villa, Wake editions, New York (Autumn 1948), 25.

C276 Article: "What Is Modern in Modern Poetry?" *The Tiger's Eye*, I:4 (1948), 1-13.

The modern poets are heroic, because they have tried to make us understand in terms of our imagination the inhuman environment we have made for ourselves.

•C277 Poem: "What I Expected," *Turnstile One* (1948), 79-80.

C278 Poem: "Judas Iscariot," *Nation*, 167(Dec. 25, 1948), 728.

1949

C279 Article: "Life of Literature," *Partisan Review*, 16(Jan/Feb. 1949), 56-66.

C280 Article: "Situation of the American Writer," *Horizon*, 19(March 1949), 162-79.

C281 Poems: "Faust's Song" and "Ice," *Horizon*, 19(March 1949), 161.

C282 Poem: "The Angel," *New Statesman and Nation*, 37(March 5, 1949), 225.

C283 Poem: "The Angel," *Nation*, 168(March 19, 1949), 336.

C284 Poem: "O, Omega, Invocation," *New Statesman and Nation*, 37 (March 26, 1949), 297.

C285 Article: "Dylan Thomas," *New Statesman and Nation*, 37(June 18, 1949), 650-52.

Review of *Dylan Thomas* by Henry Treece (Lindsay Drummond, 7s.6d.).

C286 Poem: "O, Omega, Invocation," *Nation*, 168(April 2, 1949), 392.

C287 Poem: "Word," *New Yorker*, 25(April 9, 1949), 37.

C288 Article: "The Riddle of Shaw," *Nation*, 168(April 30, 1949), 503-505.

Review of *16 Self Sketches* by Bernard Shaw and *Days with Bernard Shaw* by Stephen Einsten.

C289 Article: "London Gray, New York Gold," *Nation*, 168(May 14, 1949), 558-560.

English life is an experiment in socialism and in spite of its grayness seems to be better than New York gold.

C290 Article: "What's Wrong with Unesco?" *Nation*, 168(June 18, 1949), 686-87.

Unesco suffers from many disadvantages on account of the enormous pretensions of the aim and the title. Better to build many, small, efficient organizations in different countries of the world than a single top-heavy monster.

C291 Article: "Reflections on the Literary Life," *New Statesman and Nation*, 40(Aug. 12, 1949), 170-71.

C292 Article: "Oxford and Germany," *Partisan Review*, 16(Sept. 1949), 924-36.

Excerpt from Spender's autobiographical work in progress.

C293 Article: "Jewish Writers and the English Literary Tradition," *Commentary*, 8(September 1949), 216-18.

C294 Article: "Writers in America—I," *Nation*, 169(Oct. 15, 1949), 373-75.

C295 Article: "Writers in America—II," *Nation*, 169(Dec. 3, 1949), 543-44.

These comments are based upon Spender's visit in thirty states and forty universities and colleges in 1947 and 1948. The deepest American experience is the writer's loneliness which is the major feature of American writing.

C296 Poems: "Cold" and "Angel," *Voices*, II(1949), 137.

1950

C297 Article: "Goethe, the Great European," *The Listener*, 43:1096(Jan. 26, 1950), 151-152.

"How close he is to the threshold of our epoch."

C298 Article: "Inner Meaning of Fuchs Case," *New York Times Magazine* (March 12, 1950), 13.

The British traitor's brilliant but sick mind demonstrates the need for constructive faith.

C299 Article: "The Pattern of Error," *New Statesman and Nation*, 39 (March 18, 1950), 306-308.

Review of Collected Shorter Poems: 1930-44, by W.H. Auden (Faber, 15s.).

C300 Article: "Christopher Fry," *Spectator*, 184(March 24, 1950), 364-65.

Fry as a promising poetic talent of the theatre.

C301 Article: "The Horizon Decade," *World Review* (Incorporating *Review of Reviews*), New Series 15(May 1950), 22-31.

The *Horizon* magazine against the reality of war gave young people strength for survival.

C302 Article: "Personified Corsair," *The Listener*, XLIII(June 22, 1950), 1071.

Review of *Trelawny* by R. Glynn Grylls.

C303 Article: "Reflections on the Literary Life," *New Statesman and Nation*, 40(Aug. 12, 1950), 170-71.

About writing reviews.

C304 Letter: "American Symbolic Realism" *The Listener* XLIV(Sept. 14, 1950), 348.

Protesting against absurd judgments of Mr. Geoffrey Gorer.

C305 Article: "Task of an Autobiographer," *The Listener* XLIV(Sept. 14, 1950), 349-350.

C306 Article: "Dostoevsky's Ninth Symphony," *New Statesman and Nation*, 40(Sept. 16, 1950), 278-79.

Review of *Dostoevsky: The Making of a Novelist* by Ernest J. Simmons (Lehmann, 18s.).

C307 Article: "The Problem of Freedom Today," *The Listener*, XLIV (Dec. 21, 1950), 779-80.

Our life is made up of both freedom and necessity.

C308 Article: " 'Horizon' and Cyril Connolly," *Atlantic Monthly*, 186 (Dec. 1950), 78-80.

Spender with Peter Watson and Cyril Connolly helped to establish the English Monthly, *Horizon*. Here he narrates the story of its beginning, its growth, its success, and the decision to suspend its publication.

1951

C309 Aritcle: "Does the English Writer Have a Chance?", *Saturday Review of Literature*, 34(Jan. 13, 1951), 22-23+.

After the war the situation of art and literature has changed. The young writer should assert his independence against growing collectivization and other dangers.

C310 Article: "Russell and Logan," A Portrait of Logan Pearsall Smith, Drawn from His Letters and Diaries, Selected and Introduced by John Russell, *New Statesman and Nation*, 41(March 17, 1951), 310-312.

Review of the book.

C311 Article: "Reflections on the Literary Life," *Partisan Review*, 18:2 (March/April 1951), 251-56.

C312 Article: Autobiography of an Individualist, Christopher Isherwood. *Twentieth Century*, 149(May 1951), 405-11.

C313 Article: "English Intellectuals and the World of Today," *Twentieth Century*, 149(June 1951), 482-88.

C314 Article: "To Think of Peace as Well as War," *New York Times Magazine* (August 12, 1951), 12.

The way to avoid the great dangers of "Saber-rattling and timorous pacifism."

C315 Article: "Seriously Unserious," *Poetry*, 78(Sept. 1951), 352-56.

Review of Auden's *Nones*. Praises Auden's classical precision and detachment." "In Praise of Limestone" is one of the great poems of this century.

C316 Letter: "Fear Neurosis," *New Statesman and Nation*, 42(Sept. 22, 1951), 311.

Reply to Dr. Alex Comfort's letter.

C317 Article: "Let Us Not Be Monolithic, Too," *The New York Times Magazine* (Oct. 7, 1951), 24+68-71.

The democracies must have unity but not rigid conformity to meet the Soviet challenge.

C318 Article: "Shelley, M.P,." *New Statesman and Nation*, 42(Nov. 3, 1951), 500.

Review of *The Young Shelley: Genesis of a Radical* by K.N. Cameron (Gollancz 21s.).

C319 Article: "British Intellectuals in the Welfare State," *Commentary*, 12(November 1951), 425-30.

How the new climate of economic crises and political uncertainty affects science and culture.

C320 Article: "Thoughts on British Elections," 173(Nov. 10, 1951), 390-391.

Analyses the recent November elections in Britain and suggests ways to alter the situation.

C321 Article: "L'Univers Concentrationnaire," *New Statesman and Nation*, 42(Nov. 17, 1951), 566-68.

Review of *A World Apart* by David Rousset and *Peter Moen's Diary.*

C322 Article: "Character of Lloyd George," *Twentieth Century*, 150 (December 1951), 511-16.

C323 Article: "My Credo: On the Function of Criticism," *Kenyon Review*, 13:2(1951), 207-17.

1952

C324 Article: "Thomas Mann," *New Statesman and Nation*, 43(Jan. 12, 1952), 46-47.

Review of *The Stature of Thomas Mann*, edited by Charles Neider (Peter Owen, 21s.).

C325 Article; "Chosen People," *New Statesman*, 43(May 31, 1952), 642.
About converted Italian Jews.

C326 Article; "New Novels," *The Listener* 48(Oct. 30, 1952), 735.
Review of *Recollection of a Journey, The Finanical Expert, A Cry of Children,* and *In the Making.*

C327 Poems: "To My Daughter" and "One Flesh," *New Statesman*, 44 (Nov. 22, 1952), 608.

C328 Article: "Spectre de la Rose," *New Statesman and Nation*, 44(Nov. 8, 1952), 554-55.
Review of *The Last Years of Nijinsky* by Romola Nijinsky (Gollancz, 15s.).

C329 Article: "New Novels," *The Listener*, XLVIII(Nov. 13, 1952), 821.
Review of *Torment, The Strange Children, Martha Quest,* and *The Trial of Bébé Donge.*

C330 Article: "New Novels," *The Listener*, XLVIII(Nov. 27, 1952), 905.
Reivew of *Young Men Waiting, Bubu of Montparnasse, Rowan Berry Wine,* and *Madame de.*

C331 Article: "New Novels," *The Listener*, 48(Dec. 11, 1952), 999.
Review of *The Grass Harp, Many Are Called,* and *The Queerfella.*

C332 Article: "The German Muse," *New Statesman and Nation*, 44(Dec. 20, 1952), 760-61.
Review of *The Poems of Hoelderlin*, translated with a critical study by Michael Hamburger, *German Lyric Poetry* by S.S. Prawer, *Hoelderlin* by L.S. Salzburger and *Storm and Stress* by H.B. Garland.

C333 Article: "New Novels," *The Listener*, 48(Dec. 25, 1952), 1087.
Review of *A Bag of Stones, The Man from Madura,* and *Two Adolescents.*

1953

C334 Article: "New Novels," *The Listener*, 49(Jan. 15, 1953), 115.
Review of *Invisible Man, The Producer, The Witch-Diggers,* and *The Courting of Susie Brown.*

C335 Article: "New Novels," *The Listener*, 49(Jan. 29, 1953), 195.

Review of *The Mountains Remain, Drum Singers, Blanket Boy's Moon, The Blue Hussar*.

C336 Article: "Speaking for Spain," *New Republic*, 128(Feb. 2, 1953), 18-19.

Review of Garcia Lorca by Roy Campbell (Yale; $2).

C337 Article: "One Man's Conscience," *New Republic*, 128(March 16, 1953), 18-19.

Review of *Such, Such Were the Joys*, a collection of essays by. George Orwell, in which he states simply and clearly all his main ideas.

C338 Article: "German Romanticist," *New Republic*, 128(March 30, 1953), 27.

Review of *Poems* by F. Hoelderlin, translated by Michael Hamburger (Pantheon, $3.50).

C339 Poem: "Nocturne," *Sewanee Review*, 61:2(April/June 1953), 181-82.

C340 Article: "The Predatory Jailer," *New Republic*, 128(June 22, 1953), 18-19+.

Review of *The Captive Mind* by Czeslaw Milosz. Recommended for immediate reading. It is a master-piece explaining mainly how the communists succeed in enslaving the minds of the intelligentsia. This cannot be stopped unless the rights of human individuals are held to be sacred.

C341 Article: "W.H. Auden and His Poetry," *Atlantic Monthly*, 192(July 1953), 74-79.

Discusses the evolution of Auden's poetic ideas with the sympathy of a friend and the insight of a critic.

C342 Article: "New Orthodoxies," *New Republic*, 128(July 27, 1953), 16-17+.

C343 Article: "New Orthodoxies," *New Republic*, 129(Aug. 3, 1953), 15-17.

Discusses in three series three orthodoxies which influence writing and to some extent all the arts.

C344 Article: "Rilke and the Angels; Eliot and the Shrines," *Sewanee Review*, 61(October 1953), 557-81.

Modern poet as hero?

C345 Article: "American Diction v. American Poetry," *Encounter*, edited by Stephen Spender and Irving Kristol, 1:1(Oct. 1953), 61-65.

Review of *American into English* by G.V. Carey (Heinemann, 6s.) and *Selected Poems* by Wallace Stevens (Faber, 12s.6d.), and *Poems* by Elizabeth Jennings (Fantasy, 5s.).

C346 Article: "Misery and Grandeur of Poets," *The Listener*, L(Oct. 8, 1953), 608.

Review of W.B. Yeats and *Sturge Moore, Their Correspondence, 1901-1937*, edited by Ursula Bridge.

C347 Letter: "Encounter," *The Listener*, L(Oct. 15, 1953), 645.

Regarding a review of the first number of *Encounter*.

C348 Article: "On Literary Movements," *Encounter*, I:2(Nov. 1953), 66-68.

"Good signs in literary England today of what might be called a rebellion of the Lower Middle Brows."

C349 Article: "Ghosts of a Renascence," *Encounter*, I:3(Dec. 1953), 2-3.

Editorial comment on ideas like "individualism," "renascence" etc.

1954

C350 Letter to a Young Writer: "Brilliant Athens and Us," *Encounter*, II:3(March 1954), 4-5.

An editorial addressed to Henry James Joyce Junior.

C351 Article: "English Painting in the Fifties," *New Republic*, 130(April 19, 1954), 16-17.

Comments upon the death of outstanding talent in English painting & compares it with contemporary literature.

C352 Article: "Is There a London Literary Racket?", *Twentieth Century*, 156(July 1954), 49-53.

C353 Poems: "Missing My Daughter" and "Archaic Head," *Sewanee Review*, 62(October 1954), 621-22.

C354 Poems: "Archaic Head," "One," and "Dog Rose," *London Magazine*, 1:9(October 1954), 25-26.

1955

C355 Article: ARGO RECORDS of Hopkins, Keats, Lorca, T.S. Eliot and others, *London Magazine*, 2:3(March 1955), 104-108.
A Review.

C356 Article: "Inside the Cage," *Encounter*, 4:3(March 1955), 15-22.
Notes on the poetic imagination today.

C357 Article: "Notes from a Diary," *Encounter*, 5:5 (Nov. 1955), 48-49.
About prisoner, anti-Americanism etc. About postwar Germany, the Thirties etc.

C358 Article: "Notes from a Diary," *Encounter*, 5:5(Dec. 1955), 54-55.
About post-war Germany, the Thirties etc.

C359 Article: "Pages from a Journal," *Sewanee Review*, 63(Fall 1955), 614-30.

C360 Article: "Notes from a Diary," *Encounter* (Dec. 1955), 54-55.

C361 Article: "On Poetic Drama," *London Magazine*, 2:12(December 1955), 77-82.
Reviews of *The Death of Satan, A Match for the Devil,* and *The Hidden King.*

1956

C362 Article: "Notes from a Diary," *Encounter*, 6:1(Jan. 1956), 52-53.

C363 Article: "Notes from a Diary," *Encounter*, 6:2(Feb. 1956), 38-39.

C364 Poem: "Poem in Four Movements," *London Magazine*, 3:3(March 1956), 13-14.
This poem, never before published, was written in 1934. Part IV is a sketch for the last section of *Vienna.*

C365 Poem: "Mein Kind Kam Heim," *Poetry* (London-New York), 1:1 (March/April 1956), 13.

C366 Article: "Notes from a Diary," *Encounter*, 6:5(May 1956), 82-83.

C367 Article: "Notes from a Diary," *Encounter*, 6:6(June 1956), 64-65.

C368 Article: On Marianne Moore," *London Magazine*, 3:6(June 1956), 73-75.

Review of Moore's *Predilections* and *Selected Fables of La Fontaine* (Faber).

C369 Article: "Notes from a Diary," *Encounter*, 7:1(July 1956), 60-61.

C370 Article: "Looking Back on Spain," *Spectator*, 197(July 13, 1956), 57-58.

Spain was a demonstration of the fact that there was a will to fight Franco's allies, Hitler and Mussolini, by individuals, for the sake of individual values.

C371 Article: "Notes from a Diary," *Encounter*, 7:2(Aug. 1956), 70-71.

C372 Article: "Notes from a Diary," *Encounter*, 7:3 (Sept. 1956), 52-53.

C373 Article: "Notes from a Diary," *Encounter*, 7:4(October 1956), 59-60.

Note: "Notes from a Diary" was a regular feature of the magazine for comments on sundry subjects to which Spender frequently contributed.

C374 Article: "A Double Debt to Yeats," *The Listener*, 56(Oct. 4, 1956), 513-515.

Comments on the poetry of Yeats in relation to our times.

C375 Article: "Low Pressure Gauge," *The Listener*, 56(Oct. 11, 1956), 575.

Review of *Poetry Now*, an Anthology, edited by G.S. Fraser.

C376 Poem: "On a Photograph of a Friend, Peter Watson," *Poetry* (London-New York), 1:2(Winter 1956), 3-4.

1957

C377 Article: "Notes from a Diary," *Encounter*, 8:1(Jan. 1957), 61-64.

C378 Article: "Two Witty Women," *Encounter*, 8:2(Feb. 1957), 77-79.

Review of *Venice Observed* by Mary McCarthy and *The Tower of Trebizond* by Rose Macaulay.

C379 Article: "Notes from a Diary," *Encounter*, 8:3(March 1957), 69-71.

C380 Article: "The Writer in His Age," *London Magazine*, 4:5(May 1957), 49-51.

The *London Magazine* invited nine authors to answer questions about writers' engagement with the age in which they live.

C381 "Engaged in Writing" (A Short Novel, Part I), *Encounter*, 9:1(July 1957), 36-69.

C382 "Engaged in Writing (A Short Novel, Part II), *Encounter*, 9:2(Aug. 1957), 42-66.

With illustrations.

C383 "Introducing German Poets," *London Magazine*, 4:9(Sept. 1957), 48-51.

C384 Poem: "To Samuel Barber," *Poetry* (London-New York), 1:3 (Winter 1957), 11.

C385 Article: "Japanese Observations: I," *Encounter*, 9:6(Dec. 1957), 49-51.

No. II is by Angus Wilson.

1958

C386 Article: "Notes from a Diary," *Encounter*, 10:1(Jan. 1958), 56-58.

C387 Poem: "Orpheus: Adam: Christ," *Encounter*, 10:3(March 1958), 65.

This poem was suggested by a sculpture in the Byzantine Museum in Athens, portraying Orpheus as Christ in the branches of a tree which is the world. . .

C388 Poem: "Subject: Object: Sentence," *Encounter*, 10:4(April 1958), 47.

C389 Poem: "Instructions," *London Magazine*, 5:5(May 1958), 34.

New Poems for Spring 1958.

C390 Article: "Anglo-Saxon Attitudes," *Partisan Review*, 25(Winter 1958), 110-16.

"London Letter": "The young writers, with all their complaints about England, seem scarcely conscious of a world outside England. ... Yet they are engulfed by a wider context—prosperous Germany and the Common Market ...

1959

C391 Article: "Dismantling Politics," *Encounter*, 12:2(Feb. 1959), 79-81.

Notes from a diary.

C392 Article: "Robert Lowell's Family Album," *New Republic*, 140 (June 8, 1959), 17.

Review of Lowell's *Life Studies*. The brilliant characterization of the Lowell family illustrates the possibility of humanist poetry.

C393 Article: "The Most Ecstatic Poetry Ever Written," *New Republic*, 140(June 29, 1959), 15-16.

Review of *The Poems of St. John of the Cross*, New English versions, by John Fredrick Nims.

C394 Article: "Words for the Wind," *New Republic*, 141(Aug. 10, 1959), 21-22.

Review of *The Collected Verse of Theodore Roethke*.

C395 Article: "Political Truth in Practice," *The Listener*, 62(Oct. 15, 1959), 635.

Review of *Political Prisoner* by Paul Ignotus.

C396 Article: "From a Diary," *Encounter*, 13:6(Dec. 1959), 58-59.

About the International P.E.N. Conference at Frankfurt.

1960

C397 Article: "Steinberg in the West," *Encounter*, 14:4(April 1960), 3-4.

Includes a number of drawings, pp.5-9, by Steinberg.

C398 Article: "The Problem of Sincerity," *The Listener*, LXIII(May 26, 1960), 945-946.

Review of *Dante Called You Beatrice*, by Paul Potts.

C399 Article: "Poetry *vs.* Language Engineering," *New Republic*, 143 (Aug. 15, 1960), 17-18.

Review of John Ciardi's *How Does a Poem Mean.*

C400 Article: "Three Painters Haunted by Greatness," *The Listener* 64 (Sept. 8, 1960), 377-378.

About Whistler, David Bomberg, and Permeke.

C401 Article: "American Movement and English Abstraction," *The Listener*, 64(Sept. 22, 1960), 478.

Discussion of the exhibition of 'American Painting, 1930-1958' at the City of York Gallery.

C402 Article: "English Light and German Dream," *The Listener*, LXIV (Oct. 6, 1960), 559-560.

Comment on some London Art exhibitions.

C403 Article: "Odd Man Out," *The Listener*, 64(Oct. 6, 1960), 583-585.

Review of *The Natural Bent* by Lionel Fielden.

C404 Article: "Round the London Art Galleries," *The Listener*, 64(Oct. 20, 1960), 698.

Comments illustrated with a reproduction of a still life by Matthew Smith.

C405 Article: "British Culture & Co.," *Encounter*, XV-5(Nov. 1960), 56-61.
"The 'T.L.S.' submits a Company Report."

C406 Article: "Round the London Art Galleries," *The Listener*, 64(Nov. 3, 1960), 802.

Illustrated with a reproduction of 'The Head' by Evert Lundquist.

C407 Poems: "Inscription on a Stele," "Kyoto," 'Hiroshima Reubilt," "After Stefan George: Mein Kind Kam Heim," *Shenandoah*, 11:2 (Winter 1960), 53-54.

1961

C408 Article: "Times and Lives," *Encounter*, 16:1(Jan. 1961), 71-73.

Review of *Hired to Kill* by John Morris and "Sowing" by Leonard Woolf.

C409 Article: "Francis Bacon at Nottingham," *The Listener*, 65(Feb. 23, 1960), 360.

Comments on an exhibition of thiry-four paintings by Francis Bacon, "An exciting Modern painter."

C410 Article: "The Connecting Imagination," *Saturday Evening Post*, 234(April 1, 1961), 22-23+73-74.

Imaginative truth as a bridge between the inward aims of personal life and the demands of external forces and as a solution to the dilemma of modern man who has become a victim of a world of increasingly impersonal forces.

C411 Article: "Oskar Kokoschka and the 'Breakthrough'," *The Listener*, 65(June 22, 1961), 1099.

". . . a unique phenomenon, a case of genuis."

C412 Poem: "Voice from a Tomb," *Texas Quarterly*, 4:3(Autumn 1961), 64-65.

C413 Article: "The Immigration in Reverse," *Texas Quarterly*, 4:3 (Autumn 1961), 9-17.

For a special issue: "Image of Britain" comments on the change of attitude of Americans towards Europe.

C414 Article: "The Miniature and the Deluge," *Encounter*, 17:6(Dec. 1961), 78-81.

Review of *The Fox in the Attic* by Richard Hughes and *Pantaloon* by Philip Toynbee.

C415 Article: "Doctor of Science, Patient of Poetry," *Noble Savage*, 4 (1961), 14-17.

Reprinted, with permission, from *The Observer* (London), where it appeared July 2, 1961.

1962

C416 Poem: "The Generous Days (Aetat 18)," *Encounter*, 18:1(Jan. 1962), 98.

In the same number also has Spender's "An Editorial Postscript," pp.122-24.

C417 Article: "What Modern Writers Forget," *Saturday Review of Literature*, 45:3(Jan. 20, 1962), 15-17+32-34.

The modern movement in literature is described as a condemnation of the present by nostalgia for the past. The young writer has nothing more to learn from nostalgia, but he must learn to see the good as well as the bad in the modern world if there is to be a future for literature.

C418 Article: "Context," *London Magazine*, New Series, I:11(Feb. 1962), 28-30.

Answers questions on the Writing of Poetry today.

C419 Article: "For a Wider View of Poetry," *Saturday Review of Literature*, 45:20(May 19, 1962), 19-21+.

Although there is a difference between *The Waste Land* and *Ulysses*, poem-novels or narrations should be regarded as poetry, even if they are also regarded as prose.

C420 Article: "Modern German Poetry 1910-1960, edited by Michael Hamburger and Christopher Middleton," *The Listener*, 67(June 28, 1962), 1126-27.

Review of the book representing the special German contribution to the world-wide movement of modern poetry.

C421 Article: "Being Young Poets," *Encounter* 19:1(July 1962), 73-78.

Subtitle: "Who's Genteel?" Review of *The Penguin Modern Poets* etc.

C422 Poem: "Voice from a Tomb," *Twentieth Century*, 171(Summer 1962), 1712.

C423 Article: "Modern as Vision of a Whole Civilization," *Partisan Review*, 29(Summer 1962), 350-65.

The confrontation of the past with the present and the concept of wholeness seem to be the fundamental aim of modernism.

C424 Poem: "The Generous Days," *Carleton Miscellany*, 3:3(Summer 1962), 3-4.

C425 Article: "Are Poets Out of Touch with Life?" *The Listener*, LXVIII (Sept. 20, 1962), 439.

Many poets produce verbal bundles of symbols, ambiguities, influences, complexity, all wrapped up in self-conscious technique.

C426 Article: "Is a New Literature Possible?" *Saturday Review*, 45:38 (Sept. 22, 1962), 16-19.

Literature is limited by the conventions of language, but painting is free. Literature can be new to the extent to which it can go close to the purity of painting.

C427 "Letter from Edinburgh," *Encounter*, 19:4(October 1962), 66-68.

C428 Article: "In the Overlap," *Spectator*, 209(Oct. 5, 1962), 532-33.

About English literature becoming "Anglo-American."

C429 Article: "Moderns and Contemporaries," *The Listener*, 68(Oct. 11, 1962), 555-56.

Makes a distinction between "Contemporary" and modern writers. "The Obsessive Situation—I."

C430 Article: "Imagists and Realists," *The Listener*, 68(Oct. 18, 1962), 599-600.

"The Obsessive Situation—II."

C431 Article: "Experience as a Whole," *The Listener*, LXVIII(Oct. 25. 1962), 651-52.

"The Obsessive Situation—III," Last of the series of talks broadcast from BBC.

1963

C432 Article: "The Free-Lance Life," *The Listener*, 69(Feb. 27, 1962), 244-45.

Advice to young poets about free-lance writing.

C433 Poem: "Pronouns in This Time," Fragments of the Opening Sections, *London Magazine*, 3:2(May 1963), 10-20.

Incomplete.

C434 Article: "The Need for Roots," *The Listener*, 69(May 30, 1963), 922-23.

Review of Herbert Read's *The Contrary Experience.*

C435 Article: "1943: To Be or Not To Be," *Saturday Review*, 46(June 1, 1963), 26+.

Review of *Rescue in Denmark* by Harold Flender (Simon & Schuster, $4.95): Explains why the Danes accepted German occupation but resisted Nazi plans to exterminate the Danish Jews.

C436 Article: "Songs of an Unsung Classicist," *Saturday Review*, 46 (Sept. 7, 1963), 25-33.

Review of *Collected Poems: 1925-1948* by Louis MacNeice (Oxford University Press, $6.): Asks why Louis MacNeice, who is one of the best poets of the present century, is one of the most neglected.

C437 Article: "Poets and Critics: The Forgotten Difference," *Saturday Review*, 46:40(Oct. 5, 1963), 15-18.

Surveys this generation's attitudes toward poetry and criticism.

1964

C438 Article: "How Much Should a Biographer Tell?" *Saturday Review*, 47(Jan. 25, 1964), 16-19.

Questions the present tendency to reveal everything about the hero of a biography. With regard to uptodate research in the lives of artists still living, Spender observes that their right to privacy should be respected.

C439 Article: "How to Identify a Poet," *Saturday Review*, 47(Aug. 8, 1964), 14-17.

The writer of poems is, at his best, different from anyone else; his challenge is to guard the differences.

C440 Article: "Shakespeare: A Personal View," *Literary Review*, 7:4 (Summer 1964), 485-493.

C441 Poem: "Draft of the First Five Sections of Part One: 'Pronouns of This Time'," *Shenandoah*, 16:1 (Autumn 1964), 5-20.

C442 Article: "A High-Pitched Scream," *The Listener* 72(August 13, 1964), 242.

About "Books and Ideas."

C443 Article: "With Lukács in Budapest," *Encounter*, XXIII-6(Dec. 1964), 54-57.

Part of "Notes and Topics."

C444 Article: "A Change of Air," Symposium on W.H. Auden, *Kenyon Review*, 26(Winter 1964), 199-203.

It expresses one of Auden's earliest preoccupations. (Symposium with essays by various writers and a reply by Auden.)

1965

C445 Article: "Three Little Sitwells and How They Grew," *New Republic*, 152(April 24, 1965), 19-20.

Review of *Taken Care Of*: The Autobiography of Edith Sitwell. (Atheneum, $5.95)

C446 Article: "W.B. Yeats: 1865-1965," A Centenary Tribute, *The Irish Times*, special edition, (Thursday, June 10, 1965), 1+.

Evaluation of the poet for the special centenary edition.

C447 Poem: "If it were not for that," *Encounter*, 25:6(Dec. 1965), 23.

1966

C448 Article: "Age of Overwrite and Underthink," *Saturday Review*, 49:11(March 12, 1966), 21-23+.

"A timely reminder, for a civilization that too often forgets is that words, written or spoken, are meant to communicate."

C449 Article: "On English and American Poetry," *Saturday Review*, 49:17(April 23, 1966), 19-20+.

The urgent question to be asked of modern poetry: is there an English modern poetry independent of the American?"

C450 Article: "Warnings from the Grave," *New Republic*, 154(June 18, 1966), 23-26.

Review of *Ariel*: Poems by Sylvia Plath (Harper and Row, $4.95)

C451 Article: "Roethke: The Lost Son," *New Republic*, 155(Aug. 27, 1966), 23-25.

Review of *The Collected Poems* by Theodore Roethke (Doubleday, $5.95).

C452 Poem: "Isé: Voice from a Skull," *Encounter*, 27(Nov. 1966), 18.

1967

C453 Article: "The Brilliant Mr. MacNeice," *New Republic*, 156(Jan. 28. 1967), 32-34.

Review of *The Strings are False* by Louis MacNeice.

C454 Article: "T.S. Eliot's London," *Saturday Review*, 50(March 11, 1967), 58-59+.

Describes how Eliot came to be a supreme Londoner.

C455 Letter: "Mr. Spender and the CIA," *Nation*, 204(June 26, 1967), 802+.

About Spender's resignation from the editorship of *Encounter* on learning that the magazine received funds from the CIA.

C456 Article: "Writers and Politics," *Partisian Review*, 34:3(Summer 1967), 359-381.

Comments on reactionaries, socialists, and those that renounced literature and "lived and died the tragedy."

C457 Poems: "To Become a Dumb Thing" and "Bagatelles," *Transatlantic Review*, 26(Autumn 1967), 30-35.

C458 Article: "Liberal Anti-Communism," *Commentary*, 44(September 1967), 71-73.

A symposium to bring out the changes in attitudes and opinions in the liberal and intellectual communities.

C459 Article: "Uncommon Poetic Language," *Times Literary Supplement*, 3(Oct. 5, 1967), 939-40.

C460 Article: "Miracle of Romanticism," *New Republic*, 157(Nov. 11, 1967), 22-23.

Review of *Friedrich Hoelderlin: Poems and Fragments*, a bilingual edition, edited and translated by Michael Hamburger (Michigan, $10).

C461 Article: "Dame Edith Sitwell's Show," *New Republic*, 157(Dec. 2, 1967), 21-22.

Review of *Dame Edith Sitwell: The Last Years of a Rebel*, by Elizabeth Salter (Houghton Mifflin, $5).

C462 Two Poems: "The Lost Days," "Sentenced," *London Magazine*, 7:9(Dec. 1967), 28.

C463 Article: "Remembering Eliot," *Sewanee Review*, 74(Winter 1966), 58-84.

After his death there is a danger of different opposing attitudes towards him becoming crystallized.

C464 Poem: "Auden Aetat XX, LX," *Shenandoah*, 18:2(Winter 1967), 5.

1968

C465 Poem: "Fifteen Line Sonnet in Four Parts," *The Listener*, 79(Feb. 1, 1968), 136.

C466 Article: "A Morality," *The Listener*, 79(March 14, 1968), 340-342.

Review of *Brian Howard* a "biographical miscellany," edited by Marie-Jaqueline Lancaster.

C467 Article: "What the Rebellious Students Want?" *N.Y. Times Magazine*, (March 30, 1968), 56-57.

Reflecting upon student protest here and abroad, Spender says that the problem for students is to use their power within the limits of the possible, without wrecking the university.

C468 "Chairman," *Commentary*, 45(June 1968), 77-79.

Translation of Lorca's "Lament for Ignatio Sanchez Mejias."

1969

C469 Poem: "Middle East," *Times Literary Supplement*, 68(April 24, 1969), 437.

C470 Poem: "After Tibullus," *Times Literary Supplement*, 68(Sept. 25, 1969), 1062.

1970

C471 Article: "Les Baux and the Pleasures of Provence," *Travel and Camera,* Illustrated, 33(April 1970), 36-39.

C472 Poem: "If It Were Not," *The Quarterly Journal of the Library of Congress*, 27:20 (April 1970), 164.

Published by permission of *The London Magazine* which published an earlier version.

C473 Article: "Form and Pressure in Poetry," *Times Literary Supplement*, 69(Oct. 23, 1970), 1226-1228.

From the text of the inaugural lecture delivered at University College, London, October 22, 1970. Considers some modern poets confronting the problem of writing in a world "whose appearance and values are unpoetic, its tradition uncontinuous, its values fragmented."

C474 Three poems: "V.W., 1941," "Matter of Identity," "Boy Cat Canary," *The Listener*, 84(Nov. 26, 1970), 736.

1971

C475 Three Poems: "What Love Poems Say," "On the photograph of a Friend, Dead," "Sleepless," *London Magazine*, 10:11(Feb. 1971), 22-24.

C476 Article: "Writers and Scholars International," *Times Literary Supplement*, 70(Oct. 15, 1971), 1270.

Explains the aims of *WSI*, an organ of consciousness expressing the care and concern of members of the same intellectual community for one another against censorships etc.

C477 Article: "Do the Claims of Conscience Outweigh the Duties of Citizenship?" *Esquire*, 76(Dec. 1971), 158+.

Testimony of Spender: Daniel Ellsberg, a catalyst, whose act was "historic" and must lead to results which will make it impossible for an administration to conduct an undeclared war, like Vietnam. Is not Daniel Ellsberg that which lieutenant Calley is punished for not being?

C478 Article: "London Letter," *Partisan Review*, 38:2(1971), 202-207.

Contemporary conditions like inflation, strikes, unemployment etc. and the confusing remedies suggested. Compares the English situation with the American.

C479 Article: "Bob Dylan: The Metaphor at the End of the Tunnel," *Esquire*, 77(May 1972), 109-118+.

About Bob Dylan's Lyrics: Commentary by Frank Kermode & Stephen Spender. Spender calls "Bob Dylan a phenomenon, one of those voices that rose out of the corrupt entertainment world.

C480 Article: "Center of Critical Values: Excerpts from The Gateway to Science: The Weizmann Institute at Twenty-five," *Bulletin of Atomic Science*, 28(Oct. 1972), 2-6.

C481 Article: "The Immense Advantage," *London Magazine*, 12:4(Oct/ Nov. 1972), 29-47.

Emerson's phrase which described the advantage England had over America is here used as comment on the reversal of the situation today. European thoughts are American thoughts.

C482 Article: "A Way of Caring," Notes from a Journal," *The Atlantic Monthly*, 230:5(Nov. 1972), 83-89.

"By caring I mean the pursuit of knowledge and the determination to pursue knowledge." Notes from a journal kept in fits and starts— October 1944, Christmas 1952, May-June-July. Sept. 1955.

1973

C483 Article: "A Certificate of Sanity," *London Magazine*, 12:6 (Feb/ March 1973), 137-140.

Review of *Virginia Woolf*, a Biography by Quentin Bell (The Hogarth Press, In two volumes, £3 each).

C484 Article: "W.H. Auden (1907-1973)," *Partisan Review*, 40:3(1973), 546-48.

The greatness of Auden as a poet whose death represents the disappearance of more than personal loss to many people besides his friends.

C485 Article: "America and England," *Partisan Review*, 40:3(1973), 349-369.

Modern English literature measured against American achievement.

C486 Article: "Can Poetry Be Reviewed?" *New York Reviews of Books*, 20(Sept. 20, 1973), 8+.

C487 Article: "W.H. Auden (1907-1973)," *New York Reviews of Books*, 20(Nov. 29, 1973), 3+.

Address by Spender at Oxford in honor of Auden.

1974

C488 Article: "A Parallel World," *Partisan Review*, 41:4(1974), 553-562.

Comments on Aleksandr I. Solzhenitsyn's *The Gulag Archipelago, 1918-1956*, An Experiment in Literary Investigation I-II (Harper and Row, $12.50): a book "about a parallel world of murder, torture, slavery, labor camps, imprisonment under the most terrible conditions."

C489 Article: "Notebook—I," *London Magazine*, 14:4(Oct/Nov. 1974), 80-87.

The first of the series Spender wrote for the magazine.

1975

C490 Article: "Notebook II," *London Magazine*, 14:5(Dec. 1974/Jan. 1975), 87-93.

C491 Article: "Notebook—III," *London Magazine*, 14:6(Feb./March 1975), 59-64.

C492 Article: "Notebook—IV," *London Magazine*, (April/May 1975), [40] -46.

C493 Article: "Notebook—V," *London Magazine*, (June/July 1975), 28-37.

C494 Article: "Notebook—VI," *London Magazine*, (Aug./Sept. 1975), 47-56.

D

MANUSCRIPTS

BY

STEPHEN SPENDER

Note

This section records manuscripts in the possession of The Bancroft Library, University of California at Berkeley and Humanities Research Center, University of Texas at Austin.

As some of the manuscripts have not been dated, attempt is made to present them in their alphabetical order. Numbers assigned to "notebooks" are arbitrary.

D1	**The American**	**N.D.**

Loose sheets, typed and holographic, pp. 5. An article on "The American" by Henry James.

D2	**Arable Holdings**	**N.D.**

Loose sheets, handwritten, pp. 3. Signed. Review of "Arable Holdings" by F.R. Higgins (Dublin).

D3	**Autumn Journal**	**N.D.**

Handwritten manuscript with revisions. pp. 5. signed.

Review of "Autumn Journal," a poem by Louis MacNeice (Faber).

Written on graph paper. Later published in *Poetry* (London), November 1940. pp. 86-87.

D4	**Auden at Milwaukee**	**N.D.**

Loose sheets; photocopy.

D5	**Blue Notebook—I**	**1949**

Blue exercise book: workbook containing drafts of poems, pp. 1-120. Front and back of the cover also has drafts. Notebook is 23.5 x 18.5 cm. Hard-boards in blue cloth. Dated: Summer 1949 (June 3, Portland).

Contents: Drafts of poems:
1. Within a country of dervishes,
2. My beloved friend, you ask me to write to you,
3. When I was a boy I evoked ghosts,

4. Here my concentration with her silence (Many drafts).
5. O map, spotted with dark cities . . . .,
6. Verlaine and Rimbaud; "Naked under absinthe like x-rays,"
7. Ears stopped with wax, arms tied behind my back,
8. Rome, March 1950: "But that way . . ."
9. June 1950: "a sketch for a play"
10. Nocturne,
11. Such interprenetration,
12. O that girl O that girl,
13. Such sensuous pattering,
14. Civilization,
15. That was the day you came,
16. They lift him through the channels and the crowd,
17. Whoever longs as I do now.
18. After a French poem of Rilke,
19. Another,
20. Outside the Registry Office.

D6   Blue Notebook—II   1945

Blue exercise book II in purple, 23.5 x 18.5 cm. Blue cloth on hard boards with child's drawings on the cover. On front in Spender's hand: Notebook / August 1948 / [Signed] : Stephen Spender.

Written on both sides of the page. Opens with a poem on Dickens; numerous drafts of "Judas Iscariot"; then a poem "written in Cincinnati, I think," after Rimbaud. Idea for a Radio Play: "Shelley would have loved the wireless." Cover has child's drawings.

D7   The Burning Cactus   N.D.

Long loose typed sheets with corrections, 24 leaves. Manuscript of THE BURNING CACTUS, a story by STEPHEN SPENDER. Right hand top in hand: *Life & Letters.*

D8   By the Lake   N.D.

Loose sheets, written on one side of the paper; handwritten manuscript, pp. 53, of "By the Lake," a story.

D9   Collected Poems, 1930-1950   N.D.

A large folio notebook of unruled white paper. Handwritten manuscript with revision of many poems, pp. 172.

D10 **Collected Poems of W.B. Yeats** N.D.

Loose sheets; handwritten manuscript, pp. 5. Review of *The Collected Poems of W.B. Yeats* (Macmillan, 10s.6d.).

D11 **The Common Reader** N.D.

Typed copy and galley proofs from *Criterion Review* of Spender's review of *The Common Reader, Part Two.*

D12 **The Dead Island** N.D.

Notebook with ruled pages, 33 x 22 cm., hardboards in dark green with black spine. Manuscript pages, 121.

Contents: 1. Various sketches for Parts I & II of *The Dead Island*, 112 pp. Spender's note added later: "The Dead Island" from *The Burning Cactus* 1935. Early rough draft unpublished." 2. The other end of the notebook consists of a rough unpublished draft of his second story, "The Cousins," pp. 9.

D13 **Diary** 1925

Handwritten manuscript, notebook, 20 x 12.5 cm., purple cover, torn spine, gold border on front, 3 blank leaves, 30 pp.

Entries from July 3, 1925-July 27, 1925; entries from Tuesday, July 7th to Monday, July 12th are in code language; last entry, Monday, July 27th.

Contains, along with autobiographical details, notes on symbolism, creation and worship, beauty and truth, and epigrams on a variety of subjects, poems: "We never shut our pet bird in a cage, "Forgive me, if this once my spirit broke." An interesting couplet:

"Whoever wrote autobiographie
But needs must pack it full with many a lie?"

D14 **Diary of Journey to Israel** N.D.

Hard-bound notebook in black, 30.5 x 20 cm., ruled paper, hand written in ink, pp. 77.

Diary of Spender's journey to Israel on which his book, *Learning Laughter*, was based.

D15	Early Work Poems	1936-38

Large folio pages, loose, unbound. Manuscript material, 183 pp.

First page is a sketch for a Book of Poems, with a list of 36 poems and epilogue. Poems classified under: "Love," "Subjects," "Miscellaneous," "Autobiography," "Spain," "Epilogue." Many early variants.

D16	Edith Sitwell	N.D.

Loose typed sheets, pp. 12.

Contents: Article: "Images in the Poetic World of Edith Sitwell."

D17	E.M. Forster	1970

Copy of Spender's article on E.M. Forster: "In Memoriam." Published in *The New York Review of Books*, XV:2 (July 23, 1970), 3-4.

D18	From My Journal	1929

Loose sheets, 31 x 20.5 cm., written on one side of the paper, pages 155-169, 187-203.

Contains: "Five characters: Part Four (November 1929); "From My Journal—I (November 10).

D19	The Future of Shelley	N.D.

Loose sheets, 25 x 20.5 cm., stapled together, 20 pp. MS. in Spender's hand-writing in ink.

First draft of the essay later published under the title of "Shelley" by the British Council.

D20	Germany	N.D.

Loose sheets, handwritten, pp. 2.

Review of a book on Germany by Leland Stowe.

D21	Germany	N.D.

Loose sheets, handwritten, pp. 3., signed.

Reivew of *Germany, Prepare for War* by Professor Banse.

D22   Gertrude Stein   **N.D.**

Loose sheets, handwritten article on Gertrude Stein, pp. 3.

D23   The Good Gray Poet   **N.D.**

Loose leaves, handwritten in ink, pp 4. Manuscript with emendations, written on thick handmade paper.

Review of Fausset's critical study of Walt Whitman.

D24   The Holy Devil   **N.D.**

Mimeographed copy, pp. 31.

The Holy Devil (Rasputin's End): Opera in Three Acts: Libretto by Stephen Spender and Nicolas Nabokov; music by Nicolas Nabokov.

D25   The Immense Advantage   ˙**N.D.**

Loose sheets and notebook typed as well as handwritten manuscript.
Draft of his essay "The Immense Advantage."

D26   Instead of Death   **1945**

Instead of Death, Volume One: The Younger Poets. Typed ms. 25.5 x 20 cm., 201 pp. In gold on the box: STEPHEN / SPENDER / INSTEAD / OF / DEATH / – / AN / AUTOBIOGRAPHICAL / NOVEL / UNPUBLISHED / AUTHOR'S / CORRECTED / TYPESCRIPT / 1945.

A letterhead of The Hogarth Press, accompanying the manuscript is dated 3/3/45 with the note: MS. *Instead of Death* by Stephen Spender forwarded to John Lehmann, 601 Carrington House, Hertford Street, W1. Inside on p. 1 of the MS. in the left-hand top corner a note by John Lehmann: "This was apparently never published–but partly autobiographical with Stephen Spender's own convictions.

D27   Journal   **1932**

Ruled notebook cardboard, 30.5 x 21 cm. Pages unnumbered. Written pages, 1-23.

Journal begins Nov. 4, Barcelona; entries on Nov. 5, 7, 17, 18, 19, 26, 29, 30; Dec. 6, 9, 14 and Feb. 1.

Contains notes on style, genius, symbols for the heat of the sun etc. Also has poems: "Oh love, forgive me for the ideal without scruple," and on the last page: "Possibility, possibility of a new life."

D28   Journal   1939

Ruled notebook bound in cloth with: Journal/1929/Stephen/Spender, on front. 32.5 x 20.5 cm. Pages unnumbered, written pages 104; some are blank.

Contains: entries on September 3, 4, 5, 6, 8, 9, 10, 12, 15, 19, 26, 28, 29; October 1, 19, 20, 21, 23, 24, 25, 26, 27; November 16.

Also notes for "A Look at the Worst," Summing up thoughts on the War; notes for "The Poet's Task" and drafts of a poem; "You also have your cities/sunk in the commerce of the world."

D29   Journals   1944-62

Loose sheets, typed MS. with corrections.

Extracts from Journals; 1944, 1950 (American Notes), 1952, 53, 55, 56, 57, 60, 62; also pages from journals "extracted by William Abrahams": 1944, 53, 55; published in *Atlantic Monthly*, November 1972.

D30   Lawrence and James   N.D.

Loose sheets, typed with corrections by hand, pp. 10; accompanied by an incomplete holograph of the same.

An article on D.H. Lawrence and Henry James.

D31   The Left Wing Orthodoxy   N.D.

Typed manuscript, 12 pp., with corrections, signed.

The Left Wing Orthodoxy—the task of the writer in relation to society described as "New realism."

D32   Leishman's Translation of Rilke   N.D.

Loose sheets, handwritten, pp. 2, signed.

Review of Leishman's translation of Rilke's poems.

D33   **Looking Back on Life**   N.D.

Loose sheets, handwritten, pp. 3, signed.

Review of *Looking Back on Life* by George Robey (Constable, 7s.6d.).

D34   **Love-Hate Realtions**   N.D.

Loose sheets, typed transcripts with corrections, manuscript in three folders.

Typed manuscript of *Love-Hate Relations* (English and American Sensibilities).

D25   **Mary Stuart**   N.D.

Typed manuscript with corrections, 26 x 20.5 cm., 100 pp. Acts divided by blank yellow sheets. Bound in blue paper; spine taped in deep blue. (*Mary Stuart* by Schiller, freely translated and adapted by Stephen Spender).

D36   **Miss Ruth Fry**   N.D.

Loose sheets, handwritten, pp. 4.

Review of Miss Ruth Fry's study of the Quaker Movement.

D37   **Modern Germany**   N.D.

Loose sheets, hand written, pp. 6.

About Modern Germany.

D38   **Modern Literature**   N.D.

Loose sheets, handwritten, pp. 5.

An essay on Modern Literature, Political Situation and Freedom.

D39   **Modern World**   N.D.

Loose sheets, handwritten, pp. 5.

On the modern world in relation to poetry, power, and civilization.

D40 My Life as German and Jew N.D.

Loose sheets, handwritten, pp. 4.

Review of Jacob Wassermann's *My Life as German and Jew*.

D41 Notebook for an Essay N.D.

Ruled notebook, 24.5 x 19 cm., 49 pp.

"Essay on Modern Society and Truth": Sketch for the essay in *The God That Failed*, describing his disenchantment with communism. On the last two unnumbered pages: a poem, "our six weeks old daughter lies," and a rough sketch of a train.

D42 Notebook for Another Essay 1965-67

Red Lion-brand exercise book, 26 pp., writing by hand in ink and pencil on one side of the paper.

Contains: an essay, a reaction to communist experience in Kerala; two drafts of a poem: "To wake up with the morning and to feel . . ." and "Each morning . . . we feel"; the remaining pages have rough pen and pencil sketches, doodlings etc. Bottom of the first page: "Journal of 1965 / For the MARTIN BUBER / appeal from / Stephen Spender / Nov. 1967.

D43 Notebook: 1940 1940

Exercise book, white unruled paper, 23 x 18 cm. Hardboard in blue with brown leather for the spine.

Contains: Two pencil sketches, drafts for "The Fires of England: Destruction and Resurrection," "Dialogue between Superman and the Devil," "The happy few loose from their fixed time and space," "Flowing like a river, Eye," "O solitude of light," "Covered, covered with that will," "Dancing burning image of self projected," "O slave of time, free in eternity," "Upwards you must reply in mind."

D44 Notebook: "Scraps" N.D.

Notebook with blue boards in red spine, marked "SCRAPS." Ruled pages with red margin, 26 x 20.5 cm. 57 leaves.

Contains autographed manuscript written in ink: 1. Sketches of *Trial of a Judge*; 2. The first version of the story, "The Burning

Cactus," called "The Cactus Field"; an essay on Virginia Woolf's *The Common Reader*, Part II; an essay on "Poetry and Revolution"; and a short unpublished sketch called "Karl."

D45   Sketches for *Ruins and Visions*   [1940]

Notebook with ruled pages as in a ledger book, 32 x 20.5 cm., hard-bound in blue paper with black spine. 97 pages of holograph. *Contains*: 1. Sketches for poems in *Ruins and Visions*, 1940, consisting of 78 pages of text; 2. on the other end of the notebook, "Dialogues for a Play" with characters: General, Financier, Superman, Leader etc., 19 pages.

D46   Notebook—III   1966

Notebook begun April 7, 1966. Exercise book ruled and bound in leather, 25 x 20 cm., pp. 1-153. Notes were added later in purple ink (made in Berkeley, May 15, 1970).

Contents: Drafts of poems:

1. When we talk I imagine silence (April 30, 1966),
2. April 16, 1966. Isé: A poem begun 1959. Two versions published: "Here where the whole Pacific seemed a pond,"
3. Descartes,
4. Sketch for another Sonnet-unfinished, May 2.
5. To become a dumb thing,
6. The town walls seemed all one wall,
7. Getting up in a foreign inn,
8. From 1961 Notebook—Travelling from the last place to the next,
9. Close to you here looking at you I see.
10. *Unfinished*: Always these hiding summer days
11. I knew it now/through us traverse
12. Sketch for a poem on a photograph of Peter Watson. Many versions over many years, unfinished.
13. A Voice from a Tomb
14. Being alone, I call to mind a figure,
15. Filigree mosquito,
16. From a notebook 1948: "You said you always like them to be rough."
17. From a notebook: "For this for which you care the most,"
18. Flowering almond tree, begun in 1944.
19. This bed she lies in is a boat, (Recollection of Lizzie 3 years old),
20. We cannot hold on to the world (about Virginia Woolf: many

sketches),
21. Bagatelles,
22. From an earlier notebook
    Jan 1967, Mouton,
    "I wonder whether anyone"
    Jan. 4: "In the middle of a war"
    Feb. 1: "You slept so quiet . . ."
23. The gay man with putty features
24. In your oxford room,
25. W.H. Auden Aetat XX, LX,
26. Out of the envelope
    Feb. 8, 1967: To Rose Macaulay "Reading your travel book posthumous."
    Pencil sketch of vineyards at Mouton.

D47   Notebook—IV   **N.D.**

Hardbound exercise book; on front: "University / Manuscript / Book"; 26 x 20.5 cm., pp. 1-102.

Contents: Drafts of poems:
1. Shadowless light . . . (sketch for Spiritual Explorations,)
2. In me a world of man. In me a will (many sketches),
3. Ode to the flowers: First sketch of "Almond Blossom in War time,"
4. Her wonder colored eyes,
5. The body has its saintliness,
6. After the errands, the orders, the irrelevances,
7. Surely it is enough,
8. Tribute to Prague, translated from the seifest. etc. etc.

D48   Notebook—V   **1959**

Large exercise book ruled. Hard-boards in blue with brown leather for spine. 32.5 x 20.5 cm., on the first page in pencil: "If found please return to / STEPHEN SPENDER / ENCOUNTER / 25 Haymarket, London S.W.1 / £10 reward. Sketchbook dated July 1959.

Contents: Drafts of Poems:
1. Sketches for a long poem: "Pronouns in our time,"
2. Draft of "If it were not for that lean executioner,"
3. Draft of "A Voice from a Skull,"
4. May 24, 1961: A Sketch written in Venice in 1950?—"Buying this notebook in a Venice shop,"
5. "Travelling from the last place to the next,"
6. Sketch for "Lost Days,"

7. There was an hour was twenty hours you lay,"
8. If you are underestimated,
9. Sketch for "The Generous Days,"
10. "Smooth the sheet down: then kiss her forehead,"
11. The moon sinks and the Pleiades.

D49   Notebook—VI   N.D.

Notebook bound in hard boards in cream colored cloth, title and author on white paper pasted on front. Pages unnumbered, handwritten, 1-130 (about).

Contains: A sketch for Lieutenant Oliveiro: A Play in Four Acts and Twelve Scenes. Dedicated to Cecil Day Lewis.

D50   Notebook—VII   1955

Notebook with white sheets bound in hardboards in wall-paper with brown leather for spine and decorative end-papers. Done by Bookbinders; Chas. W. Poole & Sons, Bookbinders etc., Victoria Road, Chelmsford. Presented by H.S. (Humphrey Spender) to Stephen on his birthday (Feb. 28, 1955). Handwritten manuscript, pp. 1-139.

Contains: ENGAGED IN WRITING / A COLLAGE / LITERATURE ENGAGÉE / for: Names illegible. sd. Stephen Spender, 1956-1957.

D51   Notebook—VIII   1956

Notebook bound in soft blue paper, spine taped in deep blue. On front with label pasted: ENGAGED / IN / WRITING / by / Stephen / Spender, type-script with corrections, pp. 1-173.

Draft of *Engaged in Writing*, 1956. Dedicated to Nicholas Nabokov.

D52   Notebook—IX   1941

Wire-bound "century notebook," 20.5 x 16.5 cm.

Contains: Notes for Poems: 1941 [in red written by Spender]. Drafts:

1. As clouds are filled with each other,
2. Oxford English Club: Notes for a talk,
3. You, whom such fragments . . . surround,
4. I too am one who sees each day . . .

5. I know a wild race.

Most of the notebook is filled with child's drawings.

D53	Notebook—X	N.D.

Soft-bound in beige cloth, colored edges, 22.5 x 14 cm. Hand written manuscript.

Contains: 1. Sketch for a play called *Towards the Island* (113 pages); 2. Journal of "Journey to India," March 17-19 (6 pages).

D54	Notebook—XI	N.D.

Ruled ledger book, hardbound in blue with black spine, 22.5 x 5.18 cm., written pages, 84.

Contains: Draft of a novel: *The Backward Son*.

D55	Notebook—XII	1965

Wirebound exercise book, ruled pages, 28 x 22 cm. Handwritten.

Notes for lectures at Beloit, Wisconsin, 1965: 1. what was modern in 1914 (27 leaves), 2. The 1930's and after (16 leaves), 3. The Situation of Modern Poetry Seen from Today (23 leaves).

D56	Notebook —XIII	1942

Ruled leatherbound black notebook, 20.5 x 16.5 cm.

Notes for Fire Service 1942 (commenced in December 1941, in the form of a Journal).

D57	Notebook—XIV	1940-41

Hardboards in pink, ruled paper, 22 x 17 cm.

Contents: Notes for poems 1940-41: 1. Some pages torn off, 2. Prose passages—beginning with, "Hammer Your Thoughts into Unity," 3. Present fears / are less than horrible imaginings, 4. We cannot hold on to the world. 5. And now that woman profound and wise, 6. Michael, Michael, and all Michaels (many drafts), 7. Thinkers and airmen—all such, 8. Shining edge of a plough, 9. Flowers grow in the electric light, 10. Children who fear the dark and fear the dreadful, 11. It happens every when and where, 12. I am glad I met you on the edge, 13. In this room like a bowl filled with light, 14. She walked by the river, 15. The early summer prepares its green heart, 16. Pen, ink and paper, 17. The calm that burns in the dark shrines, 18. How can I piece together, 19. There were a hundred ways a hundred ways, 20. O you whose childhood lies about you.

D58   Notebook—XV, XVI   1945

Notebooks, ruled paper, black leather-bound 18.5 x 11.5 cm.

Contents: I. German Diary, July 6, 1945: entries on July 6, 7, 8, 11, 16, 20, 21, 22, 23, 24, 25. II. German Journal, Vol. II; noted: "The diary is a day post-dated throughout, as I write entries in the evening or in the morning for the previous day and date them the following day."

Entries on September 7, 8, 9, 10, 11, 12, 13, 14, 15, 16, 17, 18, 19, 20, 21, 22, 23, 24, 25, 26, 28, 29, 30, and October 1, 2, 3, 4, 5, 6.

D59   Notebook—XVII   1945

Hard-bound in ivory leather, ruled paper, 33 x 20.5 cm. Handwritten manuscript.

Contents: 1. MS. entitled "Splendour and Misery of Europe: 1945 by Stephen Spender (Germany France London): Draft of *European Witness* (82 pages); 2. Sketch for a play (20 pages).

D60   Notebook—XVIII   N.D.

Exercise book, white unruled paper, 25.5 x 28.5 cm. Cover torn.

Contents: Journal: Journey to India, pp. 54. many drawings by a child.

D61   Notebook—XIX   N.D.

Exercise book with brown cover, 25.5 x 18.5 cm., 14 pages.

Contains: Journal entries and about 24 sketches in crayon and pencil.

D62   Notebook—XX   **N.D.**

25.5 x 18.5 cm., white paper.

Contains: Notes for Libretto of Rasputin, Composer: Nicolas Nabokov.

D63   Notebook—XXI   **1965**

24.5 x 19 cm., hardboards in glazed woven cloth.

Contains: Journal entries for September (1965) 27, 26, 29, 30; October 1, 4, 6, 12, 13, 14, 16, 18, 19, 20, 22, 25, 26, 27, 30, 31; November 1, 6, 7, 8, 9, 10, 11, 18, 19, 21, 28, 29; December 8, 16.

D64   Notebook—XXII   **1955**

Notebook of white paper with brown cover, 25.5 x 18.5 cm.

Contains: Sketches for poems: Sept. 1955:
1. Why do they call it dark? It is too bright.
2. A day that makes all squares and circles,
3. Another feature of becoming older,
4. Who always moved away . . .
5. Journal entries dated March 26, 28, 30, April 2,
6. Some enter into the facade,
7. The lovers walk under the trees,
8. Here there are appetites and feeding them,
9. Dear me, dear dust enclosed in the dark,
10. Make yourself imagine a field—if you dare,
11. Pencil sketches,
12. To a Japanese translator,
13. These are walls that separate,
14. Out of the envelope,
15. He saw his life was a trick,
16. Utter stillness rules the ocean,
17. And that we think life ought to be,
18. Sketches in pencil.

D65   Notebook—XXIII   **1944, 67**

Notebook with torn cover, 23 x 18 cm. Notebook of 1944, worked on in 1967.

Contents: Sketches of poems:
1. On the gray cold stone platform,

2. I am conditioned by this time,
3. I am the victim of all your arrangements (rewritten in June 1967),
4. The lamp, the chair, the slant ceiling,
5. When the foundations quaked and the pillars shook,
6. Your love and my love (Many drafts),
7. No one is perfection, yet,
8. Oh with your eager profile . . .,
9. A man-made world.
10. The hydra-headed, the writhing nest of the ocean,
11. What a wild room,
12. We are enmeshed by burning wire,
13. Flowering almond tree,
14. There are some days when the sea lies like a harp,
15. With your sculptured features like a prow,
16. Upon the table under the ceiling,
17. The core of the day,
18. O fuse my singing heart of victory (many versions),
19. Judas Iscariot,
20. I envy the painter the palate of his eyes
21. She came in from the snowing air,
22. Once I lay awake conscious,
23. O their opening O,
24. To speak true, our relationships,
25. The world was silent as the peak of rocks,
26. Within a city whose inhabitants,
27. They wrung their peace out of this war.

D66	Notebook—XXIV	N.D.

Brown covered exercise book 25 x 20 cm.

Rough draft for an essay on literature.

D67	Notebook—XXV	1969

Notebook, hard-bound in green leather with label: Flowers on the front. 30 x 21.5 cm.

Final drafts for a new collection of poems, July 1969:

1. The generous days,
2. If it were not,
3. I read a book "Hoelderlin Characters" (Different drafts),
4. Lamp. Table. Slant ceiling (different drafts),
5. The boy came home,
6. Sketch for cantata from the war 1944.

7. Child Falling Asleep in Air Raid,
8. My English writing runs behind your eyes,
9. It is through / A green shoot grew,
10. Identity,
11. Vocation,
12. What lives in a liquid gesture (different drafts),
13. The Fascist Exhibition in Rome (1934),
14. Out of the / Enormity of Space,
15. Remembers (from Storrs notebook) "The thing I most remember in your childhood,"
16. A time and place,
17. Dear scattered flesh (many drafts), "Dear friend . . . proves,"
18. We cannot hold on to the world,
19. That woman entering the room,
20. Question of identity,
21. Pledges of Blessing—Goethe,
22. In a Cafe,
23. When we talk I imagine silence (different drafts),
24. There was a time I'd race across the town (different drafts),
25. The Young Poets,
26. The Chalk Blue Butterfly (different drafts),
27. Jewel-winged Almond Tree (many drafts),
28. Mein Kind Kam Heim (different drafts),
29. Moon,
30. Zero,
31. Driving through Connecticut,
32. Hoelderlin—Heidelberg,
33. Honey now I've loved thee,
34. Dream No Dream (different drafts),
35. D.H. Lawrence was born a perfect little Oedipus,
36. I see through those circumferences (different drafts).

D68   **Notebook—XXVI**   **1949**

Black leather notebook, 19.5 x 12.5 cm. Handwritten manuscript.

Essay on Goethe, written for the Goethe Centenary 1949.

D69   **Notebook—XXVII**   **N.D.**

Handwritten manuscript of Preface to *Love-Hate Relations*, and Printer's copy of *Love-Hate Relations / Inter-related Reflections on English and American Sensibilities*; Galley proofs corrected by the author.

Hardboards in wall paper with yellow leather spine, 23.5 x 17.5 cm.

Contains: Drafts of several poems:

1. And still I feel their breath upon my cheek!
2. We are such stuff as dreams are made on, these dreams which strike open our eyes . . . . . .,
3. Ballad of the Exterior Life,
4. Poet,
5. Gardner,
6. The Young Squire,
7. The Stranger,
8. Our six year old daughter lies (many drafts),
9. One draft of "Nocturne." Many pages decorated with a child's drawings.

Hardboards in blue vinyl; on front, label pasted "Pronouns in Our Time," dated 1964. The rest not legible. 29.5 x 21 cm.

Opening page has a quotation from Paul Valery to Gide (Dec. 3, 1891). Several drafts:

1. In the middle of a war (Fair copy April 8, 1964),
2. Everyone I tried to think (Fair copy April 26),
3. So even King George in his place,
4. A careful box of instruments (April 22),
5. I know one day,
6. At boarding school by elder brother,
7. So every one must know he is (April 25),
8. And in the North my brother Michael (May 1),
9. Lying awake alone (May 8/9, 1964),
10. I know that I must tell the world (March 9-10),
11. I tried to think it out (May 10),
12. Proof of Selected Poems (May 15),
13. Even the greatest know they are none (May 15),
14. O Yes! O yes! Ye people (many drafts),
15. O then at the crowd's center (many drafts),
16. Delirious Oratory (Aug. 17, Saint Jerome),
17. Apotheosis of Stephen (Try to make a rough unthinking form-less free associative scribbled draft to the end); loose sheets clipped to the note-book: what gives edge to remembering etc.

Notebook cardboard bound, covered with wall paper design 21.5 x 17 cm.

On the top of the page: Randall Jarrell died October 15. Then:

1. Under the wars there is the ground of peace (many drafts),
2. They are not buried under pasts (many drafts),
3. Ladies and Gentlemen, this sphere the earth is a clock dial (many drafts).

Hardboards in green flowery wall paper with white spine, unruled white paper, 25 x 17.5 cm.

Contains: Fair copy:

1. 1941: we cannot hold on to the world,
2. Lost days (For John Lehamann),
3. If it were not,
4. The Generous Days (4 sections),
5. What love poems say,
6. Four sketches for Herbert Read:
   i. Innocence,
   ii. Young officer,
   iii. Conferencier,
   iv. Anarchist,
7. Bagatelles
   i. After the Inscription on a Greek,
   ii. Sentenced,
   iii. Mosquito,
   iv. Descartes,
   v. Present absence,
   vi. For Humphrey House,
   vii. A Political Generation,
   viii. After Tibullus,
   ix. Temple,
   x. To My Japanese Translator (shozo),
8. To W.H. Auden on his Sixteenth Birthday,
9. Fragment on a Cantata in Time of War.
10. Questions of Identity,
11. To Become a Dumb Thing,
12. Photograph of a Dead Friend,
13. Voice from a Skull (4 sections): Futami-ga-ura, Ise, Shima (Peter Watson).

White unruled paper, hardboards in wall-paper design with black spine. 26 x 19.5 cm.

Contains: Fair copy of poems:

1. The Generous days,
2. If it were not,
3. Lost Days,
4. Voice from a skull, 4 sections (Futami-ga-ura, Ise-Shima),
5. For W.H. Auden on His Sixtieth Birthday,
6. Fifteen line sonnet in four parts,
7. Fragments of a Birthday Cantata Written in Time of War,
8. Child Falling Asleep.
9. Memories of Japan:
   i.   Temple,
   ii. To my Japanese Translator (Shozo).

Note in the MS. book given to Ann and Roderigo Moynihan, poems in this order:

1. Steam heat,
2. Art Student,
3. Boy Cat Canary,
4. The D.H. Lawrence Myths,
5. Being a Grand Father,
6. What love poems say,
7. Auden at Milwaukee.

Note from a verse diary (January 3 and 4, Florence:

1. I looked at Matthew's child (my grand daughter),
2. What love poems say,
3. Notes from a verse diary: "Dined with Auden. He'd been to Milwaukee,
4. Steam Heat (March 15, 4 A.M., 1970),
5. Art-Student (Feb. 1970).
6. The mythological nature of the life of D.H. Lawrence,
7. Boy, Cat, Canary,
8. Middle East,
9. The things I most remember you remember,
10. To become a dumb thing.
11. 1941: we cannot hold on to the world,
12. A matter of identity.

Hardbound in ivory leather, ruled thick paper, 30 x 20.5 cm.

Contains: Rejoice in the Abyss / Poems, by / Stephen Spender / To

Natasha:

1. A trance,
2. Man and woman,
3. Her dream,
4. Absence,
5. Four eyes,
6. Lines for Edith Sitwell,
7. Almond Blossom,
8. A Man-made World,
9. Sea-scape,
10. Ocean,
11. Concsript,
12. Spiritual Exercises (3 sections); on the other side of the note-book: Notes for / THE AMATEURS OF LOVE / by / Stephen Spender. pp. 52.

Opens with quotations from D.H. Lawrence and W.H. Auden.

D76 **Notebook—XXXIV** **1962**

Hard-bound in brown, 17.5 x 11 cm. About 60 pages.

South American Diary, entries dated Sept. 27, 1964 to Oct. 28, 1962.

D77 **Notebook—XXXV** **N.D.**

Black leather notebook, 19.5 x 12 cm., 59 pages.

Contains: Diary with entries dated April 1 to May 12.

D78 **Notebook—XXXVI** **N.D.**

Hardboards in orange with blue spine, 20 x 12.5 cm., about 70 pages of manuscript.

Contains: Work book with rough drafts of a play on Oliver.

D79 **Notebook—XXXVII**

Wire-bound notebook, yellow card-board cover, ruled papers, 26.5 x 20 cm.

Poetry workbook with drafts of poems:

1. Do we not appear,
2. If A is able to prove,

3. For five long years,
4. Many drafts of "Across the ocean right down there."

D80   Notebook—XXXVIII   **N.D.**

Hardboards in cream color, 23 x 18 cm. Typed manuscript.

Contains: Part Two of *TORSO*: IN JUDGEMENT." Pages begin at 66; pages numbered 1 to 50.

D81   Notebook—XXXIX   **N.D.**

Hardbound with leather spine, 32.5 x 23.5 cm. Hand written, pages about 125.

Contains: PIERNO THE UNICORN / by Stephen Spender, 11 sections. Summer 1953; end Aug. 16, 1953.

D82   Notebook—XL   **1960-62**

Notebook with cardboard cover colored yellow with black spots, 31.5 x 20 cm. About 33 pages.

Rough drafts of articles, reviews etc. (1960-62).

D83   Notebook—XLI   **N.D.**

Cardboard in black, ruled paper. 20 x 16 cm. Hand-written manuscript, pages 35 including the blue book.

Natasha's notebook on the teaching of class-singing, later used by Spender for his article on Modern Poetry, continued on in a "blue book," On the other side of the notebook, drafts of poems:
1. Burning, burning image / of self, projected in;
2. Time in one generation,
3. Shadowless light (many drafts).

D84   Notebook—XLII   **N.D.**

Ruled paper, hard cover in dark grey vinyl, 32.5 x 21 cm. Hand-written manuscript.

Contains: Script of "English and American Writers in relation to their tradition" and notes on Anglo-American Sensibilities. Written pages about 42.

D85   One Way Song   N.D.

Loose sheets, handwritten, pp. 4.

Article on Wyndham Lewis: "One Way Song."

D86   Poems of Rilke   N.D.

Loose sheets, handwritten pp. 4.

Review of *Poems of Rilke*, translated by Leishmann.

D87   Poetry in This War   N.D.

Loose typed sheets, 4 pages of prose manuscript.

Article: "Poetry in This War."

D88   Poetry and Life   N.D.

Loose sheets, hand written, 3 pages manuscript.

Article: "Poetry and Life."

D89   Poetry Workbook—I   [1948]

Notebook, hardboard in black and white design with black leather-ette spine. Label on front: Royal / compositions / Name: Goethe, translations (in blue ink); 24.5 x 19 cm. White unruled papers, unnumbered.

Contains: Rough translations from Goethe; sketches for one or two poems, including a long poem, *Returning from Vienna*, at the end, draft of a letter to the Editors, *Pravda*, Writers' Congress [1948?] , and a few untitled poems.

D90   Poetry Work-Book—II   N.D.

Hard-boards in faded green cloth, torn spine, 33.5 x 21 cm., 196 pp., 9 loose sheets.

Contents:

1. His head is caught in a net (many versions),
2. Whirring outward growth / of saw-mill worlds (many versions),
3. But supposing anxiety and guilt are real?
4. The only integrity is personal integrity
5. The corroded charred (versions),

6. Through hidden corridors unravel,
7. O shall I never reach the valley,
8. A few alone, like cows in tweeds, (versions),
9. Like quartz is she, and a silver vein (versions),
10. In the shape of a friend, sickness, a day (versions),
11. Bring me peace bring me power bring me assurance.
12. To those whose job in the street is to stare, offers (versions),
13. Supposing then you change (versions),
14. Romantic poetry was not only an escape, but a statement,
15. All I can warn today—more I shall learn,
16. I will confess to you,
17. [ink-sketch],
18. Destruction invents,
19. The uncreative chaos offers,
20. Dissection of empires, multiplication of crowns; and others.

| D91 | **Powys** | **N.D.** |

Loose sheets, handwritten pages, 3

Review of a book by Mr. Powys.

| D92 | **Process of Art** | **N.D.** |

Loose sheet, handwritten page, 1.

One paragraph on "The Process of Art and the Direction of Life."

| D93 | **Quaker Ways** | **N.D.** |

Typed manuscript with corrections, 4 pp. signed.

Review of *Quaker Ways* by Anna Ruth Fry (Cassell, 8s 6d.).

| D94 | **Red Front** | **N.D.** |

Handwritten manuscript of 3 pages and signed.

Review of *The Red Front* by Louis Aragon, translated by e.e. cummings (Chapel Hill: Contempo Publishers).

| D95 | **Roderick Hudson** | **N.D.** |

Loose sheets, handwritten, pp. 9

Article: on "Roderick Hudson."

D96   The Soldiers' Disease   **N.D.**

Loose typed sheets, pp. 24. About 8000 words.

"The Soldiers' Disease," first story Spender wrote, n.d.

D97   Spanish Journal   **1932**

Extracts from a Spanish Journal-II. Typed script, pp. 1-5. Signed: Stephen Spender; typed from the handwritten Journal for 1932 beginning with an entry on Nov. 26, with slight alteration.

D98   The Temple   **N.D.**

Loose sheets, 33 x 21 cm., ruled paper. 180 pages.

Contains: Fiction entitled *The Temple*: Part One: A Journal (July 1929); Part Two: (Four Dreams): July-August 1929):
1. Ernst Soliloquizes,
2. The Trip to the Baltic,
3. Joachim Soliloquizes,
4. Variety;
Part Three (September 1929):
1. Koln,
2. The tour down the Rhine:
Part Four (November 1929):
1. From my journal,
2. Joachim Awn Heinrich,
3. Ernst and Willy,
4. From my journal,
5. Joachim;
Part Five: Epilogue (1931).

Note: This story has an alternate version: Five characters: Part Four (November 1929) from pp. 155-169; 187-203.

D99   Thomas Mann   **N.D.**

Loose sheets, handwritten pages 2.

Review of *Thomas Mann: A study* by James Clough.

D100 **Tolstoy** N.D.

Loose sheets, handwritten pages 4. Signed.

Review of a book on Tolstoy by the Countess Alexandra.

D101 **Torso** 1927

Notebook, 17.5 x 11.5 cm., hardbound in black paper with spine in deeper black. Ruled paper. Handwritten manuscript, dated June 1927.

Contents of the Story:

1. Motive,
2. The Pensionnat and Donavld,
3. The Walk,
4. Lunch,
5. A Regency—Mrs. Maygon passes,
6. Breakfast,
7. Maygon,
8. Retrospective,
9. Donavld's fears,
10. The letter,
11. His thoughts are turned elsewhere,
12. A crisis,
13. Fireworks on the lake,
14. Finale: Afterward the lake is tormented by the rain.

Note: Opening Notice: "All the characters and incidents in this book are purely imaginery."

From page 252 to the last page, including the inside of the cover, there are some unidentified poems written in Spender's own hand.

D102 **Trial of a Judge** 1937

Handwritten manuscript in loose leaves, 82 folio pages.

First and early draft different from the printed version: THE TRIAL OF A JUDGE / A TRAGIC STATEMENT / IN FIVE ACTS / by / STEPHEN SPENDER.

D103 **T.S. Eliot** N.D.

Loose typed sheets, unassorted, with numerous corrections.

Contains critical comments on T.S. Eliot etc.

D104   **T.S. Eliot**   **N.D.**

Loose sheets, handwritten pages 4.

An essay on T.S. Eliot.

D105   **Unidentified**   **N.D.**

Loose sheets, handwritten pages 2.

Part of an unidentified narrative.

D106   **University College School**   **N.D.**

Loose sheets, handwritten pages 16.

An essay on "University College School," where Spender studied.

D107   **Work Book—I**   **N.D.**

Large folio book, 172 pp.

Collected Poems, written in Spender's own hand.

D108   **Work Book—II**   **N.D.**

Hard cover in black 32.5 x 20 cm., manuscript of 108 + 4 pages.

Contains 43 versions of poems written in ink and pencil. Many drafts of different poems.

D109   **Work Book—III**   **N.D.**

Hard boards in dark green cover with black spine. 118 pages of handwritten manuscript.

Contains early versions of poems, including *Vienna.*

D110   **Work Book—IV**   **N.D.**

Large folio size notebook hard-bound in black and white design. Tattered cover with label: Notes for Gollancz book.

Contains rough drafts of prose and poetry. Also poems by another hand and signed J.H. Madge and Godwin Ewart.

D111   Work Book—V   1948

Exercise book with hard cardboard cover, 24.5 x 19 cm., front carries a white label with "Royal Compositions" printed on it.

Name: Spender / Sketches begun Feb / 1948 / written in ink.

10 loose leaves of manuscript containing rough drafts of poems with many corrections and revisions.

D112   Work Book—VI   N.D.

Large folio size note-book bound in black card board.

Contains: Sketch of Spender's introductory essay on Henry James for his volume: *The Destructive Element:* I. Life as Art and Art as Life. The other end of the notebook contains a poem: "Orpheus ... Eurydice ... Hermes"; an article: "The Artistic Future of Poetry (6 pp.); and an essay on "The Letters of D.H. Lawrence (14 pp.).

D113   Workers' Point of View   N.D.

Loose sheets, handwritten pages, 6. signed.

Review of *The Workers' Point of View: A Symposium,* with a preface by C.T. Cramp (Hogarth Press, 4s. 6d.).

D114   W.H. Auden   1973

Loose sheets filed together.

Contains:

1. Galley proofs of "W.H. Auden, a memorial address by Stephen Spender, delivered at Christ Church Cathedral, Oxford, on October 27, 1973. Privately printed for Faber and Faber, London;
2. Type script with corrections: "W.H. Auden 1907-1973";
3. Typescript of the memorial address;
4. Handwritten MS. of the same;
5. ISIS, "Marxists from Oxford": Stephen Glover on Marxist Writers of the Thirties, pp. 19-21 (June 15, 1973),
6. Notes on W.H. Auden (April 1, 1947), in a notebook, hardbound with decorations on front 22 x 18.5 cm.

D115   Yeats   N.D.

Loose sheets, handwritten pages 2.

Article on W.B. Yeats.

DI

MANUSCRIPTS

OF

INDIVIDUAL POEMS

BY

STEPHEN SPENDER

DI—1 [Untitled poem] : "Abrupt and charming mover."
Typed ms., one page, July 1932, autographed.

DI—2 [Untitled poem] : "After they have tired of the brilliance of cities."
Typed ms., two pages, n.d., unsigned.

DI—3 "Churchill": [A poem] : "This man who saw all and bore all."
Handwritten, two pages, n.d., unsigned.

DI—4 [Untitled poem] : "For on this stage there were heroes, fools, victims, the chorus."
Handwritten ms., one page, n.d., unsigned. Includes revisions.

DI—5 [Untitled poem] : "From a tree choked by ivy, rotted."
Typed ms., one page, n.d., autographed: Stephen.

DI—6 [Untitled poem] : "here at the centre of the turning year."
Typed ms., corrections by hand, one page, n.d., unsigned.

DI—7 [Untitled poem] : "Here man wakes, conscious of work, whilst wave after wave."
Typed ms., one page, June 1932, signed: S.H.S.

DI—8 [Untitled poem] : "If it were not too late."
Handwritten ms., in ink, one page, n.d., autographed.

DI—9 [Untitled poem] : "I hear the noise of evening."
Handwritten ms., with multiple revisions, two pages, n.d., signed: Stephen Spender.

DI—10 [Untitled poem]: "In railway halls, on pavements near the traffic."

Typed script, one page, June 1932, signed: Stephen Spender. On *verso* of DI—7.

DI—11 [Untitled poem]: "It is not what they stole nor what they spoiled."

Handwritten ms., two pages, n.d., unsigned.

DI—12 [Untitled poem]: "Ladies and Gentlemen, You know."

Photocopy, two pages. "This poem was written by Mr. Spender on the occasion of the White House Conference on International Cooperation, November 28-December 1, 1965. It was read by Mr. Spender as a draft and given to the participants in the Conference as a souvenir, but not for reproduction. © copyright: Stephen Spender.

DI—13 "My Cousin Maccabeus": "My cousin Maccabeus, tall and strong."

Typed ms., with multiple corrections by hand, one page, n.d., unsigned.

DI—14 [Untitled poem]: "Not palaces, an era's crown."

Typed script, one page, n.d., autographed. On *verso* of DI—1.

DI—15 "The Conscript": "Upon the turf's edge flashing like a knife."

Typed script, one page, n.d., unsigned.

DI—16 [Untitled poem]: "The eyes seen vividly across the traffic."

Typed on the same page as DI—15, Page one, dated June 1932, signed on right hand corner of the page: S.H.S.

DI—17 "The landscape near an Aerodrome": "More beautiful and soft than any moth."

Typed script, one page, n.d., signed: S.H. Spender.

DI–18 [Untitled poem] : "The light in the window seemed perpetual."
Typed script, one page, n.d., signed.

DI–19 [Untitled poem] : "These are the fray that falls away from movement."
Typed script, one page, dated: June 1932, signed.

DI–20 [Untitled poem] : "The shapes of death haunt life."
Typed, one page, n.d., unsigned.

DI–21 "The Uncreating Chaos": "To the hanging despair of eyes in the street, offer."
Typed, two pages, n.d., both pages signed.

DI–22 "Untitled poem": "The waste of life is not in quietness."
Handwritten, one page, n.d., unsigned.

DI–23 "Untitled poem": "Those fireballs those ashes."
Typed, one page, n.d., signed: S.H.S. On *verso* of DI–19.

DI–24 "Two Kisses": "I wear your kiss like a feather."
Typed, one page, n.d., signed: Stephen Spender.

DI–25 [Untitled poem] : "You must live through the time when everything hurts."
Typed, one page, n.d., signed.

DM

BIRTH OF A POEM

(SKETCH FOR SPIRITUAL EXPLORATIONS)

Sketch for Spiritual
Explorations.

Shadowless light
God of crystals, ~~across~~ window-panes, x-ray
and tragic operations,
Descend and penetrate
~~Clean water struck ~~
~~Of touching wheels~~
My darkness, covered by the night
Of warring nations,
Trampled by wheels, broken & lost ways.

I am who was born, cry, love, must die,
Came naked, never lost his nakedness
Alone under his habit, knew needs of mind & body
Of common inexplicable simplicity
Of such strength that ~~torture~~ all custom seemed to lie
~~that the~~ In buildings and machines, ~~wonders~~ which die
In a star of streets interpret,
~~The~~ wish, ~~the~~ fear, ~~the~~ need, ~~the~~ loveliness.

That under the stars I was small
I wanted the night to be a face
With a mind that forgave me at the end
When I went out into the darkness
And I wished my neighbours to ~~forget~~ confess

Birth of a Poem

There are about thirty drafts of the poem before it is finally published as "Transparent Light" in *Spiritual Exercises*, privately printed, 1943, and as "Light" in Part III: "Spiritual Explorations" of *Poems of Dedication* (London: Faber and Faber, 1947). The following is a selection of early sketches, which, it is hoped, will give an idea about the poetic process by which the final shape and form of a poem is acquired.

I.   Shadowless light,
        Brood on window panes, clenched in crystals, tragic
            in operations
        Slant down and penetrate
                diffused mist
        Our world of confusion and wheels
        Broken lives leading to lost ways
        Turning
        ~~Revolving~~ upon a ~~planet~~ star within a night
        Slit with the threshing frost of stars
        Glittering cold remote outside our minds
        the close prison of our engines

        We were born, loved, must die
        Dawned naked and still walk in nakedness
        Ashamed under our clothes, with mind and body
        Of childlike incommunicable simplicity
        Our heads open onto the distances
        Our minds look for an end and a beginning
        Our eyes like angels through universe
        Travel
        Our minds the things of the universe
        Casting for an end and a beginning
        Our eyes

II.   Shadowless light

        Winging
        ~~angel~~ through window panes, clenched in
            crystal, tragic in operation
        O penetrate groaning
        Our world of darkness and wheels
        Broken laws leading to lost ways
        ____?____ a ~~planet~~ star ~~within~~ surrounded
                by a night

Slit with   the throbbing frost of stars
of stars-indifferent
glittering remote outsdie minds
Shut in a prison of their engines . . .

III.   Shadowless light
         Slanting through windowpanes, springing
                                    from crystals
         Tragic in operations,
         Enter and penetrate
         This forest our world, as ___?___ of wheels
         Broken lives leading to lost ways
         Our-life-upon a-star within-a-night
         Placed-on a-stars revolving in a night
         Rounded with distances and slit with stars
         glittering-throbbing in frost of black oblivion
         Remote from us by us forgotten
         In the closed prison of our engines.

IV.   Shadowless Light

         River through windows, fountain in crystals
         knife in tragedy
         Descend & penetrate
         Darkness of our flesh
         Prisoned in engines
         Revolving in the circle of a night
         Slit with the throbbing frost of stars
         Gods to our forefathers
         Lost to us.

V.   Shadowless sun.

         Cascade through windows.
         In crystals, knife
         Of tragic operations:
         Imprisoned shining in the one world:
         Descend from your mountain
                                    air rarified
         and penetrate the dark flesh-of-our life,
         The wheels, the lives, the words, the wars, machines
         A word, a fog, a night, in which we lie

198

Imprisoned in our bones and engines
On a ~~land world~~ map revolving in a sky.
Slit with the throbbing frost of stars
Glittering, remote, cold, unseeing light
                    ~~(light of oblivion)~~ -
Guides and gods of our forefathers
Forgotten by and forgetting us.

VI.   Not even the sun,
That angel slanting through windows, that rose
Hidden in crystals, that knife
Tragic in operations, shadowless one
knotted in curtained shadows,
can unravel and penetrate
Flesh slain on this altar of life
In the exhibition of ~~ruins and engines~~
                        wheels and ruins,
within the primitive forest where we die
Imprisoned in our palace of engines
Upon a map revolving in a sky,
Slit with the throbbing frost of stars
Shaking their glittering, icy, oblivions,
                        antique spears
Involved in the pattern of Venus & Mars
Forgotten by us, and far far far
                        from our wars.

VII.   Shadowless Sun,

Angel slanting through windows, rose
Hidden in crystals, knife
Tragic in operations, one
~~Unravelled from the knot of shadows~~ -
~~Ravelled in a knot of shadows~~
Knotted in many shadows
Unravel now, and penetrate
~~Our house, tragedy, flesh and life~~
Our flesh laid on this altar of life
~~Under the ruins of wheels, ways, machines~~ -
In the exhibition of wheels and ruins
Within the forest, the darkness where we lie
Imprisoned in our bones and engines
In a continent of the world revolving
                        in the sky.

VIII.   Not even the sun
         That angel slanting through windows; that rose
         Springing from crystals; that knife
         Tragic in operations — O shadowless one,
         Knotted centre of the world's shadow!—
         Not even Apollo can penetrate
         The here murdered on this altar & life
         The black sacrifice of a man's life,
         Among the wheels and roads and ruins
         In the modern mind where we all die
         Imprisoned in our fairy palace of engines.
         We are a map revolving in a sky,
         Slit with the throbbing frost of stars
         Clanking their glittering, icy, mountainous, antique spears
         Lost in the circle of Venus and Mars
         Forgotten by us, far far far from our wars.

IX.   Not even the sun
         That angel slanting through windows; that rose
         Surgent in crystals; that knife
         Tragic in operations — O shadowless one
         Solvent of the world's shadow! —
         Not even that bright light can penetrate

         The pitch black sacrifice of life
         Slain among the wheels and roads and ruins
         In the modern mind where the young die
         Imprisoned in our palace of engines.
             We are a map revolving in a sky
         Slit with the throbbing frost of stars
         Remote in blackness glittering their silver spears
         Involved in the pattern of Venus and Mars
         Forgotten by us, far far far from our wars.

X.   Not even the sun
         Wings aslant through windows; rose
         Surgent in crystals; tragic knife
         In operations — O shadowless one
         Solvent of the world's knotted shadows! —
         Not even that radiant light can penetrate
                      (golden)
         The stifling pitch sacrifice of life
         Among the wheels and ruins
         On the crossroads of the minds, where theyoung die

Enclosed/In their speeding engines.
We are on a map revolving in sky
Slit with the throbbing frost of stars
Remote in darkness, glittering their
                              mineral spears
In the shining speech of Venus & Mars
Forgotten by us, far far far from our wars.

XI.   Not even the sun
        Angel through windows; rose
        Surgent in crystals; tragic knife
        In operations — O shadowless One
        Solvent of the world's knotted shadows!
        Not even that bright light can penetrate
        The black sacrifice of life
        Amongst the wheels and roads and ruins
        of the mind, where the young men die
        Enclosed in their palaces of engines

            We are a map revolving in a sky
        Slit with the throbbing frost of stars   diamond
                                        silver   spears
        Remote in darkness, glittering their mineral
        of Venus and Mars
        Forgotten by us, far far far from our wars.

XII.   Not even the sun
        Angel through windows; rose
        Surgent in crystals; tragic knife
        In operations   O shadowless one,
                            knotted
        Solvent of the world's shadows!
        Not even that bright light can penetrate
        The knotted sacrifice of life
                black
        On an altar of wheels and roads and ruins
        In the mind, where the young men die
        Tied? in their palaces of engines.
        shut

            We are a map revolving in a sky slit
        with the throbbing frost of stars
        Remote in night: stars glistening with spears
        In the diamonded sleep of Venus & Mars,
        Forgetting, together, far far far from our wars.

201

XIII.   Annunciatory sun
         Angel through windows, rose
         Which dawns in crystals, tragic knife
         Descending in operations, shadowless one
         Solving the crowding shadows;
                     ~~enclosing~~
         O ~~Bright light,~~ concentrate, penetrate separate
         The knotted sacrifice of life
              ~~dark~~   ~~engines~~
         Among the wheels and wings and ruins
         of this generation imprisoned in engines.
         In the night slit with stars
         Glistening diamonded spears that speak
         Inaccessible glittering, silent greek
         Forgetting, forgotten, far from our wars.

XIV.   Annunciatory sun,   a
         Angel through window, rose   b
         Which surges in crystals, tragic knife   c
         Brilliant in operations - O shadowless one   a
         Who drawing back the curtained shadows, —   b
         Concentrate, separate, disclose
                     tangled   b
         The knotted sacrifice of life   c
         Here among the wheels and wings and ruins   d
         Of the young, tied to destructive engines   d
                   The blood stained night, slit with stars   c
         Has diamonded spears which speak   f
         Inaccessbile, glittering, silent Greek   f
         Lost/In the dream of Venus and Mars   e
         That/Heartless oblivion, far far far from
              our wars   c

XV.   Shadowless light
         God of crystals, window-panes, x-rays
         and tragic operations,
         Descend and penetrate
         my darkness, covered by the night
         of warring nations
         Trampled by wheels, broken and lost ways.

         I who was born, cry, love, must die,
         came naked, never lost his nakedness

                          202

Alone under his habit, knew needs
                of mind and body
Of common inexplicable simplicity
Of such strength that all custom seemed to be,
The buildings and machines, which did not
In a star of streets interpret
My wish, fear, need, loneliness—

That under the stars I was small
I wanted the night to be a face
With a mind that forgave me at the end
When I went out into the darkness
and I wished my neighbours to confess
That they were my similars, without the grace
of the inanimate   __?__

XVI   Shadowless light
        god of crystals, window-panes, x-rays
        And tragic opeartion,
        Descend and penetrate
        my world tangled in darkness and wheels
        And rails that lead into lost ways
        Roared/ in by wings of confused wills

        For I am who was born, cried, love, must die,
        Dawned naked, never lost his nakedness
        Alone under his habit, knew needs of mind and body
        Of common inexplicable simplicity
        Shuddered at the black night, white
                        with the frost
        knew the pain of distances,
        The impossiblity of imaginining a beginning
        or a world without beginning
        Was appalled at an end
        And more still at the lack of end—
        And was this not enough
        horror of a life time, agony of wonder
        And delight of wonder, called in every shape
        of doom we build, reflected
        In every artificial city and lake
        Our need, our loss, our hope our dread?

XVII   Shadowless light
           God of crystals window-panes x-rays
           and tragic operations,
           Descend and penetrate
           Our world tangled in darkness and wheels
           Broken rails leading to lost ways
           Revolving round us in this night
           of darkness slit with the uncaring stars
           Roared over by the wings of confused wills.

           For we are who were born, cried, love, are
                      loved, must die
           Dawned naked, ever knew our nakedness
           Alone under our habits, mind and body
           Of common inexplicable simplicity
           Who knew the pain of the great distances
           The dread of watching through the night
           And through all time to look for a beginning
           And finding ? our own horror
           Incapable of end or of beginning.

           And was this not enough
           The agony of our uncertainty
           The people on the plains under the seasons
           And filled within with their diversity
           Is this not enough
           To make all life an image
           of the agony of our uncertainty
           Filled with our human diversity
           So that the towers, the laws, the customs
           Are images.

XVIII   Shadowless light,
           God of window-panes, crystals, tragic operations,
           Descend and penetarte
           Our world of confusion and wheels
           of broken roads leading to lost ways
           Revolving in a night
           Slit with the throbbing frost of stars
           covered by the roaring of dark wings.

           We were born, loved, love, must die,
           Dawned naked, and still go in nakedness
           Alone with our habits, with mind and body
           of common inexplicable simplicity.

Our heads open upon the distances,
Our hearts are pierced with roots of need
Our sight seeking an end and a beginning
And striking at the end against a wall
     not?
our   indivisible final blindness.

Our flesh and blood of total ignorance
In many separate knots of flesh
Coagulates in the tribes upon the plain
The life-time gap of time and place
Each knot of separate sense is knit
Into the situation which binds all
That separateness and certainty of death.
While in each body as on a drum
Pulses the tingling blood of sound
And the word trembles over all the skin.

What is lit but the consciousness
of what we are and are not? What should our lives
Image except the truth that is our seeing
The sensual knowledge and the vast ignorance?
The dance within our veins flow through the streets
And the palatial wonder of our minds
Open on towers and monuments that cast
An image upwards onto death
     ?   reflect down on our minds of water?

It is enough, it is enough
In the slight morsel of our lives
Nibbled from the cages of a tree
Each life a caterpillar in a leaf
It is enough to be true
To what we are   O light of life,

XIX.   Shadowless light
       God of window-panes, crystals, tragic operations,
       Descend and penetrate
       Our world of confusion and wheels,
       Broken roads leading to lost ways,
       Revolving in a night
       Slit with the throbbing frost of stars
  ?   The remote fire shining in cold skies
       Sweep over the blind wings of our will.

We were born, loved, love, must die,
Dawned naked and still go in nakedness
Alone under our habits with mind and body
Of common inexplicable simplicity,
Our heads alive to the high distances
Our hearts pierced with hiding roots of need.
Our minds in searching an end and a beginning
Straining against the blindness of the eyeball
Indivisible particle of inner night.

Our flesh and bones of ultimate ignorance
In many separate knots of life
Coagulate in the tribes upon the plains
With their seventy years and their six feet of space
Each knot of consciousness is knit
Into the situation of the whole—
Separation and a seal of death.
What do we hold
But our bodies hearts each other
Our knowledge what we are not.
Stretched on the bone the parchment skin
Tingles with the blood of sound
When the word trembles on us like a drum.

God, who illuminates
With grandest wave our indivisible
Night, what do we know
But the small we are, the huge we are not?
What can the wing of our lives
Be except the pattern of our being?

            ?
Grains god, burning sun,
Final wave that illuminates
The terrible skeleton and the last darkness,
what do you show except the little grain
of what we are the everything we are not?
What should we do, transparent flame
But play the certain life we are
And build the towers to what we are not?
Making monuments that cast
                ?
Upwards an image into death
As that reflects down on our minds of water?

Surely it is enough

TRANSPARENT LIGHT
(From *Spiritual Exercises*)

Transparent light,
Piercing through eyes, and mind, and windows
Of the body, the will, the house; your knife
Shines over the locked flesh, where power's
Barriers enclose
Ruined ruinous malicious life.
Your fate, bright
With lightning compact in the dark hours,
Will strike down, unlock, expose
The feud, the hideous will, the piteous heart
Of the leaders and people hidden in night,
The gods and the kings mad,
The prince fanged with revenge, poisonous
                         and bad,
Lost and lolling among the shadows.

But to the unborn lend your healing powers,
To the son returning from the sword-bright wars,
Restore his winged steed,
Assist him to rise, demonstrate what towers,
What aeroplanes, what roads, your shining grace needs.
Tell him he does inherit
The past streaming into the present,
The illustrious tradition intellect must guide
Modify, transform, for heirs apparent,
Generation of his generation, to ride.
Tell him he does inhabit
His body your body, his spirit your spirit,
And let your purposes his purposes
Unfold through buds of him their flowers;
Through walls he builds and towers
O be your will transparent
Make his hands burn with your burning roses.

Light

No. VIII: *Spiritual Explorations*, Part III of POEMS OF DEDICATION
(LONDON: Faber and Faber, 1947). pp. 46-47.

Light
Light
Burning through eyes and windows
Of the body the will the house

Knife
Knife
Thread-suspended over clasped locked flesh
Where the demoniac powers
Dreaming of power, enclose
The ruinous and to-be-ruined life

Bright
Bright
With lightning compact in dark hours
Strike down tear apart unlock expose
The feud the kiss the will the heart
Of this people imprisoned in night
Their gods mad
Their princes fanged with revenge poisonous and bad
Lost and lolling among the shadows.

Strike to the womb the unborn with new power
Speak to the boy back from the sword-bright war
And with his wounds unbandage his light eyes
Show him as he is
Show him your own existence as you are

Teach him his blindness teach him to rise
Show him his body and what winged steed
Fulfilments of your grace and his grace need.

Show him the words that bleed
out of the past and through the present
To the future of his heirs-apparent
Words and Pegasus he must guide
For generation of his generation to ride.

Tell him he does inhabit
Himself yourself, his spirit your spirit,
And let your purposes his purposes
Unfold through buds of him their flowers.

Through walls he builds and towers
O be your truth transparent
Make his hands burn with your burning roses.

Both the poems, "Spiritual Exercises" and "Spiritual Explorations" should be studied in their entirety to find out how "shadowless Light" finally branches out into many dimensions.

R

RECORDINGS

BY

STEPHEN SPENDER

R1   **Twentieth Century Poetry in English**

The Library of Congress Recording Laboratory, PL9: "Contemporary recordings of poets reading their own poems; selected and arranged by the Consultants in Poetry in English and issued by the Library of Congress under a grant from the Bollingen Foundation."

Side B: Spender reading: "An Elementary School Class Room in a Slum," "The Landscape Near an Acrodrome," "The Pylons," "An 'I' can Never Be Great Man," "I Think Continually of Those Who Were Truly Great," "A Stopwatch and an Ordnance Map."

R2   **Caedmon Treasury of Modern Poets Reading Their Own Poetry: TC-2006**

Spender reading: "I Think Continually of Those Who Were Truly Great" and "Seascape."

R3   **Stephen Spender Reading His Poetry (New York: Caedmon Publishers, 1956), TC-1084**

Recorded in New York, October 20, 1956.

Contains Spender's Poems: "My Parents Kept Me"—"What I Expected"—"Who Live Under the Shadow of a War"—"Thoughts During an Air Raid"—"Two Armies"—"Memento"—"The Express" —"Hoelderlin's Old Age"—"The Room Above the Square"—"A Stopwatch and an Ordnance Map"—"Song"—"From Elegy for Margaret, I, IV, VI"—"Seascape"—"He Will Watch the Hawk with an Indifferent Eye"—"An 'I' Can Never Be Great Man"—"Beethoven's Death Mask"—"The Double Shame"—"Ice"—"Words"— "To My Daughter"—"Dylan Thomas, November 1953."

R4   **The Poet Speaks**

Recorded in association with the British Council and the Poetry Room in the Lamont Library of Harvard University (26 August 1964):

London: Argo Record Company Ltd., 1967.

Spender reads: "Earth Treading Stars," "Seascape," "To My Daughter."

R5   World's Great Poets

Reading at the Festival of Two Worlds, Spoleto, Italy, Produced by Vincent R. Tortora, copyright, 1968, Applause Productions, Inc. New York.

Spender reads: "Word," "The Express," "Bagatelle," "If It Were Not So," "To My Daughter at the Age of Five," and "I Think Continually of Those Who Were Truly Great."

R6   Casette: Stephen Spender

Stephen Spender—I (Modern Literary Voices): A discussion of anti-poetic subjects in today's poetry, 28 minutes. 020/10166 The Center for Casette Studies, Inc., 8110 Webb Ave., N. Hollywood, California, 91605.

Spender discusses the following questions: 1. What, according to Spender is "anti-poetic" about modern Life? 2. Why does Spender call his poem, "The Express," perverse? 3. How did Spender's visit to an elementary School class in a slum affect his work for BBC? 4. What qualms does Spender have about one of his most popular poems, "I Think Continually . . ."?

On this program Spender reads seven of his poems and discusses both the external landscape and the inner world with the poet-teacher Louis Simpson.

R7   Casette: Stephen Spender

Stephen Spender—II (Modern Literary Voices): A discussion of Poetry as a political tool). The Center for Casette Studies, 8110 Webb Ave., N. Hollywood, CA.

The following questions are disucssed: 1. What is the origin of the title of Spender's poem "Ultima Ratio Regum"? 2. Why does Spender feel that death tends to become an unreal abstraction during war? 3. What difficulties did Spender encounter in trying to write "the truth" about war? 4. How does Spender's love poetry differ from that of his contemporaries?

Stephen Spender's poetry is a record of the international and political movements of the Thirties and Forties, and he has always been interested in the effect poetry could have on the political world. Spender reads three of his war poems on this program: "Two Armies," "Ultima Ratio Regum," and "Thoughts During an Air Raid." Also included are four love poems.

R8   Phonotape

McGraw Hill Sound Seminars, 53 minutes, track one-702 feet; track two—511 feet.

Stephen Spender: "Poetic Vision and Modern Literature."

R9   Phonotape

23215: track one—630 ft; tarck two—511 ft.

Stephen Spender: Poetry of Stephen Spender.

R10   Houghton Mifflin Literary Masters LP Program

3-7992, mono: Spender reads his poems: "Word," "The Hawk," "Not to You I Sighed," "An I Can Never Be a Great Man," "Beethoven's Death Mask," "My Parents Kept Me From Children That Were Rough," "What I Expected, Was," "Who Live under the Shadow of a War," "The Express," "The Landscape near an Aerodrome," "The Prisoners," "I Think Continually . . .," "An Elementary School Classroom," "Elegy for Margaret," "Song," "Four Short Poems about Children."

S

CRITICISM OF THE WORKS
OF
STEPHEN SPENDER
INCLUDING
SELECTED BOOK REVIEWS
AND
UNPUBLISHED DISSERTATIONS

i.   Ashley Sampson in *Saturday Review*, 155 (Feb. 4, 1933), 122.

Much that is beautiful and true is here; shows reserves of strength not expended in these poems.

ii.   G.W. Stonier in *New Statesman and Nation*, 5(Feb. 4, 1933), 136.

Spender's poetry is conditioned by T.S. Eliot but gravitates towards D.H. Lawrence.

iii.   Allen Tate. "A New Artist," *New Verse*, 3(May 1933), 21-23.

iv.   Edward Roditi in *Spectator*, 150(May 19, 1933), 722.

Spender offers a varied array of qualities, is less restricted, more complete and universal than many of his contemporaries.

v.   Horace Gregory in *Nation*, 136(June 14, 1933), 675.

Shows promise of being the best lyric poet of his generation in England. His talents lie in ease of movement, freshness and clarity. Fond of generalizing his emotions.

vi.   J.B. Fletcher in *Poetry*, 42(July 1933), 225-228.

A man of fastidious taste, of mature discrimination but is psychologically inhibited "unable to take fire, to go mad with indignation, aspiration or ecstasy." Remains one degree aloof and disdainfully remote.

vii.   *Times Literary Supplement* (July 6, 1933), 463.

Mr. Spender is likely to enter very graciously into the poetic history of our time.

viii.   John A. Holmes, "A Dissenting Opinion," *Poetry*, 42(Sept. 1933), 355-56.

Takes exception to Mr. Fletcher's review of Spender's Poems. Tries to show that the poems have a totality of purpose: "Stephen Spender, best of the young British poets, master of new expression, sharply aware of his world and his time, sure in purpose and noble in spirit, deserves far better treatment in Poetry's pages . . ."

ix.   Archibald MacLeish, "Stephen Spender and the Critics," *Hound and Horn*, 7(October/December 1933), 145-47.

"I am merely a spectator. I am not a judge. As a spectator I am profoundly moved by Mr. Spender's poems. He is the first new poet in many, many years who has thus moved me."

S2 S.K. Senagupta, "A New Force in Egnlish Poetry," *Calcutta Review*, (March 1934), 307-16.

S3 Malcolm Cowley, "Spender and Auden," *New Republic*, 80(September 26, 1934), 189-90.

Spender is serious, straightforward; he can use words like "love," "bravery," "honor," without having them turn mealy in his mouth. The most serious defect to be found in his poems is a sort of fogginess that sometimes makes his meaning doubtful.

S4 L. Untermeyer, "Poetry of Power," *Saturday Review of Literature*, 11(Nov. 10, 1934), 274-75.

S5 Philip Burnham, "Auden and Spender," *The Commonweal*, 21(Dec. 28, 1934), 255-57.

The lyrics express a revolutionary outlook, and since this is before the day, they are also the work of a seer. Compared to Auden, Spender seems a poor seer.

S6 Reviews of *Vienna* (Random House): 1934-35

i. I.M. Parsons, *Spectator*, 153(Nov. 9, 1934), 728.

Mr. Spender, we cannot help feeling, is in a sense too involved in his material here to see it whole and to dissociate the universal from the particular—and ultimately trivial . . .

ii. *Times Literary Supplement* (Dec. 13, 1934), 890.

In 'Vienna' Mr. Spender has tackled a problem in the real use of the imagination and in diction which is of the greatest interest today, and he has given us some lovely lines.

iii. *Chrisitan Science Monitor* (Jan. 30, 1935), 12.

Vienna shows an advance on all but the best of the "Poems": and advance in the direction of wider scope and a far stronger initial impulse.

iv. William Troy in *Nation*, 140(March 13, 1935), 312.

The theme is there, and the emotions are there, but the two do not coalesce in a way that would give an ordered intensity to the whole.

S7 M.D. Zabel, "The Purposes of Stephen Spender," *Poetry*, 45(Jan. 1935), 208-13.

M.D.A. applies Spender's statement about Yeats to him: His "poems contain a seed of inspiration derived from the external world . . . they are the beginning of something new." . . . should establish him as a writer not only of immediate values but of permanent and convincing truth.

S8 Reviews of *The Destructive Element* (Houghton and Cape): 1935-36.

i. Cyril Connolly in *New Statesman and Nation*, 9(May 4, 1935), 641.

In spite of its faults, it remains an important book. It is the attempt of a patient, intelligent, and deeply interested person to get really underneath . . . far below the critic's usual working level.

ii. V.S. Pritchett in *Christian Science Monitor* (June 19, 35), 10.

Mr. Spender has some excellent things on Kafka and Rilke and on certain young English writers . . . His only serious weakness is a humorless and sometimes prose style.

iii. Malcolm Cowley in *New Republic*, 86(March 4, 1936), 114.

A book that is full of excitement for anyone interested in the problems of contemporary writing.

vi. Louis Kronenberger in *New York Times* (Oct. 25, 1936), 24.

The aimlessness of characters gets confused with the aimlessness of the author's methods.

S9 Theodore Maynard, "When the Pie Was Opened," *Commonweal*, 22(Aug. 2, 1935), 339-41.

Now a poetic boom because of C. Day Lewis, W.H. Auden and Stephen Spender.

S10 Reviews of *The Burning Cactus* (Random House and Faber): 1936.

i. *Times Literary Supplement* (April 18, 1936), 333.

Mr. Spender's poetic originality is not absent from these pages, and the images into which he projects mood or scene, however daring and bizarre they may be are an exciting experience in themselves for the imaginative reader.

ii.   Graham Greene in *Spectator*, 156(April 24, 1936), 766.

More uneasy, less accomplished. The legend, except in the fine title story, has been insufficiently dramatized; the umbilical cord has not been cut.

iii. L.C. Hearn, in *Saturday Review of Literature*, 14(Oct. 10, 1936), 34.

There is grace and aptness in Mr. Spender's writing and also— one cannot escape it—the art of the amateur.

S11   Reviews of *Forward from Liberalism* (Random House and Gollancz): 1937.

i.   R.C.K. Ensor, *Spectator*, 158(Jan. 15, 37), 90.

The attraction of this book is its sincerity. Mr. Spender has portrayed himself and a mental portrait of generous youth.

ii. *Times Literary Supplement* (Jan 16, 1937), 35.

Sincere. "It differs from similar apologias in its general fairness, in its reluctance to admit the unpalatable tactics towards which a belief in the unique inspiration of communism and its immediate necessity drives him."

iii. F.A.V. in *Manchester Guardian* (Feb. 2, 1937), 5.

Mr. Spender's book is a characteristic product of English parlour Bolshevism . . .

iv. E.H. Carr in *Christian Science Monitor* (March 17, 1937), 10.

A young poet and openhearted. But he has marched forward from liberalism into a morass of illusions . . .

v.   F.H. Underhill in *Canadian Forum*, 17(April 37), 31.

Mr. Spender has set forth in this book his personal reasons for being a communist. It is a much more persuasive and convincing effort than that of John Strachey.

vi. Cleanth Brooks in *Poetry*, 50(Aug. 37), 280-84.

The most attractive qualities of the book are the liberal virtues of tolerance and fair-mindedness. The strongest element is the attack which is made on present-day stupidities. Has a real passion for social justice (Review of The *Destructuve Element* and *Forward from Liberalism*).

S12   James G. Southworth, "Stephen Spender," *Sewanee Review*, 45 (July/Sept. 1937), 272-83.

S13 William Troy, "Revolution by Poetic Justice," *Nation*, 144(March) 27, 1937), 354-56.

Forward from Liberalism is a bewildering farrago of historical information, political theory, personal autobiography, and unamalgamated emotion.

S14 Charles Glicksberg, "Poetry and Marxism: Three English Poets Take Their Stand," *University of Toronto Quarterly*, VI, pp. 309-325.

On the critical theories of Cecil Day Lewis, W.H. Auden, and Stephen Spender.

S15 Reviews of *Trial of a Judge* (Random House): 1938.

   i.   Nevill Coghill in *Spectator*, 160(March 18, 1938), 482.

       Extraordinary performance. The finest English poetic drama written since Otway's *Venice Preserved.*

   ii. *Times Literary Supplement* (March 19, 1938), 185.

       Has every prospect of being exciting on the stage. For the reader, it is one of the most interesting poems in recent years.

   iii. Charles Powell in *Manchester Guardian* (March 29, 1938), 7.

   iv. S.F. Morse, "Prophecy and Fact," *Poetry*, 52(August 1938), 292.

       Conceived fundamentally as a poem. The drama and the poetry separate too easily. But the poetry itself has much.

   v. Louise Bogan in *New Yorker*, 14(October 1, 1938), 76.

   vi J.G.S. in *Saturday Review of Literature*, 19(Nov. 26, 1938), 22.

       Narrow in range, yet affording sufficient subtlety and variety. *Trial of a Judge* indicates that Mr. Spender can draw his inspiration from sources outside of himself. This warrants us in thinking that we may expect to see a steady growth in his poetic stature.

S16 F.C. Flint, "New Leaders in English Poetry," *Virginia Quarterly Review*, 14(October 1938), 502-18.

Among the newcomers, Spender is the most nearly romantic. His romanticism is disclosed in his literary enthusiasms, his temperament, and technique.

S17 Samuel Baker Householder, *Some Modern Tendencies in English Poetry as Illustrated in the Works of Auden, Spender and Day Lewis*. Unpublished Master's Thesis (University of Texas at Austin, 1938).

There is unity among the "Oxford Poets." They are serious and self-conscious in their examination of the poetic function and sensitive to the world in which they found themselves.

S18 C.I. Glicksberg, "Poetry and the Social Revolution," *Dalhousie Review*, 17(1938), 493-503.

S19 Reviews of *Poems for Spain*: 1939.

  i. *The Evening Telegraph and Post*, Dundee (March 4, 1939).

  Wilfred Owen said that "the poetry is in the pity," and this motto is again applicable here, where the simple poetic statement of truth is the rule rather than the exception.

  ii. "Poets of the Left," *Manchester Guardian*, (March 21, 1939).

  The book includes poems of substance by Auden, MacNeice, and Warner, with a sprinkling also of translation from Spanish originals, some of which are truly felt.

S20 R.D. Harper, "Back to the Personal," *Poetry* 57(Oct. 1940), 46-49.

S21 Malcolm Cowley, "What Poets Are Saying," *Saturday Review of Literature*, 23(May 3, 1941), 3-4+.

Predicts revival of poetry and Spender's contribution to this revival would be through comradeship and the desire to honor greatness.

S22 Reviews of *Ruins and Visions* (Random House):

  i. Sheila Shannon in *Spectator*, 168(May 8, 1942), 446.

  Spender is full of self-pity and smug self-consciousness, and yet there is an engaging, almost touching, quality in some of his poems.

  ii. G.W. Stonier in *New Statesman and Nation*, 24(August 1, 1942), 79.

  By always edging towards greater things *Ruins and Visions*, in fact, enlarges its poetry, and in general Mr. Spender is better worth reading than the safe writer who compounds at a lower level.

   iii. Louis Untermeyer in *Saturday Review of Literature*, 25(September 26, 1942), 16.

Underneath all the uncertainties and easily discovered blemishes, there is the clear voice of something dearly held and deeply felt as true. Here blending tradition and experiment, is a voice of courage and there is no lesser word for it—nobility.

   vi. Warren Beck in *Poetry*, 61(Oct. 1942), 386.

"Standing undismayed amidst ruins, he knows where the sun rises; he can say with assurance that 'a wind blows hither,' that men shall be knit "into a life of joy again." At such an advent these poems would glow anew, for the poet, a gifted artist and a profoundly humane personality, has indeed signed them with his honor." Warren Beck calls this book "another milestone."

S23 D.S. Savage, "The Poet's Perspectives," *Poetry*, 64(June 1944), 148-58.

Study of Auden, Spender, and others as *Social* poets and the consequence of their social preoccupation on poetry, personality, and their perspectives.

S24 Reviews of *European Witness* (Reynal & Hamilton): 1946-1947.

   i. Goronwy Rees in *Spectator*, 177(Nov. 1, 1946), 456.

We should thank him for the best piece of reporting that has come out of Germany.

   ii. Alfred Kazin in *Weekly Book Review*, (Dec. 29, 1946), 4.

Spender is not ashamed to project his personality in his book . . . yet this is a troubled book, with a kind of visible embarrassment running through it, and, therefore, less than first-rate.

   iii. Noel Annan, *New Statesman and Nation*, 32(Nov. 16, 1946), 362.

It is reporting—the reporting mercifully of an intellectual—done with quiet humor, and in good writing that makes it an attractive book to read.

   iv. Edmund Wilson in *New Yorker*, 22(Jan. 4, 1947), 64.

Mr. Spender is a careless writer: his sentences do not always come out neatly and his grammar is sometimes bad . . . yet everything he writes has the charm of a natural appetite for the highest art and a natural sympathy with human beings. His approach is that of a human individual to other individuals.

v. Saul K. Padover in *Saturday Review of Literature*, 30(Jan. 11, 1947), 18.

"*European Witness*, despite some glaring faults, is a fascinating record and contains far and away the keenest observations on the German mind and character in recent literature."

S25   Reviews of *Poems of Dedication* (Random House): 1947:

i. Richard Church in *Spectator*, 178 (Jan. 3, 1947), 22.

Not always comprehensible. It is as though he looks upon the universe through eyes whose focus fluctuates. This results in intermittent clarity of image and stumbling of rhythm. The movement becomes disordered and his characteristic Shelley-like speed drops down like that of a spent meteor to be lost in a Rilke-like mist. When, however, the poet is most himself, it is a self that creates something remarkably beautiful . . . .

ii. *Times Literary Supplement* (Jan. 4, 1947), 6.

"Mr. Spender has an urgent contemporary quality. For the question how far the self is real or unreal, and what else is more deeply real is one widely discussed in our time. In a long, ambitious and not wholly successful poem called 'Spiritual Exercises' Mr. Spender . . . provides the answer . . . But Mr. Spender's attitude is fundamentally dualistic . . .

iii. George Mayberry in *New Republic*, 116(March 3, 1947), 33.

"Poems of Dedication, particularly in 'Elegy for Margaret,' reaches an intensity, almost an extravagance, of personal feeling that had been only latent in Spender's earlier work. Paradoxically, this emotion is enclosed in forms that may conveniently be labeled traditional. Altogether, it is an achievement, and one can only hope that its contribution to the stirrings of a poetic renaissance will be warmly recognized."

iv. Babette Deutsch in *N.Y. Herald Tribune Weekly Book Review*, (May 4, 1947), 7.

"What Spender really is . . . is a man who is working, not too successfully, but sensitively and responsively, toward an understanding of his and our difficult world. If the book is less immediately appealing than his previous work, it is because his technical ability has not kept pace with the increase in the scope and depth of his themes."

v. Selden Rodman in *Saturday Review of Literature*, 30(July 5, 1947), 24.

"As one who found (and still finds) Spender's first book of poems little less than miraculous, and who was impressed by the energy and warmth of the second, it is not pleasant to report that his third slight in substance, thin in texture, and blemished not infrequently with the kind of threadbare 'poetic' properties one would scarcely expect to encounter in the work of a careful third-rate poet."

S26 Reviews of *Returning to Vienna 1947; Nine Sketches* (Poem), Limited Autographed Edition (Banyan Press):

i. Richard Eberhart in *N.Y. Times* (Feb. 8, 1948), 4.

"The new work is artistically better than the poem of 1934, due, in one respect, to the detachment which allows integrity of meaning not confounded by a chaotic rush of events. 'Returning to Vienna 1947' speaks in Spender's purest power, which is personal, and in his purest lyrical language. I would not hazard a guess, however, as to the qualitative value thirteen years hence."

S27 Valentin Iremonger, "The Poetry of Stephen Spender," *The Bell*, 14(May 1947), 294.

Is marked by a failure of communication, yet possesses the essential poetic drive, "the awe-inspiring sincerity, and above all the fundamental brainwork." "He is not yet forty; there is no hurry."

S28 Reviews of *Edge of Being*: Poems (Random House): 1949.

i. Gerald McDonald in *Library Journal*, 74(June 15, 1949), 958.

"To me it is a high spot in his career, marked expecially by such poems as 'Returning to Vienna, 1947,' and 'Time in Our Time.'

ii. David Daiches in *New York Herald Tribune Weekly Book Review*, (June 26, 1949), 7.

"Though this volume contains no startlingly magnificent poems, it does contain a handful of impressive lyrics which show that Spender is still seriously concerned with the improvement of his poetic craftsmanship."

iii. Robert Fitzgerald in *New Republic*, 121 (August 8, 1949), 18.

"*The Edge of Being* is full of anxious rhetoric and uncertainty of vision. There are always nice lines and passages in Spender, and in this book there are some of a certain strength, as if the iron had entered in; but the lyric style that went to pieces ten or more years ago has not by brave efforts been reconstituted."

iv. Frank Jones in *Poetry*, 74(September 1949), 348-53.

"Mr Spender may be in a minor phase, but it is that of a major poet. If he perseveres in the directions of precision in subjects and of rigor in form, I can see no reason why he must remain, as he is nowadays, most moving when confessing failure to keep pace with the violent pressure of creative and uncreative times."

S29 Howard Mumford Jones, "The American Malady," *Saturday Review of Literature*, 32(Aug. 6, 1949), 24-27.

Comments on Spender's discussion of the American writer in an article in *Horizon*: "I am not wholly persuaded that the American malady is the commercialization of spiritual goods on an enormous scale, baleful though elephantiasis may be."

S30 Reviews of *World Within World*(Harcourt): 1951.

i. Mark Schorer in *New York Times* (April 8, 1951), 1.

"None of our writers now in his middle years is better equipped to make an interesting running commentary of his life than Stephen Spender, for few of them have at once been so consistently involved in public issues and so determined to maintain the lineaments of their individuality."

ii. Maurice Cranston in *Spectator*, 185 (April 13, 1951, 496.

"Mr Spender has married twice. He writes of these and related private matters with delicacy as well as candour, and it may be that such passages of his narrative will command the greatest respect from his readers. I suspect that everyone who reads the book will think kindlier of the author afterwards. I know that my own admiration has been quickened."

iii. *Times Literary Supplement* (April 13, 1951), 228.

Has written an exceptionally good book: one, moreover, which by its nice mixture of tact and candour is likely to give him an experience not often vouchsafed to those who make their introspections public—that of gaining, rather than losing, friends."

iv. V.S. Pritchett in *New Statesman and Nation*, 41(April 14, 1951), 426.

"Mr Spender's insights are better than his arguments and he is his best when he proceeds, as one would expect a poet to do, by vision. Like his earlier witness of Germany, this eye-witness account of himself makes the deep impression of a many-sided piece of nature wholly revealed."

v. "Humble Pie," *Time*, 57(April 16, 1951), 112.

Review of *World Within World*: "Here and there the gloom is pierced by a lively sense of humor that bursts out like a prisoner escaping from a dungeon; occasionally there is evidence of Spender's acute eyes and ears . . ."

Contains Spender's portrait with the caption: "Bumblebees in his blossoms."

vi. B.M.W. Knox in *Yale Review*, 40(Summer 1951), 738.

"It is a penetrating and honest, sometimes embarassingly honest, attempt to recreate the poet's life in the years 1928-39. It has the disadvantages as well as the merit of honesty, for it is sometimes exasperating, and occasionally dull."

S31 Storm Jameson, "I-British Literature: Survey and Critique," *Saturday Review of Literature*, 34(October 13, 1951), 24-26+.

Includes comments on Spender and the other Oxford poets.

S32 Anne Fremantle, "Stephen Spender," *Commonweal*, 54(May 11, 1951), 119-21.

Spender as *"Ce Shelley"*: "To day's poet can no longer choose between politics and the ivory tower, if indeed he ever could. Nor is the poetry any longer . . . "in the pity." Life cannot be seen whole except by the poet, such is the departmentalization required of journalists, novelists, biographers, and essayists. The only universal left is the distilled inscape of the poet . . . Mr. Spender is giving us so vulnerable and touching an account of the way one poet's mind and heart have grown, has performed a great service to life as well as to literature.

S33 Hubert Butler, "The Sense of Evil and the Sense of Guilt: Part Two —Stephen Spender and the sense of Social Guilt, *The Bell*, 17 (December 1951), [36] -45.

Compares Spender with Graham Greene as authors who "ought to be valuable as correctives to each other."

S34   Geoffrey Moore, "Three Who Did Not Make a Revolution," *American Mercury*, 74(April 1952), 107-114.

A critical study of three poets—Auden, Spender and Isherwood against the background of their politics. A note at the end about Spender on taking sides: quotations from Spender's essay in *The God That Failed*.

S35   Reviews of *Learning Laughter* (Harcourt): 1953.

    i.   Meyer Levin in *New York Times* (June 28, 1953), 4.

        "Unfortunately, Mr. Spender's book is only sketchily worked out. But even those who spend only a few weeks in Israel often manage to increase our knowledge of that land, so turbulent is the material, so stimulating the contact. Mr. Spender's rapid reportage has great sensitivity, and is usually devoid of preconceived enthusiasm or hostility."

    ii.   J.G. Harrison in *Christian Science Monitor* (July 14, 1953), 9.

        "It is interesting for several reasons. First, because, paradoxically, it reaches no conclusions. Second, because Mr. Spender's artistic and inquiring mind touches intelligently on a number of subjects. Third, because it stimulates thought regarding the world's newest republic and the tremendous problems which it admittedly faces."

    iii.   *Atlantic Monthly*, 192(August 1953), 88.

        "Some of what Mr. Spender saw he liked, while some of it worried him. His book is informative, varied, full of sharp vignettes. A crisp report that is sympathetic in tone but evades set intellectual conclusions."

S36   Reviews of *Creative Element*; a Study of Vision, Despair and Orthodoxy among Some Modern Writers (British Book Centre): 1953-54.

    i.   "Old Lamps and New," *Times Literary Supplement* (Nov. 27, 1953), 760.

        The review compares this book with Spender's *The Destructive Element*. While it is marked by almost the same kind of defects, it is more mature, and its conclusion is not different from his earlier work that "literature is a means of understanding the profoundest and most moral changes in the human mind."

ii. Walter Allen in *New Statesman and Nation*, 46(December 12, 1953), 765.

Not a good prose writer. "He is often, it seems, needlessly involved, needlessly obscure; 'thinking aloud' is the expression that comes to one's mind as one reads him. Yet from the very manner of his prose something of real value emerges, something immensely attractive."

iii. David Daiches in *Manchester Guardian* (Jan 15, 1954), 4.

Sloppily written book. "His ideas are interesting and helpful, but that only makes it more desirable that they should be expressed with accuracy and precision."

iv. William Blissett, *Canadian Forum*, 34(May 54), 44.

Some very good things in it. But the literary, moral and political elements are not successfully joined.

S37 Morton Seif, "The Impact of T.S. Eliot on Auden and Spender," *South Atlantic Quarterly*, 53(January 1954), 61-69.

The influence is summed up in Spender's own words: "Eliot's is a voice which seems to speak for many of his contemporaries in Europe. He may well be the greatest poetic influence in the world today.

S38 Reviews of *Collected Poems, 1928-53* (Random House).

i. *Times Literary Supplement* (Jan. 28, 1955), 56.

". . . out of fumblings, out of over-emphatic gestures, the great white bird of poetry suddenly takes wing."

ii. Anthony Hartley in *Spectator* (Jan. 28, 1955), 102.

"Mr. Spender's poetry is like a faulty electric light; sometimes it gives a fair illumination, sometimes the wires glow faintly red and sometimes nothing happens at all."

iii. Louise Bogan in *The New Yorker*, 31(April 30, 1955), 125.

"It is a virtue in Spender that he has moved steadily toward a controlled expression of the romantic spirit and has continued to find subjects . . . entirely suited to his gifts."

iv. Louis Untermeyer, "New Vigor in the Wastes," *Saturday Evening Review of Literature*, 38(March 12, 1955), 14-15.

"Now, in 'Collected Poems: 1928-53,' he gives us the works that trace his journey away from the eclectic and casual Auden, and away from the colleagues of his earlier revolt. It is a doggedly comprehensive collection."

v. Barbara Gibbs, "Where Thoughts Lash Tail and Fin," *Poetry*, 86(July 1955), 237-40.

Mr. Spender has committed many faults of taste and form. He has proclaimed *ad nauseam* that *honesty* (surely the most irrelvant of purposes to the artist) is his guiding principle.

S39 Justin Maynard Replogle, *The Auden Group: The 1930's Poetry of W.H. Auden, C. Day-Lewis, and Stephen Spender*, unpublished Ph.D. Dissertation (University of Wisconsin, 1956).

The persistent concern for society, and for the relationship of art and artist to it, suggests that the Auden group is historically significant as a representative of rather broad social and artistic changes that reached their peak of intensity in the 1930's.

S40 Willis D. Jacobs, "The Moderate Poetical Success of Stephen Spender," *College English*, 17(April 1956), 374-79.

"One is overwhelmed by the quantity done; yet the thought persists that we have from such an enormous mountain precious little mouse." This is a tentative examination "to discover, if may be, why his success as poet has been moderate, or, perhaps, even tepid."

S41 Reviews of *Enagaged in Writing* (Farrar, Straus): 1958.

i. Walter Allen in *New Statesman and Nation*, 55 (Jan. 25, 1958), 110.

An invigorating display of controlled exasperation, a splendid exposure of the pomposity and futility of men of letters who have dehumanized themselves into word-machines.

ii. Harold Hobson in *Christian Science Monitor*, (April 24, 1958), 7.

Fascinating and impressive book . . . Mr. Spender has brought to the task of composing complicated parodies of orations totally without content is amazing: it extorts admiration, and the result is extraordinarily amusing.

iii. Kingsley Amis in *Saturday Review of Literature*, 41(Sept. 13, 1958), 42.

"*Engaged in Writing*, although not totally a damp squib, fizzes and fuses with an inhibited energy."

iv. T.F. Curley in *Commonweal*, 69(Oct. 10, 1958), 55.

Mr. Spender's prose is not forceful or elegant, indeed it can be annoyingly slack, but it is usually a true prose . . . of these two novels, nevertheless, I think "The Fool and the Princess" a better work.

v. Phoebe Adams in *Atlantic Monthly*, 202 (October 1958), 93.

The second story is of no particular interest, but the first is a long account of a writers' congress staged in Venice and described with a comic deadpan fury quite unexpected of Mr. Spender.

S42 Ben Cami, "Stephen Spender—Engaged in Writing," *Nieuw Vlaams Tijdschrift*, 12:10(1958), 1103-1106.

Spender's clever satire shows him clearly engaged in political affairs (in Flemish).

S43 David O. Lipp, *The Myth of Weimar in the Works of Stephen Spender, Christopher Isherwood and W.H. Auden* (Berkeley: University of California, 1958). Unpublished Master's Thesis in Comparative Literature.

S44 Hugh Alan Nelson, *Individuals of a Group: The 1930's Poetry of W.H. Auden, C. Day Lewis, and Stephen Spender* (Evanston: Northwestern University, 1958). Unpublished Ph.D. Dissertation.

S45 *Stephen Spender: 1928-1959: Notes for an Account of His Writings* (Austin: University of Texas, 1959).

Bibliography classified under sections: 1. Books and Pamphlets, 2. Contributions to Books, 3. Translations, and 4. Contributions to Periodicals.

S46 Donna Gerstenberger, "The Saint and the Circle," *Criticism*, 2:4 (Fall 1960), 336-341.

Yeats, Eliot, and Spender have used the image of the turning wheel and fixed point.

S47 Mordecai Marcus, "Walden as Possible Source for Stephen Spender's 'The Express,' " *Thoreau Society Bulletin*, No. 75 (Spring 1961), 1.

Coincidence of detail and overtone between Spender's poem and Thoreau's description of the train in *Walden* is very remarkable. Both conceive the train to be symbolic of a "brilliant flight into the future."

S48 Robert Armstrong, "On my Right, Roy Campbell," *Critic*, 20:4 (Feb./March 1962), 18-21.

Details about the famous clash between Roy Campbell and Stephen Spender on a Monday evening in the winter of 1949 are presented.

S49 Reviews of *The Making of a Poem* (Norton): 1963.

i.   Benjamin De Mott in *Harper*, 226(Jan. 1963), 93.

Contains shrewd speculations about confessions and autobiography, a critique of modern cant about the necessity of despair, and amusing jottings on assumptions implicit in American diction. But the wirter's tone is . . . unvaryingly airy . . . And the note of self-congratulatory tolerance is depressingly blimpish in effect.

ii. M.L. Rosenthal in *New York Times Book Review* (April 28, 1963), 18.

"The making of a Poem" presents a colder spirit than I would have expected . . . His refusal of enthusiasm is a special kind of disengagement from a purely subjectivist absorption in esthetic values for their own sake.

iii. John Berryman, "Spender: The Poet as Critic," *New Republic*, 148(June 29, 1963), 19-20.

Candor has long been known as one of Spender's chief notes, both as a writer and as a man, and it looks forth at us, tranquil and friendly, everywhere in this collection of his recent criticism. It has come under reproach for a pose. Whether it is or not, it serves him well.

iv. Charles Tomlinson in *Poetry*, 102(August 1963), 344.

This is not a particularly distinguished book. It moves from flashily journalistic onsets . . . on to that appearance of omniscience in matters of art . . .

S50 Reviews of *The Struggle of the Modern* (University of California Press), 1963.

    i.   Donald Davie in *New Statesman*, 65 (March 29, 1963), 465.

> "I want to be on Spender's side, but I can't be—the argument is too loose at the joints, too slack or wrong whenever it descends to particulars, the tone is too casually and confidently amateur. In theory I'm with him and his moderns but when Spender makes the modern case he can only alienate just those we need to win over.

    ii.   *Newsweek*, 61(June 17, 1963), 94.

> The English poet and man of letters Stephen Spender is a splendidly sane, knowing, and modest guide among the great confusions of the modern literary scene.

    iii.   Lawrance Thompson in *N.Y. Herald Tribune Books* (June 23, 1963), 3.

> The essays do not make for easy reading. But they reward the patient effort required of anyone who will stay with Spender's provocative and exasperating prose style.

S51 Reviews of *The Concise Encyclopedia of English and American Poets and Poetry*, edited by Stephen Spender and Donald Hall (Hawthorn Books): 1963-64.

    i.   Robert Cayton in *Library Journal*, 88(May 15, 1963), 1990.

> Though the stress is on the "concise," the editors achieve a wonder of poetic criticism and biography. Highly recommended for college and high school libraries.

    ii.   C.G. in *American Literature*, 35(Jan. 1964), 566.

> A handsomely printed and ornamented collection . . . . A competent editor selected from the ranks of scholars could have improved this book with only a little effort.

S52 Justin Replogle, "The Auden Group," *Wisconsin Studies in Contemporary Literature*, 5:1(Winter/Spring, 1964), 133-150.

While the group began collecting itself in the early 20's, it was not until 1932 that Auden, Day-Lewis, and Spender could legitimately be called a literary group. Further, their early enthusiasm for individualism, their shifts to Marxism, and subsequent modifications demonstrate the group's sharing of experiences and beliefs about man and society, and reveal the thematic correspondence of their art.

S53 Peter Lowbridge, "The Spanish War," *Review: A Magazine of Poetry and Criticism*, 11-12(1964), 42-50.

In a sense no real war poetry was written. For writers of the *Left Review* poems represented fighting by proxy.

S54 K. Viswanathan, "Metaphor and Modernity in Metaphor—II," *Aryan Path*, 35:8(August 1964), 355-362.

Eliot, Spender, Day-Lewis, and Auden are among modern poets drawing upon life of their time for fresh and newly meaningful metaphors. Different though their poetry may be, it is worthwhile.

S55 David Lodge, "The Critical Moment 1964," *Critical Quarterly*, 6:3 (Autumn 1964), 266-274.

Includes comments on *The Struggle of the Modern*: Contemporary criticism is rejecting the critical orthodoxies associated with Eliot, Richards, and Leavis and is developing an independent intellectual discipline.

S56 Ellis A. Wunsch, *Stephen Spender: Critic of Modern Literature* (University of Michigan, 1964).

Unpublished Ph.D. dissertation which analyzes the nature, practice, and quality of Spender's criticism of modern literature.

S57 Reviews of *Selected Poems* (Random House), 1965.

i. Chad Walsh in *Saturday Review of Literature*, 48(Jan. 2, 1965), 28.

The intellectual and technical brilliance of W.H. Auden has overshadowed the other "Oxford Poets." Literary histories often treat Spender as a kind of footnote to Auden. He is not good in what Auden excels. But he is best in gentle, ruminative poems on love, personal relationships, and the quiet inter-course between man and nature.

ii. Webster Scott in *Christian Science Monitor* (May 20, 1965), 7.

Reads like a diary of metaphors. An autobiography searching for forms to express himself.

iii. William Stafford in *Poetry*, 106(July 1965), 294-95.

Tuneful writing. Eloquent record . . . "Where he is caught up in a current experience of his time, he is supremely moving, and delivers some of the best of all modern poems."

S58 W.H. Sellers, "Wordsworth and Spender: Some Speculations on the Use of Rhyme," *Studies in English Literature*, 1500-1900, 4 (Autumn 1965), 641-650.

Examination of Wordsworth's and Spender's poems reveals that they eschew rhyme when they wish to express great and intense thoughts and feelings, substituting various other devices to harmonize thought and effect. They use rhyme when they wish to develop other effects.

S59 James L. Potter, " 'The Destined Pattern' of Spender's 'Express,' " *College English*, 27:5(February 1966), 426-429.

A study of the successive drafts of Spender's "The Express" reveals how frequently works of literature have "to emerge from within" themselves through their "own working out."

S60 James Hazard, "Stephen Spender: The Poet and the Machine," *Wisconsin Studies in Literature*, no 3(1966), 57-66.

Spender rejected the traditionalist view that mechanical products have no relevance for poetry. He accepts the technological age and responds imaginatively to it. His poetry of the machine gains authenticity and strength through its engagement with the actual world.

S61 A.T. Tolley, *The Early Published Poems of Stephen Spender: A Chronology* (Ottawa: Carleton University, 1967), 18 pages.

This is a listing of Spender's published short poems up to 1934 arranged in a chronological order of composition.

S62 J.J. Connors, *Poets and Politics: A Study of the Careers of C.Day-Lewis, Stephen Spender, and W.H. Auden in the 1930's* (Yale University Press, 1967).

Deals with the political involvement of three left-wing English poets individually and provides a lengthy background chapter on Oxford University during the 1920's.

S63 J.R. Parbs, *Individuality and Related Themes in the Poetry of Stephen Spender* (University of Wisconsin, 1967).

Unpublished Ph.D. dissertation: The purpose of this study is to examine thoroughly the nature and development of Spender's thought in his poetry and to illustrate the relationship which exists among the several themes that have preoccupied him since 1928.

S64　W.H. Sellers, "Spender and Vienna," *Humanities Assocoation Bulletin*, 18:1(Apring 1967), 59-68.

The two Vienna poems provide a revealing index of Spender's development as a poet.

S65　A.T. Tolley, "The Printing of Auden's POEMS (1928) and Spender's NINE EXPERIMENTS," *Libarary*, 22:2(June 1967), 149-50.

Spender printed both volumes in the summer of 1928, although his own accounts are inconsistent (because he was confused as to the date of Auden's leaving Oxford.).

S66　Philip L. Gerber and Robert J. Gemmett, "A Conversation with Stephen Spender: The Creative Process," *English Record*, 18:4 (April 1968), 2-10.

Spender thinks of the topic and method of the poem at the same time, though other poets use other habits. American poets have a more public sense than do British ones etc.

S67　Margherita Leardi, "La Poesia di Stephen Spender," *English Miscellany*, 19(1968), 205-50.

Spender's first publication, *Poems* (1933) is really a manifesto of his spiritual isolation from modern life. Images, such as glass, which are recurring symbols of isolation, form the central impulse of his poetry. In the mid-30's he tried to write contemporary poetry through the use of mechanistic imagery, natural language, and sympathy for the poor, and the war-victims in Spain. In later poems he becomes private again. Unfortunately his inner world lacked enough force of real life to provide a reliable source of energy for developing his poetry (In Italian).

S68　Prescott Evarts, *The Struggle of a Poet: A Study of Stephen Spender's Development in the Thirties* (Columbia University, 1968), 229 pages.

Unpublished Ph.D. dissertation: How Spender's preoccupation with his isolation in the modern world and his desire to overcome it and change the world affects his literary development.

S69   Derek Stanford, *Stephen Spender, Louis MacNeice, and Cecil Day-Lewis: A Critical Essay* (Grand Rapids: Eerdmans, 1969), 48 pages.

Part of a series on contemporary writers in Christian perspective: "All that is most positive in Spender's poetry would seem to spring from gestures of imaginative and emotional charity . . . A sensitive agnostic." Contains a select bibliography.

S70   Reviews of *The Year of the Young Rebels* (Random House): 1969.

i.   *T.L.S.* (May 22, 1969), 558.

Probably the best book yet on student revolt—sensitive, carefully written, well-informed and thoughtful. . . . With a poet's insight into human motives, together with a natural sympathy for young rebels . . . Mr. Spender is very well-equipped to give the student revolt its due.

ii.   H.D. Beck in *American Scholar*, 38 (Autumn 1969), 725.

If students say that the older generation does not understand them, one might ask, "Who well do you understand yourself?" Spender resolves the querry . . .

S71   Dan Wakefield, "The Literature of Student Revolt: An Early Appraisal," *Denver Quarterly*, 4:3(Autumn 1969), 1-22.

Spender's *The Year of the Young Rebels* errs on the side of detachment.

S72   H.B. Kulkarni, *Stephen Spender: Poet in Crisis* (Glasgow: Blackie & Son Ltd., 1970), 194 pages.

Contents: I. Hamlet of the Thrities, II. Sticks for the Dahlias, III. Centre and Circumference, IV. Selected Bibliography. Studies Spender's works against the background of political, social, domestic, and personal crises.

S73   Rose Kamel, *The Making of a Poem: A Stylistic Study of the Pre-War Poetry of Stephen Spender* (Temple University, 1971).

Unpublished Ph.D. dissertation: Study of Spender's stylistic development and the impulses behind it.

S74   Dolores J.J. Stewart, *Politics and Imagination: The Worlds of Stephen Spender* (The University of Tulsa, 1971).

Unpublished Ph.D. dissertation: "A double commitment exists in Spender's work. On the one hand he turns to the political world and to social themes; on the other he turns to a more imaginative world and to more personal themes."

S75   A.K. Weatherhead, "Stephen Spender: Lyric Impulse and Will," *Contemporary Literature*, 12(Autumn 1971), 450-65.

S76   Reviews of *The Generous Days* (Random House): 1971.

    i.   Alan Brownjohn in *New Statesman* 82(Dec. 3, 1971), 791.

       There is something new after this long hesitation which makes me wish Spender had broken his silence earlier.

    ii. *T.L.S.* (Dec. 31, 1971), 1629.

       This collection draws, potentially, on the products of more than twenty years. But it is a slim offering from such a time span.

S77   Jeffrey C. Sekula, *The Role of Ramanticism in Stephen Spender's Criticism and Poetry: A Study in Artistic Vision* (University of Tennessee, 1972).

Unpublished Ph.D. dissertation.

S78   John Gruen, *"An Interview with Stephen Spender,"* Vogue, 160 (Nov. 15, 1972), 55+.

Spender talks about Auden, Isherwood, Virginia Woolf, women, sex, and the lessons of being alive.

S79   Reviews of *D.H. Lawrence: Novelist, Poet, Prophet*, edited by Spender, 1973.

    i.   *Economist*, 249(Nov. 3, 1973), 134.

       Lawrence's reputation as a guru will not be enhanced by this collection of essays . . . What it may well succeed in doing . . . is whet the newcomer's curiosity.

    ii. *T.L.S.* (Nov. 9, 1973), 1369.

       The vogue for "coffee-table" books may deter some readers from examining this volume.

S80   Philip Waldron, "T.S. Eliot, Mr. Whitside, and the Psychobiographical Approach," *Southern Review*, 6:2(June 1963), 138-147.

Comments, among other things, on Spender's position in this approach.

S81   Mirko Jurak, "Dramaturgic Concepts in the English Group Theatre: The Totality of Artistic Involvement," *Modern Drama*, 16:1(June 1973), 81-86.

The contribution of the Group Theatre to dramaturgical advances in England during the 30's, its experimentation and social commitment: W.H. Auden and Stephen Spender were most active in this movement.

S82   Reviews of *Love-Hate Relations: English and American Sensibilities* (Random House): 1974.

     i.   *Economist*, 251(May 25, 1974), 139.

        . . . a deeply satisfying book to read and to re-read.

     ii.   M.G. Perloff in *New Republic*, 170(June 29, 1974), 19.

        Spender's discussion of the peculiar tensions that characterize our literary scene . . . is consistently illuminating. When he can draw on his personal experience of America, he reacts with tact, insight, and sound judgment.

S83   Reviews of *W.H. Auden: A Tribute*, edited by Spender (Macmillan) 1975.

     i.   *Economist*, 254(March 29, 1975), 128.

        Spender has discharged the office of a true friend . . . the composite portrait built up in this book is a touching one . . .

     ii.   Judy Mimken in *Library Journal*, 100(May 1, 1975), 845.

        This is a lively book. It is more biography than criticism. This book may seem a luxury to some libraries because of its price.

S84   A.K. Weatherhead, *Stephen Spender and the Thirties* (Lewisburg, Pa.: Bucknell University Press, 1975), 241 pages.

Contents: 1. Spender's Two Worlds, 2. Politics in the Literary Scene, 3. Political Poetry, 4. Repudiating the Georgians, 5. Observations, 6. Technique, Imitation, and Self-Consciousness, 7. Spender's Volumes of Verse, 8. Stephen Spender—Selected Bibliography.

Note: "Spender's poetry has been neglected on account of its purity." The author wants to compensate for this neglect in this book about his works. The book tries to place the poetry in the context of other poets and considers his poetry volume by volume and lead the reader to "the heart of the matter."

INDEX

Only Spender's works and their criticism, excluding those he has edited or introduced, have been indexed. Books and pamphlets have been set in capital letters. Titles of poems and articles have been placed within quotation marks. The initial articles like a, an, and the in the items have not been considered for their alphabetical order. "r" stands for review.

INDEX

critique," S31.
"Bubu of Montparnasse (r)," C334.
"Buonaparte (tr.)," C41.
"Burning, burning image . . . ," D83.
THE BURNING CACTUS, A9; D7; S10.
"The burning cactus," C6.
"But supposing anxiety . . . real," D90.
"Buying this notebook in a Venice shop," D48.
"By the lake," D8.

C

"The cactus field," D44.
"The calm that burns in dark shrines . . . ," D57.
"Can poetry be reviewed?" C486.
"Can't we do without the poets?" BN68.
"Can we do without the poets?" BN70.
"Can unesco succeed?" C257.
"A careful box of instruments," D71.
"Case for constructive peace," C42.
"The case of Herbert Read (r)," C155.
"A catholic on the jews (r)," C126.
"Center of critical values (excerpts)," C480.
"Central heating system," A44.
"A certificate of sanity," C483.
"Chairman," C468.
"The chalk blue butterfly," A44, D67.
"A change of air," C444.
"The change of heart (r)," C141.
CHAOS AND CONTROL IN POETRY, A42.
"Character of Lloyd George," C322.
"Chief glory," C259.
"The child," C232.

"Child falling asleep . . . ," A44; D67, 74.
"A childhood," A17, BN35.
"Children who fear the dark . . . ," D57.
A CHOICE OF ENGLISH ROMANTIC POETRY (ed.), B16.
A CHOICE OF SHELLEY'S VERSE (ed.), B43.
"Chosen people," C325.
"A Christmas anthology (ed.)," C222.
"Christopher Fry," C300.
"Churchill," DI-3.
"Citizenship and C.D.," C195.
CITIZENS IN WAR–AND AFTER, A20.
"Civilization," D5.
"Close to you here . . . ," D46.
"The coast," A17.
"The cocktail party," B23.
"Cold," C296.
COLLECTED POEMS, A32, D9.
"Collected poems 1928-1953 (r)," S38.
"Collected poems of Harold Munro (r)," C13.
"Collected poems of W. B. Yeats (r)," D10.
"Collected shorter poems (r)," C301.
"Come, let us praise the gasworks," A1.
"Comment," C238.
"The common reader (r)," C11; D11, 44.
"A communication," C61.
"Concerning the label 'emigrant' (tr.)," C77.
THE CONCISE ENCYCLOPEDIA OF ENGLISH AND AMERICAN POETS AND POETRY (ed.)," B34, (reviews) S51.
"Conferencier," A44, D73.
"The connecting imagination,"

BN73, C410.

"The conscript," A25; C224, 226; D75, DI-15.

"Constant April," A2.

"The contemporary subject," BN82.

"Context," C418.

A conversation with Stephen Spender: The creative process," S66.

"The core of the day," D65.

"The corroded charred . . . ," D90.

"Covered, covered with that will," D43.

"The coward," A14, 15, 32.

THE CREATIVE ELEMENT, A29; BN95; reviews, S36.

"The creative imagination in the world today," C147.

"The creative spirit-I," C189.

"The creative spirit in new writing-II," C197.

"The cries of evening," A32.

"The crisis of symbols," C207.

"The critical moment 1964," S55.

"A czech poet (r)," C213.

D

"Dame Edith Sitwell's show (r)," C461.

"Dancing burning image of self projected," D43.

"Dante in English," C103.

DANTON'S DEATH (tr.), B9.

"Dark(ness) and light," A14, 15, 32.

"Darling of our hearts . . . ," A32.

"Daybreak," A15, 17, 32; BN18; C183.

"A day that makes all squares and circles," D64.

"The dead island," D12.

"Dearest and nearest brother," A23, 32.

"Dear friend, your world is the antipodes," A15.

"Dear me, dear dust . . . ," D64.

"Dear scattered flesh," D67.

"The death of heroes," A6.

"De la Mare," C14.

"Delirious oratory," D71.

DESCARTES, A45.

"Descartes,' ' A44; D46, 73.

"The destined pattern of Spender's 'Express,' " S59.

"Destruction invents," D90.

THE DESTRUCTIVE ELEMENT, A8; D112; reviews, S8.

"The destructive element—an excerpt," BN33.

"Deus ex machina," C107.

D. H. LAWRENCE . . . (ed.), B46; reviews S79.

"D. H. Lawrence, England and the war," B46.

"The D. H. Lawrence myths," D74.

"D. H. Lawrence: Phoenix," C48.

"D. H. Lawrence was born a perfect little Oedipus," D67.

"Dialogue between superman and the devil," D43.

"Dialogue for a play,' ' D45.

Diary, D77.

Diary 1925, D13.

Diary of journey to Israel, D14.

"Different living is not living in different places," A2, 3, 15, 32; BN12.

"The disciple: after Stefan George," A31.

"Discovered in mid-ocean," A2.

"Disinterestedness of war workers," C187.

"Dismantling politics," C391.

"Dissection of empires . . . ," D90.

"Doctor of science and patient of poetry," C415.

"Does the English writer have a chance?" C309.

"Dog rose," C354.

"Doing anything and everything is a drug," C151.

"Do the claims of conscience outweigh the duties of citizenship," C477.

"A double debt to Yeats," C374, S5.

"The double shame," A15, 17, 32; BN12, 17, 29, 37, 70, 77; C133; R3.

"Do we not appear . . . ," D79.

"Dostoevsky's ninth symphony (r)," C306.

"Draft of the first five sections of part one: pronouns of this time," C441.

"Dramaturgic concepts in the English group theatre: the totality of artistic involvement," S81.

"The dream," A23, 32.

"Dream no dream," D67.

"Driving through Connecticut," D67.

"The drowned," A17, 32; C139.

DUINO ELEGIES, B7.

"Dusk," A17, 32; BN17; C174.

"The dust made flesh," A2.

"Dylan Thomas (r)," C285.

"Dylan Thomas-November 1953," A32; R3.

E

"Each morning . . . we feel," D42.

THE EARLY PUBLISHED POEMS OF STEPHEN SPENDER: A CHRONOLOGY, S61.

"The early summer prepares its green heart," D57.

Early work poems, D15.

"Ears stopped with wax . . . ," D5.

"Earth-treading stars . . . ," A15; R4.

"Easter Monday," A14, C34.

ÉCRITS POLITIQUES, A10.

THE EDGE OF BEING, A25; reviews, S28.

"Edith Sitwell," D16.

"Elegy for Margaret," A23, 32; BN37, 56, 70, 77; R3, 10.

"An elementary school class-room in a slum," A14, 15, 32; BN9, 57; C26; R1, 10.

"Eleven bagatelles," A44.

"E. M. Forster," D17.

"Empty house," A25, 32; BN97; C273.

"Encounter," C347.

ENCOUNTERS, B36.

"The enemy to the stars (r)," C10.

ENGAGED IN WRITING, A35; D50, 51.

"Engaged in writing," C381, 382; S41.

"'English and American writers . . . ," D84.

"English intellectuals and the world today," BN67; C313.

"English light and German dream," C402.

"English painting in the fifties," BN27, 50; C351.

"An English woman in Austria," C27.

"Epilogue," BN1.

"Epilogue to a human drama," A15, 20, 25, 32; BN22, 51.

"Epistle (near the canal)," A1.

"Epithalamion," A25.

"Escapists live on borrowed time," C156.

"Essay on communist experience in Kerala," D42.

"Essay on Goethe," D68.

"An essay on literature," D66.

"Essay on modern society and truth," D41.

"Essential Housman (r)," C131.

EUROPE IN PHOTOGRAPHS, B24.

"Freud and Marx," C37.
"From a diary," C396.
"From all these events . . . ," A3, 32; B N5, 6, 36.
"From an earlier notebook: 'I wonder whether anyone . . . ,' " D46.
"From a notebook: 'For this for which you care the most,' " D46.
"From a notebook, 1948: 'You said you always like them . . . ," D46.
"From a tree choked by ivy, rotted," A23, 32, DI-5.
"From elegy for Margaret . . . ," R3.
"From England: War and the Writer," C179.
"From enshrinement of the ideal: Part IV: Gilles," A1.
"From my journal-1929," D18.
"From 1961 notebook," D46.
"From Rhineland journal," BN47.
"From September journal," BN47.
From "spiritual explorations," BN62.
"The funeral," A3, 32; BN11, 72.
"The future of Shelley," D19.

G

"Gardner," A31; D70.
"The gay man with putty features," D46.
THE GENEROUS DAYS, A44; reviews, S76.
"The generous days," BN86; C416, 424; D48, 67, 73, 74.
German diary, D58.
"German impressions and conversations," C254.
German journal, D58.
"German muse (r)," C332.
German romanticist (r)," C338.
"Germany," D20, 21.
"Germany after the war (r)," C17.

"Germany in Europe," C249.
"Gertrude Stein," D22.
"Getting up in a foreign inn," D46.
GHIKA (ed.), B37.
"Ghosts of a renascence," C349.
GOD THAT FAILED (Spender's essay in), B19.
"Goethe and the English mind," BN40.
"Goethe, the great European," C297.
"The golden bowl," BN24.
"The good gray poet," D23.
GREAT GERMAN STORIES (ed.), B32.
GREAT WRITINGS OF GOETHE (ed.), B29.
"The Greeks in the black-out (r)," C120.
"Graves superieur (r)," C146.
"Grocer's wine (r)," C88.

H

"The half of life (tr.)," C40.
"A hall of mirrors," A17.
"Hammer your thoughts . . . ," D57.
"Hampstead autumn," A14, C73.
"The happy few loose . . . ," D43.
"Have English writers marked time?" C248.
"The hawk," R10.
"Healing dreams (r)," C231.
"Hearing from its cage," A2; B3.
"Hear this voice," C78.
"A heaven-printed world," A32.
"Heine in English (r)," C71.
"Henry James and the contemporary subject," A8.
"Her dream," D75.
"Here at the centre of the turning year," DI-6.
"Here man wakes . . . ," DI-7.
"Here my concentration . . . ," D5.
"Here there are appetites," D64.

"Here where the whole Pacific . . . ," D46.

"Heroes in Spain," C53.
"Her wonder colored eyes," D47.
"He saw his life was a trick," D64.
"He will watch the hawk . . . ," A3, 15, 32; BN3, 72; R3.

"High-brow fireman (r)," C177.
"A high-pitched scream," C442.
"Hiroshima rebuilt," A36, C408.
"His figure passes," A2.
"His head is caught in a net," D90.
"Hoelderlin," C106; R3.
"Hoelderlin, Goethe and Germany," C205.

"Hoelderlin—Heidelberg," D67.
"Hoelderlin's old age," A14, 15, 32; R3.

"The holy devil," D24.
"Honey-bubblings of the boilers (r)," C121.

"Honey now I've loved thee," D67.
"Horatio hits back (r)," C258.
"The Horizon decade," C301.
"Horizon and Cyril Connolly," C308.

"Houses at the edge of railway lines," A14, BN20.
"The houses fronting the railway lines," C111.

"How can I piece together," D57.
"How much should a biographer tell? C438.

"How shall we be saved (r)," C127.
"How strange it seems," A15.
"How strangely this sun reminds me of my love," A3, 32.
"How to identify a poet," C439.
"The human condition," C99.
"Human drama," A15.
"The human situation," A14, 15.
"The hydra-headed, the writhing nest of the ocean," D65.

I

"I am conditioned by this time," D65.
"I am glad I met you on the edge," D57.
"I am that witness through whom the whole," A19, 23.
"I am the victim of all your arrangements," D65.
"An 'I' can never be a great man," A2, 3, 32; BN7, 12; C28; R1, 3, 10.
"Icarus," A15.
"Ice," A25, 32; BN9, 87; C281; R3.
"I demand the ultimate death," C70.
"Identity," D67.
"I envy the painter the palate of his eyes," D65.
"If A is able to prove . . . ," D79.
"If it were not for that . . . ," A44, C447, 472; D48, 67, 73, 74.
"If it were not so," R5.
"If it were not too late," BN14; C43; DI-8; R5.
"If you are underestimated," D48.
"I hear the cries of evening," A2, 3; BN4, 12.
"I hear the noise of evening," DI-9.
"I knew it now . . . ," D46.
"I know a wild race," D52.
"I know I must tell the world," D71.
"I know one day," D71.
"I look at Matthew's child," D74.
"Images in the poetic world of Edith Sitwell," BN34.
THE IMAGINATION IN THE MODERN WORLD, A40.
"Imagists and realists," C430.
"The immense advantage," C481; D25.
"The immigration in reverse," C413.

J

"Japanese observations-I" C385.
"Jewel-winged almond tree," D67.
"Jewish writers and the English literary tradition," C293.
"The jews we deserve (r)," C113.
JOURNAL—1932, D27.
JOURNAL—1939, D28.
Journal entries, D61.
Journal entries, D64.
Journal entries—1965, D63.
JOURNALS—1944-62, D29.
"The journey," A17, C184.
"Journey to India: journal," D53, 60.
"Judas Iscariot," A25; C278; D6, 65.
"June 1940," A17, 32; C152, 170, 201.
"June 1950: . . . ," D5.

K

"Karl," D44.
"Keats and Shelley," BN10.
"Kyoto," C408.

L

"The labourer in the vineyards," BN35, C263.
"Ladies and gentlemen," D72, DI-12.
"Lamp, table, slant ceiling," D67.
"The lamp, the chair, the slant ceiling," D65.
"Landscape," C68.
"The landscape near an aerodrome," A3, 15, 32; BN12, 29, 37, 51, 57, 61, 62, 70, 99; DI-17; R1, 10.
"La poesia di Stephen Spender," S67.
"Lawrence and James," D30.
LEARNING LAUGHTER, A28; re-views, S35.
"The left wing orthodoxy," C96; D31.
"Leishman's translation of Rilke," D32.
"Les Baux and the pleasures of Provence," C471.
"Lessons of poetry (r)," C211.
"Letter from Edinburgh," C427.
"Letter from G.O.M.," C122.
"The letters of D. H. Lawrence," D112.
"Letter to a colleague in America," C149.
"Letter to Arthur Calder-Marshall," C159.
"Letter to a young writer: brilliant Athens and us," C350.
"Let us not be monolithic, too," C317.
Letter to *Pravda,* D89.
"Liberal anti-communism," C458.
"Liberal individualism," C44.
"Libretto of Rasputin: notes," D62.
LIEUTENANT OLIVEIRO: a play in 4 acts, D49.
LIFE AND THE POET, A18.
"Life of literature," C279.
THE LIFE OF THE VIRGIN MARY (tr.), B22.
"Light," A23, DM-XXI.
"The light in the window . . . ," DI-18.
"Like quartz is she . . . ," D90.
"Lines for Edith Sitwell," BN19, 22; C202, 220; D75.
"Lines written when walking down the Rhine," C2.
"Literary London: A tight little isle," B39; BN85.
"Literature," BN89.
"Literature and public events," C194.
"The literature of student revolt: an early appraisal," S71.

"Modern as vision of the whole," BN94.

"Modern German poetry: 1910-1950 (r)," C420.

"Modern Germany," D37.

"Modern literature," D38.

"Modern poets and reviewers," C188.

"Moderns and contemporaries," C429.

"Modern satire and tradition (r)," C24.

"Modern world," D39.

"Modern writers in the world of necessity," C236.

"The moment transfixes the space which divides," C60.

"Moods and reactions (r)," C243.

"Moon," A44; D67.

"The moon sinks and the pleiades," D48.

"Morale and short term education," C186.

"A morality (r)," C466.

"A morality play with no morals (r)," C130.

"The morning road . . . ," B5.

"Mosquito," A44; D73.

"The most ecstatic poetry ever written," C393.

"Moving through the silent crowd," A3, 15, 32; C5.

"Mr. Leavis's essays (r)," C50.

"Mr. MacNeice's poems (r)," C35.

"Mr. Spender and the CIA," C455.

"Mr. Yeats's vision (r)," C76.

"Murry on Blake (r)," C20.

"Music and decay (r)," C46.

"My beloved friend . . . ," D5.

"My brother Louis (tr.)," C67.

"My child came home," BN58.

"My cousin Maccabeus," DI-13.

"My credo: on the function of criticism," C323.

"My English writing runs behind your eyes," D67.

"My life as German and jew (r)," D40.

"My parents kept me from children who were rough," A3, 32; BN12, 23, 57, 60; C25; R3, 10.

"My parents quarrel in the neighbour room," A3.

"THE MYTH OF WEIMAR IN THE WORKS OF STEPHEN SPENDER," S43.

"The mythological nature of the life of D. H. Lawrence," D74.

N

"Napoleon in 1814," A14, 15; BN18.

"Near the snow," C135.

"The need for roots (r)," C434.

"Never being . . . ," A3, 32; BN36, 72.

"A new force in English poetry," S2.

"New leaders in English poetry," S16.

"New novels (r)," C326, 329, 330, 331, 333, 334, 335.

"The new orthodoxies," B27; BN50; C342, 343.

"New poems and reprints (r)," C163.

"New poetry (r)," C57.

THE NEW REALISM, A13.

"New verse," BN14.

"New year," A3.

NINE EXPERIMENTS, A1.

"1943: To be or not to be," C439.

"The 1930's and after," D55.

"Nocturne," A15, 32; C339; D5, 70.

"No, not a word," A3, 32.

"No one is perfection, yet," D65.

"No Orpheus, no Eurydice," A17, 32; C170, 209.

"The north," BN9; C30.

"Notebook-I," C489.

"O slave of time . . . ," D43.
"O solitude of light," D43.
"O that girl . . . ," D5.
"O then at the crowd's center," D71.
"O their opening O," D65.
"The other side of the Nazi medal," C109.
"Our six year old daughter lies," D70.
"Out of the enormity of space," D67.
"Out of the envelope," D46; D64.
"Outside the eternal star-tall mountains . . . ," A19, 23.
"Outside the registry office," D5.
"Ovation for spring," A1.
"Oxford and Germany," C292.
"Oxford English club: notes for a talk," D52.
"Oxford to communism," C66.
"O yes, o yes, ye people," D71.
"O you whose childhood lies about you," D57.

P

"Pages from a journal," C359.
"Parade of the executive," A6.
"A parallel world," C488.
"Paris (tr.)," B15.
"Passing men are sorry for birds . . . ," A3, 32.
PASTOR HALL AND BLIND MAN'S BLUFF (tr.), B6.
"Past values," A14.
"The pattern of error (r)," C299.
PAUL ELUARD (LE DUR DESIR), tr., B21.
Pencil sketches, D64.
"Pen, ink and paper," D57.
"The P.E.N. shelter," C193.
"Perfection," C214.
PERHAPS, A4.
"Perhaps," A3, 15, 32.

"Personal anthology," BN47.
"Peronified corsair (r)," C302.
"Photograph of a dead friend," D73.
"Picasso's Guernica," C98.
"Pictures in Spain," C58.
"Pictures in Switzerland," C115.
PIERNO THE UNICORN, D81.
"The pilot who destroyed Germany, spring 1945," A25; BN63.
"A play on Oliver," D78.
"Pledges of blessing—Goethe," D67.
POEM, A5, S1.
"Poem: 'even whilst I watch him . . . ' " BN8, C111.
"Poem: 'if it were not too late,' " BN14.
"Poem in four movements," C364.
"A poem on Dickens," D6.
POEMS, A3; BN13; S1.
POEMS: F. GARCIA LORCA (tr.), B10.
POEMS FOR SPAIN, B8; reviews, S19.
POEMS OF DEDICATION, A23; reviews, S25.
THE POEMS OF P. B. SHELLEY (ed.), B42.
"Poems of Rilke (r)," D86.
"Poet," D70.
"The poetic dramas of W. H. Auden and Christopher Isherwood," C90.
"A poetic tribute (r)," C230.
"Poetic vision and modern literature," R8.
"Poetry and expressionism," C74.
"Poetry and life," D88.
"Poetry and marxism," S14.
"Poetry and mass observation," C79.
"Poetry and pity," A8.
"Poetry and revolution," B5; BN2; D44.

"Poetry and the social revolution," S18.

"Poetry for poetry's sake and poetry beyond poetry," BN31.

"Poetry in 1941 (r)," C160.

"Poetry in this war," D87.

"Poetry of power," S4.

"The poetry of Stephen Spender," R9; S27.

POETRY SINCE 1939, A22.

"Poetry vs. language engineering (r)," C399.

Poets and critics: the forgotten difference," C437.

POETS AND POLITICS: A STUDY OF THE CAREERS OF C. DAY LEWIS, STEPHEN SPENDER AND W. H. AUDEN IN 1930'S, S62.

"The poet's maturity (r)," C200.

"Poets of two wars (r)," C153.

"The poet's perspectives," S23.

"The poet's task," D28.

"Polar exploration," A14, 15, 32; BN75.

"A political generation," A44; D73.

"Political truth in practice," C395.

POLITICS AND IMAGINATION: THE WORLD OF STEPHEN SPENDER, S74.

"Politics and literature in 1933," C21.

"Pomp and circumstance," C114.

"Poor girl, inhabitant of a strange land," A23, 32; BN9, 70.

"The port," A2, 3, 32; C2.

"Port Bou," A14, 15, 32; B8; BN23; C95.

"Portraits by Desmond MacCarthy (r)," C7.

"The power and the hazard (r)," C72, 266.

"Powys (r)," D91.

"Prague dressed in light (tr.)," C204.

"The predatory jailer (r)," C340.

"The pre-Raphaelite literary painters," C241, 247.

"The pre-Raphaelite painters," BN100.

"Prescriptions for a masterpiece," C245.

"Present absence," A44; D73.

"Present fears are less than horrible imaginings," D57.

"Printed world," A32.

"The printing of Auden's POEMS (1928) and Spender's NINE EXPERIMENTS," S65.

"The prisoners," A3, 15, 32; BN9, 36; C5; R10.

"The problem of freedom today," C307.

"The problem of sincerity (r)," C398.

"Problems of the poet and public," C1.

"The process of art and the direction of life," D92.

"Pronouns in this time," C433, 441; D48.

"Proof of selected poems," D71.

"The purposes of Stephen Spender," S7.

"The pylons," A3, 15, 32; BN12, 51, 72; R1.

Q

"Quaker ways (r)," D93.

"Questionnaire: the cost of letters," C253.

"Question of identity," D67, 73.

"Quixote on time," B2.

R

"Rainer Maria Rilke," C91.

"Reading your travel book posthumous (To Rose Macaulay)," D46.

"September journal," BN27, 47; C128, 129, 134.
"Seriously unserious (r)," C315.
"The shadow of a war," A15.
"Shadowless light," D47, 83; DM-I, II, III, IV, XV, XVI, XVII, XVIII, XIX.
"Shadowless sun," DM-V, VII.
"Shakespeare: a personal view," C440.
"Shapes of death haunt life," A3, 32; BN5, 7, 60; C23; DI-20.
"The sharp dew frozen to stars," A3, 15, 32.
"She came in from the snowing air," D65.
SHELLEY, A27.
"Shelley, M.P. (r)," C318.
"Shelley plain (r)," C85.
"Shelley would have loved the wireless," D6.
"The sheltered muse (r)," C49.
"She walked by the river," D57.
"Shining edge of a plough," D57.
"The short poems (tr.)," C41.
"Since we are what we are . . . ," A19, 23, 32.
SIRMIONE PENINSULA, A30.
"Sirmione peninsula," A32; BN23.
"The situation of modern poetry seen from today," D55.
Sketches for RUINS AND VISIONS, D45.
Sketches in pencil, D64.
Sketches of TRIAL OF A JUDGE, D44.
Sketch for another sonnet, D46.
Sketch for a play, D59.
Sketch for a poem on a photograph . . . ,D46.
Sketch for cantata from the war 1944, D67.
"Sleepless," A44; C475.
"Smooth the sheet down," D48.
"Social purpose and the integrity of the artist," BN74.

"So even King George in his place," D71.
"So every one must know he is," D71.
"So far from gentle, he is the danger," A15.
"The solders' disease," D96.
"Some enter into the facade," D64.
SOME MODERN TENDENCIES IN ENGLISH POETRY AS ILLUSTRATED IN THE WORKS OF AUDEN, SPENDER, AND DAY LEWIS," S17.
"Song," A15, 17, 32; BN21, 77; C161, 167; R3, 10.
"Songs of an unsung classicist (r)," C436.
"Sonnet," A14; C75.
"Sonnet: 'You were born, must die,' " BN51.
"South American diary," D76.
"Souvenir de Londres," A15; B4.
"Spain invites the world's writers," C63.
"Spanish journal," D97.
"The Spanish mind (r)," C69.
"The Spanish war," S53.
"Speaking for Spain (r)," C336.
"Speaking to the dead in the language of the dead," A25.
"Spectre de la rose," C328.
"Speech," C47.
"Speech from a play," C162.
"Spender and Auden," S3.
"Spender and Vienna," S64.
SPIRITUAL EXERCISES, A19.
"Spiritual exercises," BN11, 22; C208, D75.
"Spiritual explorations," BN77.
"The spiritual future of Europe," BN88.
"Splendour and misery of Europe," D59.
"Statistics," BN1.
"Statue of Apollo," BN22; C203.
"Steam heat," D74.

"Steinberg in the west," C397.
"Stele (Athens museum)," A36.
"Stephen Spender," S12, 32.
STEPHEN SPENDER AND THE THIRTIES, S84.
STEPHEN SPENDER: CRITIC OF MODERN LITERATURE, S56.
"Stephen Spender—Engaged in writing," S42.
STEPHEN SPENDER, LOUIS MACNEICE, AND CECIL DAY LEWIS: A CRITICAL ESSAY, S69.
"Stephen Spender: lyric impulse and will," S75.
STEPHEN SPENDER: 1928-1959: NOTES FOR AN ACCOUNT OF HIS WRITINGS, S45.
STEPHEN SPENDER: POET IN CRISIS, S73.
"Stephen Spender: the poet and the machine," S60.
THE STILL CENTRE, A14.
"A stopwatch and an ordnance map," A14, 15, 32; BN20; R1, 3.
"The strange death," C29, 36.
"The stranger," D70.
"Stranger, you who hide my love," C161.
THE STRUGGLE OF A POET: A STUDY OF STEPHEN SPENDER'S DEVELOPMENT IN THE THIRTIES, S68.
THE STRUGGLE OF THE MODERN, A41; reviews, S50.
"Subject: object: sentence," A15; B36; C388.
"Such interpenetration," D5.
"Such sensuous pattering," D5.
"Summer," C239.
"Supposing then you change," D90.
"Surely it is enough," D47.
"The swan," A2, 32; B4; C2.

T

"The talking Bronco," C108.
"Tall mountains gleam," A23.
"Task of an autobiographer," C305.
UN TEMOIN DE L'EUROPE, A21.
TEMPLE, D98.
"Temple," A36; D73, 74.
"Tendencies in modern poetry," BN76.
"That girl who laughed . . . ," A2, 32.
"That was the day you came," D5.
"That which divides . . . ," A19.
"That woman entering the room," D67.
"There are some days . . . ," D65.
"There are walls that separate," D64.
"There was an hour was twenty hours . . . ," D48.
"There was a time . . ," D67.
"There were a hundred ways . . . ," D57.
"These are the fray . . . ," DI-19.
"The things I most remember . . . ," D74.
"They are not buried under pasts," D72.
"They lift him . . . ," D5.
"They wrung their peace out of this war," D65.
"Thinkers and airmen—all such," D57.
"This age in poetry," C9.
"This bed she lies in . . . ," D46.
"This way to the tomb (r)," C252.
"Thomas Mann (r)," C324; D99.
"Those fireballs, those ashes," A3; DI-23.
"Thoughts during an air raid," A14, 15, 32; BN23; C81; R3, 7.
"Thoughts on British elections," C320.
"Three days," A14; C82.

"Three little sisters and how they grew," C445.

"Three painters haunted by greatness," C400.

THREE VERSIONS FROM THE GERMAN, A31.

"Three who did not make a revolution," S34.

"Through hidden corridors unravel," D90.

"A tight little isle," BN85.

"Till death completes their arc," C95.

"A time and place," D67.

"Times and lives," C408.

"Time in one generation," D83.

"Time in our time," A25.

"To a Spanish poet," A14, 15, 32; B11; BN57, 72.

"To become a dumb thing," A44; C457; D46, 73, 74.

"To be truly free," C176.

"Tod und das Maedchen," A17; C166.

"Tolstoy (r)," D100.

"Tom's a-cold," A25, 27; C274.

"To my daughter," A15, 32; C327; R3, 4, 5.

"To my Japanese translator," A44; D64, 73, 74.

"To Natasha," A17; BN22.

"To poets and airmen," A17; BN17, 25; C154.

"To Rose Macaulay: 'reading your travel book posthumous,'" D46.

TORSO: IN JUDGEMENT, D80, 101.

"To Samuel Barber," C384.

"To speak true, our relationships," D65.

"To T.A.R.H.," A11, 32.

"To the young writers, present, past, and future," BN91.

"To think of peace as well as war," C314.

"To those whose job in the street is to stare," D90.

"To wake up with the morning . . . ," D42.

TOWARDS THE ISLAND, sketch for a play, D53.

"To W. H. Auden," A44; D73.

"Town shore at Barcelona," · C38.

"The town walls seemed all one wall," D46.

"The trance," A15, 23, 32; C203; D75.

"Translation and the classics (r)," C116.

"Transparent light," A19, DM-XX.

"Travelling from the last place . . . ," D46, 48.

"TRIAL OF A JUDGE, A11; D102; reviews, S15.

"Trial of a poet (r)," C267.

"Tribute to Prague," D47.

"Trigorin," A15.

"The truly great," A15.

T.S. ELIOT, A47.

"T. S. Eliot," D103, 104.

"T. S. Eliot's London," C454.

"T. S. Eliot, Mr. Whitside and the psycho-biographical approach," S80.

TWENTY POEMS, A2.

"Two armies," A14, 15, 32; BN16, 23, 25, 99; C54, 62; R3, 7.

"Two kisses," A14, 32; BN39, 72; DI24.

"Two landscapes of novel," C246.

"Two speeches from a play," C52.

"Two witty women (r)," C378.

U

"Ultima ratio regum," A14, 15, 32; B8, BN16, 18, 25, 26, 29, 62, 71; C33, 56; R7.

"Ultimate death," C64.

"Uncommon poetic language," C459.

"The uncreating chaos," A14, 15, 32; BN14; C33; DI-21.
"The uncreative chaos offers," D90.
"Under the wars there is the ground of peace," D72.
"Unidentified," D105.
"United nations: cultural division," C260.
"University college school," D106.
"Upon the table under the ceiling," D65.
"Upon the turf's edge," DI-15.
"Upwards you must reply in mind," D43.
"U.S. cultural influence in Europe," C265.
"Utter stillness rules the ocean," D64.

V

"Valediction," B47.
"Van der lubbe," A3, 15, C18, 19.
"Variations on my life," A14, 15, 32.
"The vase of tears," A17, 32; C124.
"Verlaine and Rimbaud . . . ," D5.
VIENNA, A6; reviews, S6.
"View from a train," A14.
"The visionary individualists," BN95.
"The vital self and secondary means," BN96.
"Vocation," D67.
"Voice from a tomb," C412, 422; D46.
"Voice from a skull," A44; D48, 73, 74.
A VOICE IN A SKULL, A37.
"Voyage," B2.
"V. W. 1941," A44; C474.

W

"Waiting," A15.

"Walden as a possible source for Stephen Spender's 'The Express,' " S47.
"Walter de la Mare," C190.
"Walt Whitman and Democracy," C185.
"War and peace-II: Rhineland journal," C240.
"The war god," A15, 17, 32; BN15; C164.
"Warnings from the grave," BN98; C450.
"War photograph," A14, 15; C56.
"The waste of life is not . . . ," DI-22.
"A way of caring," C482.
"W. B. Yeats (r)," C446.
"We are enmeshed by burning wire," D65.
"We are such stuff . . . ," D70.
"We cannot hold on to the world," A25; D46, 57, 67, 73, 74.
"We can win the battle for the mind of Europe," C268.
"We, divided, join again in belief," A23.
"Weep, girl, weep," A25.
"We fly through a night of stars," A19, 23, 32.
"Were born, must die," A32.
"What a wild room," D65.
"What I expected," A3, 15, 32; BN57; C3, 25, 277; R3, 10.
"What is modern in modern poetry?" C276.
"What lies in a liquid guesture," D67.
"What love poems say," A44; C475; D73, 74.
"What modern writers forget," C417.
"What poets are saying," S21.
"What's wrong with unesco?" C290.
"What the eye delights in no longer dictates," A5.

"What the rebellious students want?" C467.

"What was modern in 1914," D55.

W. H. AUDEN (ed.), B47; reviews, S83.

"W. H. Auden," B48; C484, 487; D114.

"W. H. Auden aetat XX, LX," D46.

"W. H. Auden and his poetry, BN83; C341.

"When I was a boy . . . " D5.

"When Petra slept with me," A15.

"When the foundations quaked and the pillars shook," D65.

"When the pie was opened," S9.

"When we talk I imagine silence," D46, 67.

"Where dons delight (r)," C119.

"A whim of time," BN1.

"Whirring outward growth," D90.

"Who always moved away . . . " D64.

"Whoever longs as I . . . ," D5.

"Who live under the shadow of a war," A3, 15, 32; R3, 10.

"Why do they call it dark . . . ," D64.

"A wild race," A17, C170.

"The will to live (r)," C100.

"Wings of the dove," A17.

"Winter and summer," A17; BN20; C169, 181.

"Winter landscape," BN1.

"Wise man and fool (r)," C142.

"Within a city whose inhabitants," D65.

"Within a country of dervishes," D5.

"Within our nakedness . . . ," A32.

"With Lukács in Budapest," C443.

"Without that once clear aim," A3, 32; BN72.

"With your sculptured features," D65.

"Women poets (r)," C173.

"Word," A15, 25, 32; BN21, 97; C287; R5, 10.

"The word dead and the music mad," C86, 93.

"Words," R3.

"Words for the wind (r)," C394.

"Wordsworth and Spender . . . ," S58.

WORK BOOK–I, II, III, IV, V, VI, D107, 108, 109, 110, 111, 112.

"Workers' point of view," D113.

"Working day," C112.

"The world was silent as the peak of rocks," D65.

"The world wears your image . . . ," C75.

WORLD WITHIN WORLD, A26; reviews, S30.

"World within world-an excerpt," BN49.

"The writer in his age," C380.

"Writers and politics," C456.

"Writers and scholars international," C476.

"Writers in America," BN90.

"Writers in America-I," C294.

"Writers in America-II," C295.

"Writers in the world of necessity," BN28, 30; C225.

"Written whilst walking down the Rhine," A2.

"Wyndham Lewis: one way song," D85.

Y

THE YEAR OF THE YOUNG REBELS, A43; reviews, S70.

"The year's poetry," C175.

YEAR'S WORK IN LITERATURE 1950–Spender's essay in, B23.

"Yeats," D115.

"Yeats as a realist," BN38.

"You also have your cities . . . ," D28.

Z